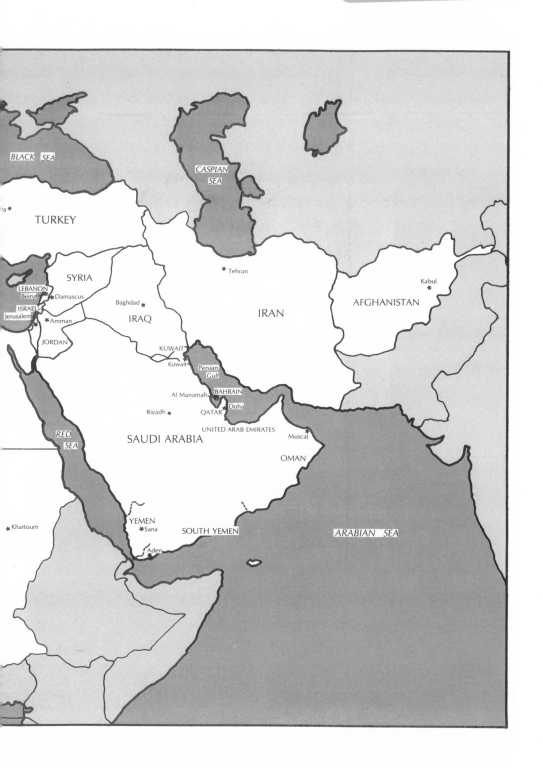

TURKEY

SYRIA

LEBANON
Beirut
Damascus

ISRAEL
Jerusalem
Amman

JORDAN

Baghdad

IRAQ

KUWAIT
Kuwait

Tehran

IRAN

Kabul

AFGHANISTAN

Persian
Gulf

Al Manamah
BAHRAIN
Doha

Riyadh
QATAR

UNITED ARAB EMIRATES

Muscat

RED
SEA

SAUDI ARABIA

OMAN

Khartoum

YEMEN
Sana

SOUTH YEMEN

Aden

ARABIAN SEA

The
Middle
East
Annual

A Reference Publication in Middle Eastern Studies
David H. Partington, Series Editor

The Middle East Annual

Issues and Events
Volume 2—1982

Edited by
David H. Partington

G. K. Hall & Co.
70 Lincoln Street, Boston, Mass.

Contents

Foreword

I am often asked what is going to happen in the Middle East. Friends who know my interest in history ask the question with a great sense of anxiety, apprehension, and expectation. Middle East events seem amazingly difficult to figure out as if determined by different laws of nature operating independently from the rest of the world. Certainly, the Middle East is subject to the same laws of nature, but the complexities of its situation derive from the successive layers of its history and culture which, although mentally discernible, are humanly intertwined.

The Middle East is the cradle of human civilization, the font for much of the world's religious thinking, and the treasure house of the accumulated wisdom of centuries of human experience, yet the present-day condition of the Middle East looks like the sands of its deserts, moving spasmodically and errantly from one site to another and making any prediction, if not impossible, extremly unwise. What one might logically anticipate does not often take place. One has to wonder why its centuries-old wisdom has been of no avail.

Comprising a great landmass stretching strategically astride North Africa and Western Asia, the Middle East is split into a variety of states of unequal power and economic and cultural standing. Unable to establish a clear and cohesive identity and subject to outside pressures politically, economically, and culturally, it seeks to assert itself and yearns to be understood. The higher aspirations of its people for a place under the sun are darkened by the clouds of international rivalry and internal factionalism. The Middle East is not at peace either within itself or with the world outside.

The distinct situation of the Middle East calls for a different approach, and perhaps a different attitude, to its study as a unique entity. It cannot, and should not, be measured with Western standards and according to Western models. It should be studied to be understood and sympathized with, not to be reduced and harnessed to anybody's political and cultural machine. The study of the Middle East in the West in general and the United

States in particular should direct itself more and more toward understanding and nothing else, for understanding, when fully achieved, carries within itself the seeds of sympathy and the potentialities of better human communication. Concern, unless accompanied by sympathy, looks suspicious, even more so in the eyes of most Middle Easteners.

The Middle East is the most obvious area in which the American public seems to be lacking in active and conscious knowledge, yet the increasing interdependence between the United States and the countries of that part of the world makes the need to look at it objectively, as a whole and in sections, increasingly urgent and necessary.

The Middle East Annual, in the statement of its editor David Partington, is meant to be a permanent reference work on the area. The editor's intention to provide the general reader and the scholar with a continuing tool of research, factual and objective, is most deserving of appreciation, for it is the kind of tool that leads to the understanding I feel is needed. It is my hope that future issues could cover as well the cultural, intellectual, and literary trends in the Middle East. That will make The Middle East Annual a comprehensive tool in addition to being objective and scholarly.

> George N. Atiyeh
> Head, Near East Section
> Library of Congress

Introduction

David H. Partington

The aim of the *Middle East Annual: Issues and Events* is to elucidate major problems of the contemporary Middle East for a readership that includes the general reader who seeks to understand the causes behind headline–seizing events, as well as researchers and college and university students. Each year five topics of major concern to the United States are selected by the editor, and recognized scholars are commissioned to address these topics in scholarly but readable, documented, and unbiased essays. Each essayist is asked also to provide a list of additional readings for further study.

The first issue of this *Annual* covered the events of 1981. It had essays entitled "The Egyptian-Israeli Peace Process, 1977–1981," by James Jankowski; "Iran's Turbaned Revolution," by Ervand Abrahamian; "Afghanistan: From Independence to Invasion," by Eden Naby and Ralph H. Magnus; "The Iran-Iraq War: Calculus of Regional Conflict," by John W. Amos II; and "Middle East Oil Producers: New Strength or New Vulnerability?" by John Gault. These topics are still very much in the news, and we anticipate that future issues of the *Annual* will take up some of them again.

The publisher intends this *Annual* to be a reference work. In addition to authoritative essays, each issue provides a detailed chronicle of the year's events. Annotated bibliographies also enhance the reference value of these volumes. We include the principal monographs published during the year, as well as a bibliography of selected journal articles.

Nineteen eighty-two was a year of problems, crises, and surprises for United States foreign policy. Against a variegated global backdrop of events such as construction of the Soviet-European pipeline, labor unrest in Poland and the apparent defeat of liberal forces represented by Solidarity, ill-defined and confusing struggles in Central America, and the seizure of the Falkland Islands by Argentina and their recapture by the British—against all this and more the major drama of the year was played out upon the Middle Eastern stage.

Three years after the conclusion of peace between Israel and Egypt, the Sinai peninsula reverted from Israeli to Egyptian sovereignty on the scheduled date of 25 April. It was not an easy transfer. Not only did Israel give up hard-won territory of strategic advantage, but some Israeli settlers on the Sinai had to be forcibly removed from their homes by the Israeli army.

The Camp David agreements of 1978 called for talks between Egypt and Israel on "Palestinian autonomy." In retrospect it seems that this aspect of Camp David was left vague so as to assure an Israeli-Egyptian peace settlement. In any event, the planned talks on this issue—which perhaps is the central problem in the contemporary Middle East—did not occur during 1982.

The issue is centered on the matter of governance of the territories seized by Israel in June 1967, commonly referred to as the (occupied) West Bank and Gaza Strip. Those territories are overwhelmingly Palestinian Arab in population, but are indubitably part of what was ancient Israel. Not only does the present coalition government in Israel rely on support from small political parties that insist on the incorporation of these areas into Israel, but Prime Minister Begin's own convictions support a policy of Jewish settlement and annexation.

The United States's approach to Palestinian autonomy is constrained both by domestic political considerations and by cognizance that considerations of oil supply, trade, and a global strategy against the Soviet Union require improved relations with the Arab world. During 1982 the dilemma posed by the Palestinian autonomy issue was personified by Secretary of State Haig, who was unwavering in his commitment to Israel's security, and by Secretary of Defense Weinberger, who avidly pursued a policy of increasing the military power of various Arab states through sales of advanced U.S. weapons, hoping to thereby strengthen the Arabs against possible Soviet aggression. These policy differences led, in part, to Haig's resignation on 25 June.

Throughout the year, the West Bank and Gaza were the scenes of often violent clashes between the Palestinian inhabitants and the occupying forces. Israel had already instituted rule by a civilian administrator, which was interpreted as a step toward outright annexation. In 1982 certain duly elected Arab mayors were expelled from office; censorship was increased; universities were forced to close—and new Jewish settlements were founded. The lack of progress in talks between Israel and Egypt, the evidence that Mr. Begin was intent on establishing new settlements, the disarray of the PLO, and the need to improve relations with the Arabs—these were some of the considerations that led President Reagan to announce a major step in American Middle East policy. Professor Donna Divine subjects the Reagan peace initiative of 1 September to a thorough analysis in this issue of the *Annual*.

The Iran-Iraq war captured few headlines in the West during the year. All efforts to mediate the dispute by delegations from the Islamic world met with the same failure that was experienced by UN delegations. Perhaps the most surprising aspect of the war was the survival of the Islamic government of the Ayatollah Khomeini. Iran not only held together but launched massive and successful counterattacks that were not halted until Iranian forces crossed into Iraq and came up against strong defensive positions. By the end of 1982 the war seemed to settle into a stalemate. The conflict posed a dilemma to the Soviet Union: although allied with Iraq, Russia also desired good relations with Iran. By the end of the year, Iraq was disappointed with the lack of support from Moscow and began to look more favorably toward the United States, with which good trading relations are maintained.

Iraq's war machine was principally funded by the Arab Gulf states whose policy is to prevent the collapse of Iraq. But the worldwide surplus of oil and the prospect of lower profits for the Gulf producers suggest that less money will be available in the future for Iraq's defense.

The Persian Gulf assumed greater importance. As a source of energy, it is uppermost in strategic planning: the United States must keep Gulf oil available to the Western world—or at least keep it from falling under the control of the Soviet Union. The United States also perceives a political threat from a militant Iran desirous of exporting "Islamic revolution" to the mainly neutral or pro-Western Arab states of the Gulf. These states, though wealthy from oil revenues, are deemed susceptible to political instability either because of their types of government, or their large populations of non-native, imported technicians and laborers. The area is also increasingly important to the United States for economic reasons: our exports to Saudi Arabia alone during the year exceeded $9 billion, and prospects are good for an increase in the trade. The United States is vitally concerned with Gulf security and provides assistance for the internal security of some states, as well as advanced weaponry in line with its strategic goals.

The Gulf states themselves have seen the need for collective security; and as OPEC, due to the temporary oil glut, is increasingly unable to control the oil market, members of the Organization of Arab Petroleum Exporting Countries are cooperating more closely. Even more significant is the Gulf Cooperation Council, and in this issue of the Annual Professor Ragaei El Mallakh provides a perceptive discussion of this new Middle Eastern entity, stressing American economic ties with the Arab Gulf countries.

Two long-standing political disputes in Africa claimed the attention of Middle East observers in 1982. In Chad, rebel leader Hissen Habré emerged victorious against Libyan-sponsored enemies and formed a new government. Libyan troops withdrew from all of Chad except the disputed area of Awzou. During the civil war, Sudan had backed Habré in order to forestall the designs of Libyan leader Qaddafi.

The other trouble spot in Africa was the Western Sahara. That conflict can be interpreted as a struggle by miserably poor indigenous inhabitants for independence—or as a strategic confrontation between Morocco and Algeria for dominance in northwest Africa. The Polisario Front of Saharan insurgents is supported in the main by Algeria and, less effectively, by Libya, while the United States gives substantial aid to Morocco both in military materiel and in tactical advice. The United States is prompted to do this not only to support King Hassan II, who is a pro-Western, moderate Arab ruler, but also to secure landing rights or support bases for the Rapid Deployment Force.

The Western Sahara conflict carried over into the Organization for African Unity when Libya attempted to seat a delegation from the Saharan Arab Democratic Republic at the OAU annual meeting in Tripoli, Libya. Morocco rallied effective opposition to this move: a quorum was not found, the OAU failed to convene, and Colonel Qaddafi was deprived of a chance to be the OAU president. In this issue of the *Annual*, the intricacies of this conflict are discussed by Professor Robert A. Mortimer.

In Turkey, the military government of general Kenan Evren moved inexorably to a nationwide referendum on a new constitution. Extremists of both left and right were rigorously pursued and prosecuted by the government, and the army proved once again to be the guarantor of Ataturk's legacy. The populace overwhelmingly approved the draft constitution, and Evren duly assumed the position of president. Professor Ilter Turan provides readers an analysis of Turkey's political processes and of the new constitution.

The most prominent event in the Middle East during 1982 was the invasion of Lebanon by Israel. Despite many clear signs of impending Israeli military action, the world was surprised when Israel launched its unprovoked attack early in June. Although the avowed objective was to protect northern Israel by clearing PLO forces out of southern Lebanon, the Israeli army quickly advanced to Beirut with the probable intention of completely destroying the PLO. Israel also overcame all resistance from Syrian land and air forces in Lebanon, inflicting heavy losses in aircraft and missile-launching sites.

As the summer progressed, Beirut was subjected to such intense bombardments from land, sea, and air that international public opinion turned against Israel. Even within Israel there were large demonstrations against the war policies of the government. Nevertheless, the Soviet Union gave no assistance to its ally Syria; the Arab states sat back and watched the PLO's death struggle; and the way was prepared for increased American intervention.

The blockade of Beirut and the damage inflicted upon it by Israel led the United States to make numerous remonstrances to Jerusalem; most went unheeded. American diplomacy, thanks largely to the untiring efforts of Philip Habib, did secure the evacuation of PLO fighting forces from Beirut, commencing on 21 August. The evacuation and dispersal of personnel to widely separated locations in the Arab world marked the termination of the PLO's ability to pursue military options.

Among the tragic consequences of this conflict were the "Beirut massacres" that occurred on 17 and 18 September when Israeli field commanders allowed Christian Phalange militiamen to enter the Sabra and Shatila Palestinian refugee camps to seek out PLO fighters. The consequent slaughter of several hundred noncombatant men, women, and children, while not the worst of recent Middle Eastern atrocities, aroused unequalled international revulsion—perhaps because some believe Israel to be guided by superior standards of morality and ethics. In Israel, outraged citizens forced Prime Minister Begin to commission a judicial inquiry into the matter of responsibility.

After the PLO forces left Beirut, the United States began an effort to bring about a peace settlement between Lebanon and Israel. These efforts were slowed by the assassination on 14 September of Bashir Gemayel, the president-elect and a Phalange leader who had held promise of being strong enough to bring a measure of unity to Lebanon. Bashir's militiamen had been supported by Israel.

After numerous delays caused by Israeli preconditions and Lebanese internal uncertainties, the first meeting to negotiate a settlement was held in

Khalde, Lebanon on 28 December. An overview of the Lebanese situation from the origins of the country's unique system of government through the year 1982 is presented by Professor Caesar Farah, who has brought years of study to his essay on what must be one of the most complicated problems of the world.

Such, briefly, are the major events of 1982 in the Middle East. In this second volume of the *Annual* we attempt to define and clarify some of the principal problems with essays on the tragedy of Lebanon, President Reagan's peace initiative, the Western Saharan conflict, the Turkish constitutional crisis, and American economic interests in Egypt and the Gulf.

I wish to thank professors Donna Robinson Divine, Ragaei El Mallakh, Caesar E. Farah, Robert A. Mortimer, and Ilter Turan for their contributions; Eric Ormsby for his painstaking work on the monograph bibliography; and members of the Advisory Board for their assistance. Special thanks are due to Ms. Karin Kiewra, Associate Editor at G.K. Hall & Co., for her work on every aspect of this volume.

19 March 1983

Middle Eastern Chronicle:
The Events of 1982

David H. Partington

This chronicle is limited to political events, or happenings of political
import, in that area of the world stretching from Morocco through India. It
also includes pertinent events in the Western capitals. All citations in this
chronicle are taken from the *New York Times*, and they are arranged in
chronological order. Readers seeking a chronicle that is subdivided by topic
and drawing upon multiple sources are referred to the quarterly issues of the
Middle East Journal.

1 January   Israeli forces place the Druze village of Majd al-Shams on
the Golan Heights under curfew and search the homes of
pro-Syrian residents.

2 January   President Hosni Mubarak of Egypt dismisses the cabinet and
names Ahmed Fuad Mohieddin as prime minister.

The U.S. ambassadors to Egypt and Israel are called home to
discuss the Palestine autonomy talks.

Foreign Minister 'Ali Akbar Velayeti of Iran returns from
talks with Syrian officials on ending the Iran-Iraq war.

3 January   A new cabinet is appointed in Egypt; posts of foreign and
defense ministers do not change.

The oil pipeline from Iraq to Tripoli, Lebanon, is blown up
after a week of operation following a six-year shutdown.

Iraq protests Israeli violation of its airspace.

Lieutenant General R. Eytan is appointed to an unprecedented fifth year as Israeli chief of staff.

4 January   The Saudi government denies that Prince Saud al-Faisal has
said that Saudi Arabia would accept Israel if it returned all

1

Arab land under occupation and recognized Palestinian rights.

President Mubarak of Egypt installs the new cabinet.

7 January Militia battles occur in Beirut between Shiites and the Organization of Communist Action in Lebanon.

8 January In the United Nations a resolution calling for voluntary sanctions against Israel for annexing the Golan Heights is drafted as an alternative to Syria's resolution calling for harsh sanctions.

Shiite and Communist groups continue fighting in Beirut.

The government of Sudan closes the country's four universities after student riots caused by increases in the price of gasoline and sugar; foreign conspiracy is blamed for the rioting.

London Bahais report that six Bahais were recently executed in Iran.

9 January The State Department says the U.S.-Israeli strategic cooperation agreement remains broken because of the Golan Heights annexation by Israel.

Syria endorses recent resolutions of the Arab League's Labor Organization calling for anti-U.S. actions.

Libyan officials visit Accra, capital of Ghana.

The Egyptian chief of staff leaves for the U.S. to discuss arms purchases.

10 January Mohammed Khamenei, a member of the Iranian Parliament and brother of President Ali Khamenei, is wounded in an assassination attempt in Tehran.

11 January In Beirut efforts to extricate bodies from the wreckage of the Iraqi embassy, blown up on 15 December, cease after sixty-one bodies are recovered.

Residents of Yamit in the Sinai renew opposition to the compensation offered by Israel: the average urban family would receive $135,000.

President Zia ul-Haq lifts censorship in Pakistan but retains the ban on reporting political news.

Ghana restores diplomatic relations with Libya.

Saudi Arabia, in rectifying a statement by Foreign Minister Saud al-Faisal, says Israel will not be recognized except with the agreement of all Arab states and the Palestinians.

12 January U.S. Secretary of State Alexander Haig arrives in Cairo to hold talks with President Mubarak; on the agenda are ways to end the impasse between Egypt and Israel over Palestinian autonomy.

Sudan and Chad agree to reinstate normal diplomatic relations.

Amnesty International accuses Pakistan of an increased number of violations of human rights during the past year.

13 January

In Cairo Secretary Haig says he received assurances from President Mubarak that Egypt will intensify efforts to proceed with Palestinian autonomy talks.

In Israel, Foreign Minister Yitzhak Shamir says no further concessions will be made in the Palestinian autonomy talks.

The first lot of sixty F–15 fighters purchased by Saudi Arabia last year leaves the U.S.

A delegation of the Council of Europe investigates restrictions on personal liberty in Turkey and may recommend suspension, but not expulsion, from the council.

In Los Angeles, a public ceremony of mourning is held for Bahais slain recently in Iran.

14 January

Secretary Haig holds talks in Jerusalem with Prime Minister Begin and ministers Shamir and Sharon. The Israelis assure him that they will endeavor to end the stalemate in the talks on Palestinian autonomy; Haig reaffirms American support for Israel's security.

France announces it will rebuild the Iraqi nuclear reactor that Israel destroyed 7 June 1981.

Pakistan seizes 480 persons associated with the Zulfikr organization.

15 January

In the UN Syria fails to get Security Council members to call for sanctions against Israel for its annexation of the Golan Heights.

Secretary of State Haig concludes his visit to Israel.

Tehran confirms the execution of Shokrollah Peknejad, a leader of the outlawed National Democratic Front.

16 January

After two days of talks in Moscow, Syrian foreign minister Abdel Halim Khaddam reaches an accord on the need to counter Israel's annexation of the Golan Heights.

The Arab May 15 Organization for the Liberation of Palestine claims credit in Beirut for bombing a restaurant in West Berlin.

18 January

Israeli defense minister Ariel Sharon requests in Cairo that the Sinai border be redrawn around the town of Rafah; both Egypt and Israel agree on ways to safeguard Israeli shipping through the Suez Canal.

The Lebanese Armed Revolutionary Faction claims credit in Beirut for assassinating a U.S. military attaché in Paris.

Reports in Damascus confirm an agreement with the USSR for the supply of military equipment to Syria.

Ethiopia claims to have eradicated the Eritrean secessionist movement.

The government of Greece announces it will resume repairing commercial and military ships of the Soviet Union.

19 January Israeli jets fly over Syrian positions in the Bekaa Valley of Lebanon and over Beirut.

Egypt and Israel reach agreement on most points regarding the return of Sinai to Egypt.

Members of an Israeli group opposed to the withdrawal from Sinai start a three-week tour of the U.S. to gain support for their position.

Turkish and Soviet officials sign an agreement in Ankara for increased trade.

Turkish authorities seize fifty-one members of underground, revolutionary organizations.

In Kabul, government forces round up male Afghans for military service.

A Soviet general is killed in Afghanistan when his helicopter is destroyed by Islamic guerrillas.

The Kuwaiti Parliament rejects a proposal that would give women the right to vote.

20 January Prime Minister Begin, in a five-page letter, assures President Reagan that Israel will not attack Lebanon without "clear provocation."

In the UN, the U.S. vetoes a Security Council compromise resolution calling for sanctions against Israel for the annexation of the Golan Heights.

Turkey advises France that a forthcoming trial of a French-Armenian assassin may cause public disturbances.

21 January Syria accuses the U.S. of encouraging Israel to destroy the chances for peace in the Middle East by vetoing the Security Council's resolution on sanctions.

The U.S. State Department regrets the recent decision by Greece to service Soviet ships.

22 January Elias Freij, mayor of Bethlehem, urges the Palestine Liberation Organization (PLO) to recognize Israel.

An earthquake hits Kerman province in Iran.

24 January Cultural exchanges between Israel and Egypt begin with the visit of sixty Egyptian students to Israel.

The first contingent of Libyan nationals arrives in Poland for special military training.

Colonel Qaddafi of Libya makes a surprise visit to Tunisia while Tunisian president Bourguiba is in the U.S.; the week-long visit ends on this date.

Rashad Shawa, mayor of Gaza, urges the PLO to recognize Israel and start a dialogue with the U.S. before Israel occupies all of the West Bank.

Reports in Lebanon allege that Israeli ships sank seven Lebanese fishing boats.

An Armenian terrorist is sentenced in France for trying to kill the Turkish ambassador to Switzerland in 1980.

25 January   The Israeli Parliament rejects the Begin government's plan to pay over $250 million to the five thousand Israelis to be displaced from Sinai.

Egypt asks the USSR for sixty-six technical experts.

The Reagan administration resubmits to Congress a proposal to sell communications satellites to an Arab consortium.

26 January   Prime Minister Begin of Israel survives a vote of confidence, fifty-five to fifty-two.

Iran and Iraq agree upon reciprocal visits by families of prisoners of war.

Zia ul-Haq, president of Pakistan, asserts his country will not manufacture nuclear weapons.

27 January   Secretary Haig arrives in Israel to resolve differences over the issue of Palestinian autonomy.

28 January   Secretary Haig confers in the morning with Prime Minister Begin in Jerusalem and in the afternoon in Cairo with President Mubarak on the Palestinian autonomy issue.

In south Lebanon, major clashes occur between Shiites who favor Khomeini of Iran and Lebanese Leftists.

The Council of Europe rejects efforts to expel Turkey for human rights violations.

King Hussein of Jordan calls for volunteers to assist Iraq in its war with Iran.

The Turkish consul in Los Angeles is murdered by Armenian terrorists.

29 January   Pakistan and India begin four days of talks in New Delhi to prepare a no-war pact.

30 January   President Mubarak of Egypt departs on a ten-day trip to Europe and the United States.

An unsuccessful coup in Syria is reported; Syrian sources deny it.

Armenian guerrillas say they will not attack sites in France, because they are assured of a fair trial and political prisoner status for four Armenians who were jailed in Paris for the attack on the Turkish embassy on 24 September 1981.

31 January   The Israeli cabinet agrees to the participation by four European countries in a multinational Sinai peace-keeping force.

The Reagan administration is reported to have offered both Egypt and Israel more military aid, with Egypt to receive more than Israel to assist it to reach parity; total U.S. assistance to Israel, however, will surpass that which is obtained by Egypt.

France contracts to expand the training facilities of the Saudi navy.

India and Pakistan agree to set up a panel on mutual ties.

1 February   The border between Egypt and Libya is reopened after three years, making it easier for the estimated two hundred thousand Egyptians who work in Libya to visit their homes.

Turkish military authorities release former premier Bülent Ecevit from prison; his three-month term for making a public statement is reduced by one month.

India and Pakistan end four days of talks on the need for a nonaggression treaty.

2 February   President Mubarak of Egypt arrives in Washington, D.C.

The Egyptian government says its border with Libya will remain closed; the border opening on 1 February was an exception.

Iran releases Andrew Pyke, a British businessman held without formal charges for seventeen months.

3 February   President Mubarak of Egypt confers with President Reagan in Washington. In public statements Mubarak calls for a Palestinian "national entity" and asks the U.S. to enter a "meaningful dialogue" with the Palestinians.

Israeli defense minister Ariel Sharon claims the Arabs are guilty of sixty violations of the cease-fire that was agreed upon last June between Israel and Palestinian forces in Lebanon.

France agrees to purchase natural gas from Algeria (after stopping purchases last year) at a higher price; Algeria agrees to purchase more manufactured goods from France.

Libya claims two U.S. jet fighters "buzz" a Libyan passenger plane over Greece.

4 February   President Mubarak concludes talks with President Reagan; both leaders vow to pursue Middle East peace through the agreements reached at Camp David.

Greece protests U.S. interference with a Libyan airliner over its airspace; U.S. denies any "buzzing."

5 February In a speech before the Washington Press Club, President Mubarak says he will pursue improved relations with Israel.

The U.S. reveals its intention to ask Saudi Arabia's assistance in plans to coordinate security aid to Persian Gulf nations.

The UN General Assembly adopts a resolution calling Israel's annexation of the Golan Heights an act of aggression and urging all nations to isolate Israel; the U.S. lobbied openly against the resolution, the USSR and Syria lobbied for it.

6 February Israel condemns the Security Council resolution condemning its annexation of the Golan Heights.

U.S. defense secretary Caspar Weinberger arrives in Saudi Arabia for talks on Persian Gulf security.

The Turkish military government publishes new regulations that bar contact, without official permission, between Turkish institutions and visitors who represent foreign organizations.

The Turkish military government prepares to legalize abortions in Turkey; this is seen as consonant with Kemal Atatürk's belief in the equality of the sexes.

In Tehran the deputy minister of industry and mines is assassinated.

7 February Israel's Defense Ministry announces it is planning to produce its own design of jet fighter, to ease dependence on the U.S.

Egyptian chief of staff 'Abd al-Nabi Hafiz begins a five-day visit to Israel.

The Gulf Cooperation Council warns Iran not to pursue subversive action in the Persian Gulf region.

The foreign ministers of seven African states prepare a cease-fire plan for the conflict in the Western Sahara.

Defense Secretary Weinberger expresses his opinion in Saudi Arabia that the USSR, soon to be an oil-importing nation, will move through Iran and Afghanistan to Iraq in order to seize Middle Eastern oil fields.

8 February At a special meeting of the Organization of African Unity assembled in Nairobi, Morocco rejects the suggestion that it negotiate directly with the Polisario Front about the Western Sahara.

Defense Secretary Weinberger, in meetings with Saudi officials in Dahran and Riyadh, encounters fundamental policy differences: Weinberger's policy is based on opposition to the USSR; Saudi Arabia sees Israel as the main threat to the Middle East.

9 February

Reports in Israel indicate that plans are being made for a large-scale invasion of Lebanon to eliminate recent PLO reinforcements.

Defense Secretary Weinberger concludes his visit to Saudi Arabia; a U.S.-Saudi Joint Committee for Military Projects was agreed upon.

President Mubarak of Egypt visits West Germany, concluding a ten-day tour of Washington and European capitals.

10 February

The U.S. State Department reports that a revolt has occurred in the Syrian city of Hama. Eight thousand government troops, led by Rif'at As'ad, are besieging the city and shelling it. The Muslim Brotherhood is held responsible for the revolt.

Israel's Parliament rejects the recent UN resolution condemning Israel for annexing the Golan Heights.

The PLO announces it still abides by the truce; Yasir Arafat asks Arab states that adjoin Israel to allow the PLO to base guerrillas on their land.

Egypt agrees to purchase nuclear power equipment from Canada.

Defense Secretary Weinberger visits Jordan to discuss the sale of U.S. military equipment.

Iran announces major gains against guerrilla groups.

Reports are received in Khartoum that former defense minister Hissen Habré will move his five-thousand-man army toward Chad's capital, Ndjamena, if the Organization of African Unity fails to make progress toward a peace settlement.

Pakistan announces it will continue the twenty-eight-month ban on political activity.

11 February

Egyptian courts rule that one thousand persons jailed in September 1981 by Anwar Sadat be released.

Secretary of State Haig confers with King Hassan II in Morocco; landing rights for the U.S. Rapid Deployment Force on Moroccan airfields is discussed.

The Organization of African Unity declares it will withdraw its peace-keeping forces from Chad by 30 June if the president, Goukouni Oueddei, does not arrange a cease-fire with the rebels. The OAU also insists on legislative and presidential elections by that date.

12 February

Arab foreign ministers meet in Tunis to discuss Israel's annexation of the Golan Heights.

Syrian authorities say the central government has regained control of the city of Hama.

13 February   Defense Secretary Weinberger, in Munich after meeting with King Hussein of Jordan, says he will urge President Reagan to sell more weapons to Jordan.

The U.S. and Morocco agree on a joint military commission.

Zev Chafets, director of the Government Press Office in Israel, severely criticizes U.S. news media for biased reporting in the Middle East.

14 February   The Israeli cabinet secretary warns the U.S. of the consequences of selling weapons to Jordan.

15 February   Prime Minister Begin of Israel, backed by all parties, publicly appeals to President Reagan not to accede to Defense Secretary Weinberger's plan to sell advanced weapons to Jordan.

16 February   President Reagan assures Prime Minister Begin that the U.S. is committed to maintaining the military superiority of Israel over adjoining Arab countries.

Israeli authorities close Bir Zeit University in the occupied West Bank for a two-month period after two days of disturbances on campus.

17 February   Demonstrations and strikes occur in the occupied West Bank by those who protest the closing of Bir Zeit University.

Richard Fairbanks, new U.S. special envoy to the Middle East, arrives in Israel to discuss the issue of Palestinian autonomy.

The foreign minister of Jordan, Marwan al-Kassem, warns in Paris that if the U.S. fails to sell weapons to Jordan, others will.

18 February   Syrian tanks have shelled and destroyed much of the city of Hama, where members of the Muslim Brotherhood rebelled recently.

The Iranian Press Agency reports that the Ayatollah Khomeini would be replaced by an elected ruling council if he were no longer able to fulfill his duties.

20 February   The Israeli army disperses a demonstration by two hundred Israelis and fifty Arab students protesting the closing of Bir Zeit University.

In Tripoli, Lebanon, a battle continues for the second day between Syrian-supported militias and Palestinian-Muslim leftists.

| 21 February | Special envoy Fairbanks meets with Egyptian foreign minister Kemal Hassan Ali to discuss talks on Palestinian autonomy. |

Battles continue to rage in Tripoli, Lebanon, between the Syrian-sponsored Arab Democratic party and the al-Fatah-backed Popular Resistance Movement.

22 February UN officials say they hope to send an additional one thousand peace-keeping troops to southern Lebanon; the UN troops, known as the United Nations Interim Force in Lebanon, have been in southern Lebanon since 1978.

In Addis Ababa, foreign ministers of the Organization of African Unity open a weeklong meeting; Morocco protests the seating of a Polisario Front delegation.

23 February The Syrian government accuses the Muslim Brotherhood of causing internal troubles in Hama, where civil disturbances have raged since 2 February.

In the UN debate begins on increasing the size of the peace-keeping force in Lebanon.

The Israeli Parliament discusses coverage of Middle Eastern news by Western newsmen.

Two car-bomb explosions in Beirut kill seven and injure sixty; two anti-Syrian groups claim responsibility.

The vice-president of Moral Majority says in Jerusalem that his group will organize tours of Israel so that American citizens can become "well-informed, educated friends of Israel."

24 February Six Arab states of the Persian Gulf agree on a collective security pact.

25 February Moshe Arens, new Israeli ambassador to the U.S., says Israel may take military action in southern Lebanon.

The Israeli army seals off four Druze villages in the Golan Heights area.

The UN Security Council approves the addition of one thousand men to its peace-keeping force in southern Lebanon, bringing the number of troops to about seven thousand.

Washington sources say the Saudi defense minister, Prince Sultan, has signed an agreement stipulating conditions for the Saudi operation of AWACS radar planes.

The U.S. bans oil imports from Libya.

India cancels plans to send a delegation to Pakistan to discuss ways to improve relations, because of objectionable statements made by a Pakistani official.

26 February	In Beirut U.S. special envoy Philip Habib begins talks with President Elias Sarkis on strengthening the cease-fire.
	Israeli defense minister Sharon orders all roads to Sinai closed to prevent militants from entering to protest against the negotiated transfer of the area to Egypt.
	Turkish military authorities arrest forty-four left-wing intellectuals, teachers, and journalists.
27 February	In Addis Ababa Morocco protests the admission of the Polisario Front into the Organization of African Unity.
	Greek Prime Minister Papandreou visits Cyprus and declares that the Turks must leave.
	Pakistan authorities arrest fourteen hundred persons on charges of subversion.
	In the Beirut suburb of Ouzai a car bomb kills eight and wounds twenty.
28 February	The Israeli cabinet announces that Egyptian president Mubarak will not be invited to visit Israel unless he plans to visit Jerusalem.
	Special envoy Habib arrives in Israel from Lebanon to discuss the cease-fire in effect in southern Lebanon.
	The Organization of African Unity ends a weeklong meeting in Addis Ababa; more than one-third of its fifty-one members boycotted the final session in order to protest the admission of the Polisario Front.
	Jordan announces it will seek advanced weapons from the U.S. Hawk antiaircraft missiles and F–16 or F–5G fighter airplanes are requested.
1 March	The Egyptian ambassador to the U.S., Ashraf Ghorbal, expresses his nation's urgent concern over Israel's threat to cancel a planned visit by Egyptian president Mubarak to Israel; Ghorbal also raises the possibility of an Israeli invasion of southern Lebanon.
	Defense Secretary Weinberger confirms that the U.S. obtained an agreement from Saudi Arabia on conditions for the use of AWACS being sold to that country; Prince Sultan, Saudi defense minister, denies any agreement.
	Olof Palme, UN special envoy, reports he has failed for the fifth time to bring about a cease-fire between Iran and Iraq.
2 March	In a talk before the Jewish Agency, Prime Minister Begin says he will not visit Egypt unless Egyptian president Mubarak includes Jerusalem in a forthcoming visit.
	A contingent of Jordanian volunteers leaves Baghdad for the Iranian front.

In Turkey, military authorities close down a magazine published by former president Ecevit.

3 March

Israeli troops forcibly remove Jewish squatters from northern Sinai; the right-wing Tehiya party is protesting the Israeli-Egyptian peace treaty that calls for Israel to return the Sinai Peninsula to Egypt on 25 April.

In Cairo, the supreme military court dismisses the entire defense team of former president Anwar Sadat's brother, who is indicted on criminal charges.

Iran decides to sell art treasures of the former shah to support the war against Iraq.

French president Mitterrand visits Israel and Jerusalem.

4 March

U.S. State Department officials express the fear that Israel may launch attacks on southern Lebanon and doubt that the U.S. can dissuade Israel from that action.

French president Mitterrand, in addressing the Israeli Parliament, urges Israel to consider Palestinian rights and the idea of a Palestinian state; he also says the PLO must recognize Israel.

The Department of State confirms it is easing restrictions on the sale of aircraft to Syria and to Southern Yemen.

Colonel Qaddafi of Libya warns the U.S. not to enter the Gulf of Sidra.

6 March

Two Arab youths are wounded in Nablus by Israeli soldiers after a rock-throwing incident.

Five of twenty-four Muslim fundamentalists on trial for Anwar Sadat's murder are sentenced to be executed.

The Islamic Conference Organization decides to send envoys to Tehran and Baghdad to attempt to mediate the conflict between Iran and Iraq.

Informal talks by the Organization of Petroleum Exporting Countries (OPEC) may have led to an agreement to support oil prices by cutting production.

7 March

Morocco urges African leaders to reverse the recent decision by the Organization of African Unity to admit the Polisario Front as a member; the Moroccan secretary of state for foreign affairs, 'Abd al-Haqq Tazi, says Morocco and eighteen other OAU members may block the next OAU meeting, which is scheduled for August in Tripoli, Libya.

Special envoy Habib returns to Israel after a week of meetings in Arab capitals on the Middle East situation.

President Assad of Syria accuses the U.S. of providing support to Muslim militants who oppose his rule.

Reports in Washington indicate that Iran is receiving large arms shipments from Israel, the USSR, and Europe.

8 March

Foreign Minister Ali of Egypt and Defense Minister Sharon of Israel make helicopter flights to survey the Sinai boundary in an effort to resolve remaining boundary problems.

Turkey denies that exiled Iranian military groups are staging in eastern Anatolia.

9 March

In Lebanon, special envoy Habib tells the country's leaders he has striven to avert a possible Israeli invasion.

The president of Somalia, Mohammed Siad Barre, arrives in Washington on the three-day visit during which he shall seek economic and military aid.

10 March

Disturbances continue in Nablus in the West Bank.

Libyan leader Qaddafi begins a four-day visit to Austria.

The U.S. Congress passes a joint resolution condemning the Soviet occupation of Afghanistan; in signing the document, President Reagan dedicates the next space shuttle flight to the Afghan insurgents.

11 March

Israeli troops continue ousting squatters from Sinai.

The Organization of African Unity initiates an effort to enforce a peace settlement in Chad; Kenya's foreign minister, Robert J. Ouko, departs for Chad accompanied by various OAU officials.

12 March

Colonel Qaddafi of Libya holds talks on economic matters in Vienna with Chancellor Kreisky of Austria.

13 March

Jordan announces it will prosecute for treason those Palestinians living in the West Bank who cooperate with the village leagues recently established by Israel.

Turkey accuses Greece of a policy of "faits accomplis" in the Aegean and vows it will not accept any action detrimental to Turkey's interest in the Aegean.

Military authorities in Israel impose a curfew on Bitunya in the West Bank after a supporter of the Israeli-sponsored village leagues escaped an assassination attempt.

Colonel Qaddafi of Libya ends a four-day visit to Austria, a visit that aroused internal Austrian criticism and the displeasure of the U.S.

14 March

An Arab member of the Israeli village league resigns.

In Tehran, a leading clergyman in the construction "crusade" is assassinated.

The Afghanistan Communist party opens its first national conference in Kabul after seizing power in April 1978.

In Pakistan, police quell a major street demonstration in Peshawar, the first in two years, planned by the National Democratic party to protest the assassination of a former provincial governor.

15 March   President Mubarak of Egypt cancels a trip to Israel because Prime Minister Begin insists that he visit Jerusalem.

Algeria places orders for forty-seven hundred trucks from Renault despite an Arab League boycott of the company.

France begins the delivery of ten missile boats to Libya.

Soviet generals visit India on a good will mission.

16 March   Turkey acknowledges that fifteen persons have died from torture since the military takeover on 12 September 1980; security officials who were responsible for these deaths have been convicted and sentenced, according to the minister of state, Ilhan Oztrak.

In Kabul the national conference of the Afghanistan Communist party ends with calls to purge dissidents and to appropriate estates of rich landowners.

A captured Red Brigade leader in Italy affirms ties with the PLO.

17 March   The U.S. Navy secretary announces that the fleet will probably conduct exercises in the Gulf of Sidra, off Libya, within the next six months.

U.S. forces enter Sinai as part of a multinational peace-keeping force.

Iran announces plans to develop nuclear technology.

A forty-member Syrian delegation to Iran returns after a five-day visit.

18 March   King Hussein of Jordan claims in an interview that divisions within the Arab world and Israeli occupation of the West Bank dangerously increase the likelihood of war.

President Saddam Hussein of Iraq initiates a new peace overture to Iran by sending an envoy to President Ahmed Sekou Toure of Guinea, who is heading a nine-member Islamic mission to mediate an end to the Iran-Iraq war.

Israel ousts the elected mayor of El Birah, Ibrahim Tawil, dissolves the town council, and installs an army colonel in Tawil's place, because Tawil refused to deal with the civilian administration.

The mayors of five major Arab cities in Israel call a three-day strike to protest Israel's action in El Birah.

19 March   Arab protesters begin a three-day strike in El Birah, Israel.

20 March	In El Birah, Israeli troops fire into a crowd of violent demonstrators and kill one youth and injure several persons.
	The Lebanese cabinet decides to create a special force to protect embassies and foreign diplomats.
	OPEC conferees in Vienna agree to cut production by seven hundred thousand barrels a day; price is set at $34 per barrel.
	Reports from Chad confirm major government losses inflicted by the forces of Hissen Habré at Oum-Hadjer on 13 March.
	In Cairo, President Mubarak approves death sentences for five persons convicted in the assassination of Anwar Sadat.
	The Revolutionary Guards in Iran stage numerous raids on the Fedayeen-i Khalq and capture forty leaders.
	The U.S. indicts several persons in an alleged plot to smuggle armaments to Libya.
21 March	Arab West Bank mayors decide to extend the general strike against the Israeli occupation.
	Colonel Qaddafi frees three French citizens imprisoned in Libya for spying.
	Pakistan increases restrictions on public protests.
22 March	President Mubarak of Egypt sends a high-ranking foreign policy adviser, Usamah al-Baz, to Israel to resolve disputed points in the Sinai border settlement.
	The fourth day of a general strike in the West Bank brings continued violence.
	An Iraqi diplomat is slain in Beirut. Iran begins a major offensive in the Dizful area; Iraqi forces retreat.
23 March	In Israel, a vote in Parliament on motions of no confidence that were introduced over Prime Minister Begin's Sinai policies is tied fifty-eight to fifty-eight; Begin offers to resign, but the cabinet votes twelve to six to keep him in office.
	Greece assures Turkey it is not pursuing oil explorations in the Aegean; Greece reiterates charges of Turkish violations of Greek airspace.
24 March	Jordan and Israel accuse each other at the UN of responsibility for the current upheavals in the West Bank.
	Iran and Iraq report heavy fighting for the third day in Khuzistan.
	In Peshawar, Pakistani police quell a demonstration by twenty-five thousand teachers.

In Bangladesh the army seizes control; martial law is imposed as the army chief of staff names himself head of the state.

25 March
Violence continues in the West Bank general strike; two Arab mayors are dismissed: Bassam al-Shaka of Nablus and Karim Khalaf of Ramallah.

Bangladesh military rulers set up courts to try former civilian officials on charges of corruption.

26 March
Menachem Milson, civilian administrator of the West Bank, says Israel's policies in suppressing the general strike are a moral crusade to suppress the influence of the PLO.

Turkey condemns recent Israeli actions in the West Bank but refuses to break diplomatic relations.

The U.S. officially joins the peace-keeping forces in Sinai, by sending twenty-four hundred U.S. soldiers; the troops are now drawn from eleven nations.

The U.S. consulate in Bombay is attacked by persons who protest U.S. aid to Pakistan.

Two hundred persons are arrested in Bangladesh on charges of corruption.

27 March
Israeli Arabs protest in Nazareth in sympathy with Arabs in the West Bank.

28 March
The Israeli cabinet votes to continue its policy toward the West Bank.

Leaders of Israeli Arabs prepare for a general strike to protest Israel's occupation of the West Bank.

29 March
The president of Israel, Yitzhak Navon, warns Israeli Arabs not to strike in support of the West Bank Arabs.

Prime Minister Begin's ruling coalition survives another vote of confidence motion in Parliament, by fifty-nine to fifty-seven.

30 March
Israel Arabs start a general strike on Land Day, a date that commemorates the 1976 protests against seizures of Arab land.

Iraq confirms that its army is retreating in Iran.

31 March
The Israeli government rejects a declaration issued on 30 March by the European Economic Community that condemns Israel for its treatment of West Bank Arabs.

The foreign secretary of Great Britain, Lord Carrington, confers in Israel on differences between the Israeli and Western European positions on the Israeli-Palestinian problem.

The head of the village league of Tarqimiyah, who had defied PLO warnings against cooperating with the Israeli government, is wounded in an assassination attempt.

The embassy of Israel in Paris is hit by machine gun fire.

The foreign minister of Kenya, Robert J. Ouko, says the Organization of African Unity will seek funding from the UN to support its peace-keeping actions in Chad.

1 April

British foreign secretary Lord Carrington, who is visiting Israel, is denied permission to talk with two Arab former mayors of West Bank towns who were dismissed last week by Israeli occupation officers.

Turkish authorities arrest twenty-nine persons believed to be part of Dev Sol, a leftist terrorist group.

2 April

In the Golan Heights, disturbances occur when native Druze residents protest the efforts of Israeli authorities to force them to accept Israeli identification cards.

In Beirut a conference of over one hundred delegates from fifteen countries opens to develop a campaign against the presence of Syrian troops in Lebanon.

Iran's foreign minister, 'Ali Akbar Velayeti, proposes that an Islamic army be formed to oust Israel from Arab territories gained since 1967.

3 April

A PLO spokesman says the organization is committed to maintaining the present truce in Lebanon.

An Israeli diplomat in Paris, Yacov Barsimantov, is assassinated; Israel blames the PLO.

4 April

The Conference of Lebanese Christians meeting in Beirut approves the following resolutions: (a) to recover territory and sovereignty; (b) to denounce the PLO; (c) to demand the immediate withdrawal of the Syrian army; and (d) to set up international solidarity groups for Lebanon and a committee to be headed by Bashir Gemayel.

Egypt sends its UN ambassador to a twenty-one-nation commission in Kuwait that is to plan a conference of nonaligned nations for next September in Baghdad.

5 April

Israel's foreign minister, Yitzhak Shamir, threatens punitive action against PLO bases in Lebanon.

At the meeting of the labor ministers of OAU states in Salisbury, Zimbabwe, Morocco and eight other countries boycott the meeting to protest the presence of the Polisario Front.

Bangladesh authorities detain two Soviet diplomats.

7 April	At a meeting of nonaligned states in Kuwait, an Egyptian proposal that Israel and the PLO give each other mutual and simultaneous recognition is rejected by Syria, Algeria, and the PLO.
8 April	The nonaligned states meeting in Kuwait condemn Israel and plead for the U.S. to review its Middle East policies, but do not condemn the Egyptian-Israeli peace treaty.
9 April	U.S. officials report there is mounting Israeli military movement near the Lebanese border.
	Reports from Iran say that former foreign minister Sadiq Ghotbzadeh was arrested two days ago.
	The Armenian Secret Army claims responsibility for an attack on a Turkish diplomat in Ottawa.
10 April	Lebanon's president, Elias Sarkis, appeals to the ambassadors of the U.S. and the USSR to avert a feared Israeli invasion.
	Syria shuts off the pipeline that carries Iraqi oil to the Mediterranean Sea.
	In Turkey former prime minister Bülent Ecevit is arrested by the ruling military authorities for false statements made against the interests of Turkey.
11 April	PLO leader Yasir Arafat says in Beirut that he expects an Israeli invasion of Lebanon within forty-eight hours; Arafat says he will not break the truce now in effect.
	The U.S. ambassador to Israel, Samuel W. Lewis, receives assurances from Prime Minister Begin that no decision has been made on invading Lebanon.
	A lone Israeli invades the Dome of the Rock mosque in Jerusalem, damages the walls with gunfire, and kills two Arabs before security forces subdue him; Prime Minister Begin calls the attack the deed of a mentally ill person.
	In an Easter message, the Maronite patriarch calls for Lebanese Christians and Muslims to unite to secure Lebanon for the Lebanese.
12 April	Violent demonstrations take place in the occupied West Bank and Gaza over the attack on the Dome of the Rock mosque by an American-born Israeli soldier; seventy are injured.
	High-level Israeli officials confer with the U.S. assistant secretary of state, N.A. Veliotes, in Jerusalem and urge him to prevent an Egyptian drift away from the Camp David agreements.
	The U.S. State Department announces that the deputy secretary of state, Walter Stoessel, will travel to the Middle East

to ensure that Israel will leave the Sinai as scheduled on 25 April.

Lebanon informs the Security Council of massive Israeli military preparations on the Israeli-Lebanese border.

Syria declares its readiness to repel any Israeli invasion of southern Lebanon.

The U.S. agrees to replace and improve the Soviet-built turbines of the Aswan High Dam on the Nile River.

13 April   King Khaled of Saudi Arabia calls on Islamic nations to hold a one-day strike to protest the recent violation of the Dome of the Rock mosque in Jerusalem.

Muslim nations in the UN denounce the lax security by Israel that led to the attack on the Dome of the Rock; Israeli representative Yahuda S. Blum contends the Security Council is summoned "to exploit the misdeeds of one . . . individual to fan the flames of religious hatred and incitement."

Iraq reports four violations of its airspace by Syrian planes.

14 April   Fifteen Islamic countries observe a general strike in protest of the Dome of the Rock incident; the pumping of oil along the Persian Gulf is not affected.

Iraq claims that Syria confiscated two hundred thousand tons of its crude oil that was loaded at Baniyas.

Iranian leftists (the Paykar) sack the Iranian consulate in Geneva.

15 April   Shiite militiamen and leftists engage in severe fighting in Beirut: twenty-seven are killed and sixty-nine are wounded; Bashir Gemayel, military leader of the Maronite Phalangists, applauds the Shiite action against Palestinian leftists.

Protests and demonstrations continue in Gaza.

Five persons convicted in the Anwar Sadat murder trial are executed in Cairo.

Former foreign minister of Iran, Sadiq Ghotbzadeh, is accused of planning a rocket attack on the house of Ayatollah Khomeini.

16 April   President Mubarak of Egypt assures Israel that Egypt will abide by the agreement on the Sinai.

Protests occur in Jerusalem, the West Bank, and Gaza.

Iran launches an offensive against the Kurds.

17 April   The U.S. and Egypt decide to set up committees to consider remaining problems in the transfer of Sinai to Egypt.

Rival Muslim militias clash south of Beirut; twenty are killed, and forty-five wounded.

A U.S. military attaché is wounded by sniper fire in Beirut.

The head of Turkey's military government, General Kenan Evren, says Turkey will be returned to a parliamentary democracy after a new constitution is approved by referendum; until then, no political activity will be allowed.

India places orders for the French Mirage fighter-bomber; manufacturing will be transferred to India. The order is seen as a move away from reliance on Soviet weapons.

18 April   President Mubarak of Egypt affirms that the Camp David accords are the "only existing basis" for peace in the Middle East.

The anti-Zionist Jewish sect Neturei Karta supports the Supreme Muslim Council in denouncing the Begin government for creating a hostile atmosphere conducive to last week's attack on the Dome of the Rock.

The deputy prime minister of Syria, Walid Hamdoun, calls upon Iraqis to overthrow their government.

Mahmoud Abdel-Fattah, chief representative of the Polisario Front in Algiers, warns the U.S. that it may seek weapons from the USSR if the U.S. increases its aid to Morocco.

UN special envoy Diego Cordoves travels from Kabul to Tehran to discuss the mediation of the Afghan situation.

Ayatollah Khomeini, speaking on Armed Forces Day, orders Iranian military commanders to purge dissidents from the ranks.

19 April   The Israeli army begins evicting Jewish protesters from a northern Sinai settlement.

Afghan insurgents inflict heavy losses on Soviet and government troops in two separate battles near Kabul.

20 April   The government of Israel imposes restrictions on news coverage of the Sinai withdrawal.

Israel reports that one of its planes flying over the Golan Heights was attacked by a Syrian missile.

The U.S. vetoes a UN resolution condemning Israel for the Dome of the Rock incident.

A high Algerian official says his country seeks better relations with the U.S., but warns that U.S. plans to increase aid to Tunisia and Morocco will lead to regional instability.

In Iran, former foreign minister Sadiq Ghotbzadeh confesses on television his connection with a plot to kill the Ayatollah Khomeini.

21 April   In apparent retaliation for the death of a soldier from a land mine, the Israeli air force bombs villages in Lebanon held by the PLO; the PLO maintains the cease-fire; Syrian jets are engaged.

The U.S. urges the PLO not to retaliate for the Israeli bombing attacks.

The Israeli cabinet votes unanimously to withdraw from Sinai on schedule.

The Ayatollah Shariatmadari, a leading Iranian theologian, is placed under armed guard.

22 April   Radical Arab states and the PLO begin discussion at the UN on means to expel Israel from the international body.

The Organization of African Unity convenes a three-day meeting in Nairobi to discuss members' differences over admitting the Western Sahara to OAU membership.

The Reagan administration requests increased military aid for Tunisia and Morocco.

In Paris, a car bomb explodes outside the office of *al-Watan al-'Arabi*, a Lebanese, pro-Iraq weekly; France declares two Syrian diplomats persona non grata.

25 April   Israel completes its withdrawal from Sinai; Defense Minister Sharon asserts that the Sinai will be Israel's final territorial concession for peace.

President Reagan assures both President Mubarak of Egypt and Prime Minister Begin of Israel that the U.S. is "firmly committed to further progress" in carrying out the Camp David accords.

26 April   President Mubarak of Egypt praises the return of Sinai as a "magnificent achievement" for peace by Israel; he also suggests that Israel's policy of settlements in the West Bank leads to doubts about the future.

27 April   Arab states in the UN abandon their plan to expel Israel.

28 April   Violent demonstrations by Arabs in the West Bank and Gaza occur.

The UN censures Israel for repressing Palestinian Arabs.

The U.S.-Turkey Joint Defense Group agrees on the need to develop Turkey's security potential, to ensure regional stability.

29 April   Violent protests by Arabs continue in the West Bank.

In Ankara, former prime minister Bülent Ecevit goes on trial for making a public statement.

30 April   Israeli authorities dismiss an elected mayor in the West Bank; Wahid Hamidallah of Anabta is the fourth elected mayor to be ousted in the West Bank.

Iran opens a military drive in Khuzistan against the Iraqis.

1 May In an Egyptian Labor Day speech, President Mubarak says the Israeli withdrawal from Sinai ushers in a new period of economic endeavor.

Iran claims gains against Iraqi forces in heavy fighting in Khuzistan.

Greece accuses Turkey of provocations in Thrace by inciting Muslims of Turkish origin to civil disorder in furtherance of irredentist aims.

2 May Twenty-six Arab mayors in the West Bank and Gaza send a letter of protest to Defense Minister Sharon demanding the reinstatement of four mayors deposed in March, the lifting of the civilian administration of Menachem Milson, and calling for a Palestinian state in the occupied area.

The Israeli cabinet resolves that the national airline, El Al, not fly on the sabbath, in deference to Agudat Israel, a political party that is essential for the ruling Likud coalition.

A fourteen-year-old Arab girl is shot in Hebron by an Israeli settler in the occupied West Bank after a series of rock-throwing incidents.

Iraq asserts it has repulsed two Iranian counterattacks in Khuzistan.

3 May Prime Minister Begin, in a speech at the opening of the summer session of Parliament, insists that Israel will demand sovereignty over Gaza and the occupied West Bank when the five-year period of transitional autonomy under the Camp David accords is over.

The Reagan administration offers new jet fighter planes to Jordan.

The Iranian government raids hideouts of the Mujahedeen-i Khalq and kill or capture over fifty Islamic socialists.

4 May An Egyptian foreign ministry official, Usamah al-Baz, says Egypt is eager to discuss Palestinian autonomy, but recent new settlements in the West Bank impede the peace process of Camp David.

Israeli army units quell disturbances by students in the Gaza Strip; an eighteen-year-old female student is killed. The unrest is seen as a consequence of Prime Minister Begin's statement that Israel will assert national sovereignty in the occupied territories after the five-year transition period of Palestinian autonomy set by Camp David.

Shaykh Zayed, president of the United Arab Emirates, travels to Saudi Arabia to confer on means to resolve the Iran-Iraq conflict.

The foreign minister of Algeria, Mohammed Ben Yahia, dies in a plane crash near the Iran-Turkey border; Iran blames the Iraqi government for the crash.

In Tehran, a raid by the Mujahedeen-i Khalq on the Khomeini Loan Center kills twenty.

The honorary Turkish consul general in New England is assassinated in Somerville, Massachusetts; the Justice Commandos of the Armenian Genocide claim credit.

5 May   Demonstrations continue in the West Bank, with an increase in Arab deaths; the Labor party protests the use of live ammunition by Israeli security forces.

Iranian helicopters raid the Iraqi city of Fuka.

6 May   West Bank mayors plan to launch a civil disobedience campaign in an attempt to force the reinstatement of four mayors dismissed by Israel.

Six Muslim leaders in the West Bank are sentenced to six months in jail for advocating a holy war against Israel.

President Assad of Syria will seek additional military equipment from the USSR to achieve a strategic balance with Israel.

President Mubarak of Egypt flies to Sudan.

Iraqi troops attack Iranian positions on the west bank of the Karun River in Khuzistan.

In Los Angeles, nineteen-year-old Hampig Sassounian, an Armenian of Lebanese nationality, is indicted for the assassination of Kemal Arikan, the Turkish consul general.

7 May   Iran launches a new drive against Iraqi positions and retakes a twenty-two-mile-long portion of the border.

An Israeli soldier, American-born Alan H. Goodman, is indicted in a Tel Aviv district court on one count of murder and five counts of attempted murder during the attack on the Dome of the Rock mosque in April.

8 May   State prosecutors in Cairo demand death sentences for 299 persons for the assassination of Anwar Sadat.

Battles occur in Tripoli, Lebanon, between the Syrian-sponsored Arab Democratic party and the anti-Syrian Popular Resistance Movement; twelve are killed and fifty wounded.

Israel agrees not to supply new weapons to Argentina during the Falklands crisis after present contracts are fulfilled.

Sultan Qabus bin Said of Oman starts a four-day official visit to Cairo.

Iraq admits a withdrawal of part of its forces from areas west of Ahwaz.

9 May	Israeli planes raid Palestinian bases south of Beirut; Palestinians shell northern Israel. These are the first attacks on Israel since the cease-fire of July 1981.
	The Israeli cabinet insists that Jerusalem be the site for any negotiations with Egypt and the U.S. on Palestinian autonomy.
	President Mubarak of Egypt and the sultan of Oman confer on the reconciliation of Egypt and the Arab states.
	Ahmad Talib Ibrahimi is appointed foreign minister of Algeria.
	Iran claims to have surrounded the port of Khurramshahr.
10 May	Battles continue in Tripoli, Lebanon, between pro- and anti-Syrian militias; nineteen are killed and forty wounded.
	Secretary of State Haig says the U.S. is very concerned over the recent breach in the cease-fire between Israel and PLO forces in southern Lebanon.
	Six Israeli army officers criticize government policy on Arab demonstrations in the West Bank.
	Iranian forces advance on Khurramshahr, the only major Iranian city still held by the Iraqi army.
11 May	In Israel, the Defense Ministry announces it is investigating charges that the army is abusing its powers in the occupied territories, in which fifteen Arabs have been killed during the last three months.
	Factional clashes subside in Tripoli, Lebanon, after five days, leaving 53 dead and 180 wounded.
	The sultan of Oman ends his visit to Cairo and calls on Arab states to restore diplomatic relations with Egypt.
12 May	U.S. special envoy Fairbanks meets with Egyptian president Mubarak in an effort to promote Egyptian-Israeli talks on Palestinian autonomy.
13 May	Secretary Haig begins talks in Turkey on arms sales and on the Cyprus problem.
	The U.S. is reported to desire a reinstatement of its strategic cooperation agreement with Israel, which was suspended by the U.S. following Israel's annexation of the Golan Heights on 18 December 1981.
14 May	King Hassan II of Morocco declares that his country is non-aligned; nevertheless, he is willing to sign a treaty with the U.S. should Morocco be threatened.
15 May	President Mubarak of Egypt, in a speech to Parliament, urges the safeguarding of democracy and the increasing of economic strength.

Secretary Haig reports progress made during his talks with the Greek prime minister; the major topic is U.S. military bases in Greece.

Zaire announces its intention to renew formal relations with Israel; these were broken in the 1973 Arab-Israel war.

The Eritrean People's Liberation Front claims that Ethiopia has failed in an attempt to crush the twenty-year-old movement for independence.

17 May   Egypt and Israel resume talks to settle a dispute over the Sinai border at the town of Eilat.

Israeli defense minister Ariel Sharon again warns the PLO not to violate the cease-fire.

The PLO denounces Zaire's resumption of diplomatic relations with Israel.

18 May   King Hassan II of Morocco begins a visit to Washington.

A Soviet housing project in Kabul, Afghanistan, is bombed by insurgents.

19 May   Prime Minister Begin's coalition government survives a no confidence vote by fifty-eight to fifty-seven in the Israeli Parliament; the defection of two members of the Likud coalition was balanced by the abstentions of three legislators.

King Hassan II of Morocco meets with President Reagan. The king is in Washington to discuss increased American military aid and an agreement for the U.S. to use bases in Morocco.

Iranian forces approaching the Iraqi-held oil port of Khurramshahr repulse an Iraqi counterattack.

Saudi Arabia says it will break ties with Zaire because Zaire has decided to resume diplomatic relations with Israel.

22 May   In Bahrain, seventy-three Shiite militants are convicted of participating in an attempted coup in November 1981; the attempt is believed to have been inspired by Iran.

The U.S. State Department requests Arab nations to persuade Iran to terminate the Iran-Iraq War.

23 May   Iran launches a new assault on the Iraqi-held port of Khurramshahr.

Prime Minister Begin, in a cabinet meeting, attacks the U.S. plan to supply advanced weapons to Jordan.

24 May   At a conference of "hard-line" Arab states (Syria, Libya, Southern Yemen, Algeria, and the PLO), Algeria urges Arab states to oppose bases for the U.S. Rapid Deployment Force.

President Saddam Hussein of Iraq says he would welcome Egyptian assistance against Iran.

In Beirut, a bomb explosion at the French embassy kills twelve people and injures twenty-seven.

Iran claims to have recaptured Khurramshahr and taken thirty thousand Iraqi prisoners.

Goukouni Oueddei, president of Chad, travels to Libya to seek assistance in the event that the African peace forces pull out of his country, leaving the rebel Hissen Habré in control of large areas of Chad.

25 May   Israeli planes on a reconnaissance mission shoot down two Syrian MIGs over Lebanon.

Iraq concedes the fall of Khurramshahr to the Iranian army.

The speaker of the Iranian Parliament, Hojatulislam Rafsanjani, declares it is Iran's right to overthrow Saddam Hussein of Iraq.

26 May   The president of France visits Lebanon.

U.S. authorities claim to have intercepted in New York an Israeli shipment of arms to Argentina; Israel denies this.

Greece says it will not participate further in military exercises of the North Atlantic Treaty Organization (NATO).

27 May   Morocco signs an agreement giving the U.S. permission to use air bases during Middle Eastern or African emergencies.

Iran announces a military offensive in the central front against Iraq, near the town of Sumar.

Greece accuses Turkey of border violations by Turkish jets and sends protests to NATO and the Common Market.

Secretary of State Haig announces that the U.S. will be more vigorous in seeking means to end the Iran-Iraq war.

28 May   The speaker of the Iranian Parliament, Rafsanjani, says that Iran will not accept a cease-fire unless Iraq accepts all its demands: withdrawal of all Iraqi forces from Iran; reparations for war damage; and the trial of President Saddam Hussein.

The secretary general of the Arab League, Chedli Klibi, embarks on a series of visits to black African countries to strengthen African-Arab ties against Israel.

30 May   Foreign ministers of the Gulf Cooperation Council states end a two-day meeting in Riyadh without agreeing on a policy toward Iran.

1 June   Prime Minister Begin says he would accept an invitation to Washington for meetings with President Mubarak of Egypt and President Reagan, but he will not discuss Palestinian autonomy until Mubarak agrees to negotiate in Jerusalem.

President Gaafar al-Nimeiry (Ja'far al-Numayri) of Sudan calls for a conference of moderate Arab states, including Egypt, to seek an end to the Iran-Iraq war.

Pakistan and India agree to resume the talks on mutual military buildups that broke down three months ago.

2 June

Egyptian foreign minister Ali meets Prime Minister Begin in Jerusalem; no progress is made on means to renew the Palestinian autonomy talks called for under the Camp David accords.

Organizers of an international conference on genocide, to be opened in Tel Aviv on 17 June, allege in Paris that Turkey has threatened to cut diplomatic relations with Israel and to adversely affect the lives of Jews in Turkey if the conference is convened.

3 June

The Israeli ambassador to Britain, Shlomo Argov, is critically wounded by gunfire in London; the PLO denies responsibility for the attack.

The chief of Israeli military intelligence says that Palestinian guerrillas are digging tunnels into Lebanese mountainsides to house missile launchers for attacks on Israel.

Former prime minister Bülent Ecevit is freed from jail but not acquitted of charges he had damaged Turkey's reputation in comments to European journalists.

4 June

Israeli jets bomb Palestinian guerrilla camps in Beirut and southern Lebanon; the attack is said to be in retaliation for the assassination attempt on the Israeli ambassador in London, Shlomo Argov.

President Mubarak of Egypt rejects a U.S. request to meet in Washington with President Reagan and Prime Minister Begin; Mubarak prefers a lower-level meeting on Palestinian autonomy at this time.

President Ali Khamenei of Iran demands $150 billion from Iraq and a trial of Iraq's president, Hussein, as preconditions for terminating the war with Iraq.

The Turkish military government categorically denies it would retaliate against Jews living in Turkey if Israel were to allow Armenians to participate in a conference on genocide.

5 June

Israel launches air and sea attacks on the coastal highway to Beirut; tanks and troops cross the border; the PLO shells northern Israel.

Secretary of State Haig, in Paris, terms the Israel bombing of Lebanon as serious, and hints that special envoy Habib will be sent to Lebanon.

Iraqi planes bomb the city of Ilam, killing forty and wounding two hundred.

6 June   The Israeli army invades southern Lebanon; PLO bases are believed to be the objective.

Prime Minister Begin, in a letter to President Reagan, declares that the Israeli army is under orders to push the PLO forces twenty-five miles back from the Israeli border.

Israel's ambassador to the U.S., Moshe Arens, declares that Israel's sole objective is to push PLO artillery out of range of northern Israel.

President Reagan, attending the Versailles summit conference, joins in a statement calling for an "immediate and simultaneous" cessation of fighting.

Forces under Hissen Habré encircle the capital of Chad.

7 June   Secretary Haig says the U.S. wants a cease-fire in Lebanon and the immediate withdrawal of Israeli forces.

Israeli forces continue a rapid advance toward Beirut; some engagements with Syrian troops occur near Jezzin; Israeli jets bomb suburbs south of Beirut.

Ndjamena, capital of Chad, falls to the rebel forces of Hissen Habré, former defense minister of Chad.

A Turkish diplomat in Lisbon is killed by Armenian terrorists.

8 June   Israeli forces advance thirty-two miles into Lebanon; six Syrian MIGs are reported downed.

Habib Chatti, secretary general of the Islamic Conference Organization, appeals for Islamic solidarity against Israel and calls for UN sanctions against the invader.

Foreign Minister Mohammed Boucetta of Morocco meets with President Mubarak of Egypt; the intent is to begin Egypt's reconciliation with the Arab world.

Secretary Haig says that an expanded UN peace-keeping force and a reduced Syrian presence in Lebanon should be part of a comprehensive solution in Lebanon after a cease-fire is put into effect.

The president of Chad, Goukouni Oueddei, is reported to have fled to Cameroun.

The Afghan army, with heavy Soviet support, gains control of the Panjshir Valley.

The Israeli consultate in Zurich is bombed.

9 June   Israel and Syria engage in a major air battle; Israel claims to have destroyed the Syrian missile system in the Bekaa Valley of eastern Lebanon. Israeli land forces seize Damur, eight miles south of Beirut.

The U.S. moves a flotilla of warships to the coast of Lebanon in preparation to receive U.S. evacuees from Beirut.

President Trudeau of Canada, in a letter to Prime Minister Begin, warns Israel of the risk of widening the war and says Canada sees no justification for Israel's attacking Lebanon.

The chairman of the U.S. House Foreign Affairs Committee, C.J. Zablocki, says that congressional support for Israel has diminished.

Lebanese Christian and Muslim leaders urge all Lebanese to support the government of Elias Sarkis.

10 June   President Reagan sends Prime Minister Begin a firm message to stop the Israeli attack on Lebanon; Secretary of State Haig rejects an invitation to visit Jerusalem.

Israeli forces advance to the suburbs of Beirut.

Iraq announces it will halt military actions in Iran and observe a cease-fire.

Hissen Habré, rebel leader in Chad, requests the Organization of African Unity to keep its thirty-eight hundred troops in Chad.

11 June   Israel and Syria announce a cease-fire in Lebanon; Israel continues the attack against the PLO, especially south of Beirut.

The commander of the OAU peace force in Chad orders his forces to withdraw from the country.

12 June   Israel announces its forces will cease firing in Lebanon at 9:00 P.M.; the PLO says it will agree to a cease-fire based on Resolutions 508 and 509 of the UN Security Council.

13 June   Israeli forces seize the town of Baabda, gaining control of the Beirut-Damascus highway, the last remaining exit for PLO troops in Beirut.

Secretary of State Haig says the U.S. will seek the withdrawal of Israeli forces from Lebanon as part of a long-term solution to the PLO-Israeli problem.

Charles H. Percy, senator from Illinois and chairman of the Foreign Relations Committee, strongly opposes the Israeli action in Lebanon and says it is inappropriate to increase military aid to Israel, and that priority should be given to creating a Palestinian entity.

King Khaled of Saudi Arabia dies of a heart attack and is succeeded by his half brother, Crown Prince Fahd.

14 June   President Mitterrand of France demands through Israeli foreign minister Yitzhak Shamir that Israel stop all attacks in Lebanon.

In Lebanon, President Sarkis forms a six-member board of national salvation to respond to Israeli conditions for withdrawal from Lebanon.

15 June   Secretary Haig asks Israel to accept a two-day cease-fire, during which PLO guerrillas could disarm.

Prime Minister Begin leaves Israel to visit the U.S.; administration officials hint that Reagan may not see Begin if Israel seizes Beirut.

Syria rejects Israel's demand for the withdrawal of its troops from the Beirut area.

Vice President Bush arrives in Riyadh at the head of a U.S. delegation for talks with King Fahd.

16 June   Israel assures the U.S. that it will not seize Beirut.

Hani al-Hassan, a high PLO official, calls for direct U.S.-PLO talks on the Lebanese situation.

In the West Bank two city councils are dissolved by Israel for refusing to cooperate with Menachem Milson, the civilian administrator.

The foreign ministers of Pakistan and the USSR confer in Geneva on Afghanistan.

17 June   Prime Minister Begin, at a meeting of the Conference of Presidents of Major Jewish Organizations, in New York, says that the June invasion of Lebanon was in response to the attack on Israel's ambassador in London, and Israel will remain in Lebanon so long as the PLO threatens the security of Israel.

U.S. special envoy Habib holds meetings with several Lebanese leaders in an effort to maintain the various cease-fires in effect.

Egypt's foreign minister, Kemal Hassan Ali, says the PLO leadership in Beirut is willing to cease fighting and has shown a desire to move toward a mutual recognition with Israel.

The U.S. House of Representatives approves $20 million in emergency aid for Lebanon; several congressmen are critical of Israel.

A PLO official is killed in Rome by a car-bomb explosion; the Jewish Armed Resistance claims credit.

18 June   Special envoy Habib continues talks with Lebanese leaders; attempts are made to persuade Walid Jumblatt, Druze leader and head of the National Movement, to join in the Council of National Salvation.

The UN Security Council votes ten to zero (Poland and the USSR abstain) to extend the mandate of its seven thousand troops in Lebanon until 19 August.

Prime Minister Begin of Israel addresses the UN; 102 of 157 delegations are absent.

20 June The Council of National Salvation, an emergency council composed of various Lebanese factions, meets for the first time; no progress is reported on ways to end the Israeli siege of Beirut.

The Syrian government rejects the request by President Sarkis of Lebanon for the withdrawal of Syrian troops from Beirut.

President Saddam Hussein announces that Iraqi troops have begun a pullback to the border between Iran and Iraq.

Prime Minister Begin of Israel arrives in Washington for talks with President Reagan.

21 June President Reagan and Prime Minister Begin agree in talks held in Washington that all foreign troops must be withdrawn from Lebanon.

Israeli forces attack Palestinian areas in West Beirut.

Soviet foreign minister Gromyko accuses Israel of genocide in Lebanon.

Ayatollah Khomeini says that Iraq's withdrawal from Iranian soil will not end the war between Iran and Iraq.

NATO commander general Bernard Rogers begins a three-day visit to Turkey to discuss Middle East affairs and Greek-Turkish relations.

22 June Israel launches a massive offensive against Syrian and PLO forces along the Beirut-Damascus highway.

Israel announces a cease-fire at 6:00 P.M., acceding to an American request relayed through special envoy Habib.

In New Delhi reports are received that Muslim insurgents ambushed a convoy of trucks en route to the Panjshir Valley, inflicting heavy casualties on young Afghan communists.

Prime Minister Begin in Washington receives assurances that the U.S. will insist on Israeli withdrawal from Lebanon only in the context of the withdrawal of Syrian and PLO forces and the establishment of a buffer zone in southern Lebanon; Mr. Begin is severely questioned by the Senate Foreign Relations Committee on the Israeli advance into Lebanon and the policy of West Bank settlements.

Israel suspends ABC's news transmissions by satellite after ABC sent out an interview with Yasir Arafat that had not been cleared by Israeli censors.

23 June New fighting breaks out with heavy Israeli attacks on Syrian positions along the Beirut-Damascus highway.

Israel claims that Syria broke the Lebanese cease-fire by attacking Israeli troops.

The U.S. House of Representatives votes $50 million in emergency aid to Lebanon.

A U.S. fleet of fifty warships assembles in the eastern Mediterranean.

24 June   Israel continues strong attacks on Syrian positions near the Beirut-Damascus highway.

The U.S. urges Arab and European governments to persuade the PLO to leave Lebanon.

The U.S. closes its embassy in Beirut.

25 June   Israel launches severe attacks on Palestinian positions and camps west of Beirut and gains full control of the Beirut-Damascus highway west to Bhamdun; Israel announces a new cease-fire in the evening.

President Reagan accepts the resignation of Secretary of State Haig.

The director of the Israeli Government Press Office, Zev Chafets, says Israel will forbid the use of transmission facilities by three U.S. TV networks.

In Calcutta, the American Center Library is ransacked by an anti-Israeli mob.

The American University of Beirut is shelled by Israeli naval vessels.

26 June   The U.S. vetoes a Security Council resolution for the limited withdrawal of Israeli and PLO forces in Beirut. The vote is fourteen to one, with the U.S. taking the view of Alexander Haig that the resolution does not eliminate armed Palestinians from Beirut.

Israeli planes destroy new Syrian SAM–6 missiles as they are being installed in the Bekaa Valley of Lebanon.

A large antiwar demonstration is held in Tel Aviv, Israel; twenty thousand persons take part.

27 June   Israel's cabinet issues proposals to end the war: (1) Israel will maintain a cease-fire but respond to any violations; (2) the Lebanese army will enter Beirut; (3) the PLO will surrender weapons to the Lebanese army and depart from Lebanon; (4) departing PLO will take the Beirut-Damascus highway, or an alternate route; (5) political negotiations will guarantee Lebanon's integrity and the departure of all foreign troops; and (6) the good offices of the U.S. in reaching this agreement will be accepted.

Israel confirms that cluster bombs were used in civilian areas of Lebanon.

Israeli planes drop leaflets on Beirut warning residents to flee.

Arab foreign ministers meeting in Tunis fail to agree on a collective response to Israel's invasion of Lebanon; the PLO representative asks for sanctions against the U.S.; others want an end to PLO activity in Lebanon.

The U.S. warns Israel not to launch new attacks on Beirut.

Iran reveals it has foiled a military coup.

Turkey seizes forty-four Kurds suspected of insurgency.

28 June

Usamah al-Baz, an official of the Egyptian Foreign Ministry, warns that the policies of former secretary of state Alexander Haig, if continued, will radicalize the Palestinian government.

Protests against continued Israeli attacks in Lebanon are voiced by some Israeli soldiers on leave in Jerusalem.

29 June

Common Market leaders condemn the Israeli invasion of Lebanon, assert that the PLO is a negotiating agent on the future of the Palestinians, and call for simultaneous withdrawal of Israeli and PLO forces from Beirut.

The U.S. urges Israel to allow time for special envoy Habib to negotiate the end of PLO military presence in Beirut.

Prime Minister Begin, while addressing the Israeli Parliament, offers to let the PLO personnel leave Beirut with their personal weapons.

Iraq reports that all of its troops have left Iranian soil; the Iranian government persists in demands for reparations and the overthrow of President Saddam Hussein.

Fighting between Kurds and Iranian forces near Mahabad is reported.

30 June

President Reagan says the U.S. did not give advance approval to Israel's attack on West Beirut.

The Israeli cabinet decides to allow more time for special envoy Habib to arrange an evacuation of PLO forces from Beirut.

Christian forces in Lebanon, backed by Israeli troops, engage in artillery duels with Muslim Lebanese militiamen backed by Syria.

Egyptian foreign minister Boutros Ghali confers in Paris with President Mitterrand on how to end the Beirut crisis.

1 July

Israel's consul general in New York, Naftalie Lavie, says that many of the fifty-eight hundred Palestinians taken prisoner in Lebanon by Israel will be tried as criminals.

Amnesty International calls on Israel to treat all prisoners taken in Lebanon in accordance with accepted standards.

Five European nations lodge a complaint with the European Commission for Human Rights against Turkey for political repression and torture of prisoners.

Ahmed Sekou Toure, president of Guinea, urges American investment in his country; U.S. officials interpret this to mean that Toure's Marxism has failed.

Ethiopia attacks Somalia.

2 July   Israeli defense minister Ariel Sharon says Israel may yet move militarily against Beirut if the PLO does not depart under a negotiated settlement.

France and Egypt cooperate at the UN to draft a proposal for the withdrawal of PLO forces from Beirut.

Dr. Isam Sartawi, a moderate member of the PLO council, urges mutual recognition between the PLO and Israel; the president of the World Jewish Congress, Nahum Goldmann, also urges mutual recognition.

Ayatollah Sadduqi is slain in Yazd, Iran.

3 July   Israeli armored troops seal off West Beirut.

4 July   Israeli troops tighten a blockade of Beirut; all food and water is intercepted.

The Israeli cabinet announces it will not accept any plan that provides an organizational structure for the PLO in Lebanon.

Libyan leader Qaddafi advises the PLO in Beirut to commit suicide.

Two are killed in the first protests in the West Bank since the invasion of Lebanon.

Syrian president Assad goes to Saudi Arabia to confer with King Fahd.

5 July   Israeli land and sea forces bombard Palestinian camps and residential areas of West Beirut; food, electricity, and water are shut off.

6 July   President Reagan agrees "in principle" to commit U.S. troops to a multinational force in Beirut.

The mayor of Jenin in the West Bank is dismissed for refusing to meet with Menachem Milson, the civilian administrator.

Bülent Ecevit, former prime minister of Turkey, is sentenced to two months and twenty-seven days in jail for giving interviews.

7 July   Israeli bombardment and blockade of PLO forces in West Beirut continue; water and electricity are restored.

Israeli forces use tear gas on Palestinian students during a demonstration at Bir Zeit University in the West Bank.

8 July	Israel maintains the bombardment and blockade of West Beirut.
	The Israeli deputy chief of staff says preparations are being made for a long stay in Lebanon.
	Negotiations between the PLO and the Lebanese government stall on the question of the role of peace-keeping troops in the PLO withdrawal from Beirut.
	In a letter to President Reagan, Soviet leader Brezhnev cautions the U.S. on sending troops to Lebanon.
	Israel shuts down Bir Zeit University in the West Bank.
	The information minister of Uganda, speaking in Washington, accuses Libya of arming guerrillas in Uganda.
9 July	Intense artillery exchanges occur between the PLO and Israeli forces.
	Syria rejects the proposal to send PLO evacuees from Beirut to Syria.
	The mayor of Gaza, Rashid al-Sawa, is dismissed by Israeli authorities as part of an effort to eliminate Palestinian nationalists from official positions.
10 July	Morris Draper, a deputy assistant secretary of state, talks with Syrian officials on evacuating PLO forces from Beirut to Syria.
	The French government agrees "in principle" to supply troops to a multinational peace-keeping force in Beirut.
	Israel gives documents to the U.S. purporting to show that mercenaries from many Asian countries are in the PLO.
	OPEC, meeting in Vienna, fails to agree on oil production levels.
11 July	Israel and the PLO engage in heavy artillery duels in Beirut.
12 July	Israeli officials assert that the PLO is using time gained through the stalled negotiations to fortify positions in Beirut.
	Israeli authorities arrest fifty-seven Bir Zeit University students.
	Large movements of Iranian troops to the Iraqi border are reported.
	Ethiopian forces attack Somalia on two fronts.
13 July	George Shultz, U.S. secretary of State-designate, says the legitimate aims and problems of the Palestinian people must be resolved. In Senate confirmation hearings, Mr. Shultz also criticizes Israel's invasion of Lebanon, the policy of West Bank settlements, and the dismissal of elected mayors in the West Bank and Gaza.

Isam Sartawi, a senior PLO official, speaking on behalf of the Palestinian National Council, states that the PLO is ready to offer mutual recognition to Israel and urges the U.S. to recognize the PLO.

Soviet and Afghan forces attack insurgent areas near Paghman.

14 July   Iran opens a major offensive and pushes ten miles into Iraq; the U.S. pledges neutrality, but calls for a halt in hostilities.

President Reagan writes to King Fahd to urge the Saudis to accept PLO evacuees from Beirut.

The administration seeks $65 million in aid for Lebanon.

15 July   President Mubarak of Egypt calls on Arab leaders to meet to agree on a unified policy to solve the Palestinian problem.

Iraq says the Iranian invasion of its territory has been halted.

16 July   The U.S. holds up a shipment of cluster bombs (artillery shells) to Israel while awaiting a report from the Begin government on the use of these weapons in Lebanon.

Somalia claims it has routed the Ethiopian invasion force.

Contingents of Iranian Revolutionary Guards hold an anti-Iraq demonstration in Damascus.

Iran launches a new offensive in southern Iraq, near Basra.

The U.S. offers to hold joint military exercises with Saudi Arabia and other Persian Gulf states.

17 July   The PLO offers to move its forces from Beirut to northern Lebanon; this offer is made after Syria refuses to accept PLO contingents on its soil.

Israel replies to the U.S. State Department on its use of American-made cluster bombs in Lebanon.

The draft of a new Turkish constitution is presented to the National Assembly in Ankara.

18 July   U.S. officials reveal that Israel, in its note of 16 July, acknowledges using American-made cluster bombs in Lebanon.

Syrian foreign minister A.H. Khaddam leaves Damascus for Washington, delegated by the Arab League to discuss Lebanon with President Reagan.

19 July   In Washington, Secretary of State Shultz meets the Syrian and Saudi foreign ministers; Shultz stresses the U.S. position that Arab states should provide refuge for the PLO fighters.

The U.S. suspends the shipment of cluster bombs to Israel.

Algeria reports that Polisario forces were successful in a raid on Moroccan positions on the Atlantic coast.

David Dodge, acting president of the American University in Beirut, is kidnapped.

20 July
The Syrian and Saudi foreign ministers in Washington propose that PLO forces in Beirut be moved to northern Lebanon while awaiting for evacuation to other Arab countries.

In Damascus, the Syrian information minister urges the U.S. to end political and military support of Israel's invasion of Lebanon, and reiterates Syria's position on not receiving PLO fighters.

Soviet leader Brezhnev endorses the idea of a UN force in Lebanon in order to break the Israeli siege of Beirut, but rejects the involvement of U.S. troops.

21 July
In confirmation testimony released today, Secretary of State Shultz says he adheres to the Camp David process for the U.S. approach to Middle East negotiations.

22 July
Israel renews air and artillery attacks on PLO and Syrian forces in Lebanon, claiming they are retaliatory in nature for violations of the cease-fire.

Special envoy Habib arrives in Damascus to attempt to persuade Syria to accept PLO evacuees.

Iran claims it destroyed four Iraqi divisions during its new drive against the city of Basra.

23 July
Israeli planes and artillery strike West Beirut for the second day.

President Assad of Syria, in meetings with special envoy Habib, calls on the U.S. to force Israel to leave Lebanon.

The U.S. and USSR conclude secret talks in Moscow on the possibility of a political solution to the Afghanistan problem.

24 July
Israel maintains its bombardment of West Beirut for the third day.

Israeli jets attack Syrian missile launchers in the Bekaa Valley of eastern Lebanon.

Iran says it will allow Algeria to mediate the Gulf War so long as the mediation supports its demands on Iraq.

The U.S. confirms it is airlifting arms to Somalia to help repeal an invasion by Ethiopia.

25 July
Israeli planes attack PLO areas in West Beirut.

Israel warns Syria not to introduce new weapons in Lebanon.

Ayatollah Khomeini broadcasts a warning to Persian Gulf states not to assist Iraq.

26 July
Israeli planes bomb Palestinian sections of West Beirut and destroy an ammunition dump.

President Mubarak of Egypt, speaking in Cairo, criticizes Israel's invasion of Lebanon, calls for a withdrawal of forces, and urges the U.S. to negotiate directly with the PLO.

The Reagan administration issues a statement strongly affirming its policy of nonrecognition of the PLO unless the PLO first recognizes Israel.

Special envoy Habib meets King Hussein of Jordan in London.

Colonel Qaddafi of Libya is reported to have urged groups within the European antinuclear movement to shut down U.S. bases.

27 July

Israel bombs a densely populated section of West Beirut; heavy civilian casualties are reported.

The U.S. State Department says President Reagan has suspended the shipment of cluster bombs to Israel for an indefinite period of time, but that no attempt will be made to see if Israel's use of cluster bombs has violated U.S. law.

In the UN, Egypt and France submit a draft resolution calling for mutual recognition of Israel and the PLO.

The Arab League mandate for Syria to maintain peace-keeping forces in Lebanon expires.

The opening of the meeting in Tripoli, Libya, of the Organization of African Unity is delayed due to Moroccan opposition to the seating of the Polisario Front delegation under the name of the Saharan Arab Democratic Republic (SADR).

28 July

Israel continues attacks on West Beirut by air and sea; both the U.S. State Department and the White House express regret over the heavy civilian casualties.

Arabs demonstrate in Jerusalem when three Arab-owned but vacant buildings are seized and occupied for housing by armed Jewish religion students.

Iran's speaker of Parliament threatens to increase military pressure on Iraq.

Iraq's president, Saddam Hussein, says he seeks a truce in the war with Iran.

29 July

The Arab League agrees in Jidda upon a plan for the PLO to leave West Beirut.

The Security Council votes to demand that Israel lift its blockade to allow food and supplies into West Beirut; the U.S. abstains from voting.

Iran claims military successes in Iraq east of Basra.

31 July

Iraq claims to have killed twenty-seven thousand Iranian soldiers during eighteen days of "epic battles" that started on 14 July.

1 August	Israel bombards West Beirut for fourteen hours and seizes control of the Beirut airport; a new cease-fire is granted at the end of the day.
	The Security Council demands a cease-fire in West Beirut.
	Syrian president Assad declares that the U.S. fully supported the Israeli invasion of Lebanon.
2 August	President Reagan tells Yitzhak Shamir, the visiting foreign minister of Israel, that the hostilities in Beirut must end.
	Israel moves tank reinforcements into all crossing points between East and West Beirut.
3 August	Two Israeli soldiers are jailed for beating a British woman employee of Bir Zeit University.
	The first contingent of about four thousand ethnic Turkish (Kirghiz) refugees from Afghanistan is airlifted from Rawalpindi, Pakistan, to Anatolia.
4 August	Israeli armed forces enter parts of West Beirut under cover of artillery fire; the attack occurs after intense negotiations by special envoy Habib on means to effect the evacuation of the PLO; the State Department says the Israeli assault directly threatens the peace negotiations of Habib.
	President Reagan appeals directly to Prime Minister Begin to call a cease-fire in Beirut, and urges the PLO to withdraw promptly from Beirut.
	Prime Minister Begin, saying that "nobody should preach to us," indicates that international criticism will not affect Israel's actions in the siege of Beirut.
	In the UN, Egypt criticizes Israel for the assault on Beirut and warns that the Camp David process is threatened.
	China accuses the U.S. of shielding the Israeli aggressors.
	UN general secretary Perez de Cuéllar cancels a planned trip to the Middle East because Prime Minister Begin of Israel said he would not receive him if he also met with Yasir Arafat.
5 August	The U.S. asks Israel to pull back its forces in Beirut to the cease-fire lines of 1 August; Israel rejects the request.
	Israel rejects a UN order to pull back its troops and allow UN observers on the scene.
	The PLO sends new proposals for withdrawing its forces from Beirut to special envoy Habib.
	King Fahd of Saudi Arabia telephones President Reagan to request that the U.S. prevent a full-scale Israeli attack on West Beirut.
	Soviet leader Brezhnev praises the PLO defense of West Beirut.

6 August	The PLO and special envoy Habib reach agreement on all major points for the PLO withdrawal from Beirut; Arab states maintain their reluctance to accept large numbers of PLO fighters.
	The U.S. vetoes a Security Council resolution aimed at halting all arms and military aid for Israel until it withdraws from Lebanon.
7 August	A high U.S. official finds "profound differences" with Israel after a comprehensive assessment of U.S. relations in the Middle East; the West Bank settlement policy of Israel is the major element of discord.
	Egypt and Syria agree to receive PLO evacuees from Beirut.
	Demonstrations are held in Munich to protest Israel's attack on Beirut.
	Armenian gunmen kill six and wound seventy-two in a two-hour machine gun attack at the Ankara airport.
8 August	Prime Minister Begin accepts the idea of a multinational peace-keeping force in Beirut.
	Special envoy Habib meets with French, Lebanese, and American military specialists to plan the withdrawal of PLO forces from Beirut.
	Secretary of State Shultz writes to Prime Minister Begin urging him to accept U.S. guarantees that PLO guerrillas will leave Lebanon if Israel agrees to the Habib plan for their withdrawal.
	The Organization of African Unity fails to muster a quorum of thirty-four members at its meeting in Tripoli, Libya; cause of the dispute is the effort by radical OAU members to admit the Polisario Front, a move opposed by Morocco.
	Libyan leader Qaddafi says he may set up a new organization as a rival to the Organization of African Unity.
9 August	The U.S. formally presents to Israel its plan for PLO withdrawal from Beirut.
	Israeli jets attack PLO positions in Beirut.
	Officials in Washington reveal that Israeli military units interfered with and harassed American military personnel near Beirut on 7 and 8 August; Israel apologizes.
	The American embassy in Damascus is stoned by crowds protesting the Israeli invasion of Lebanon; the Jordanian embassy is also stoned.
	The government of Greece formally protests Libyan interference in domestic affairs; Libya had criticized the Middle East policies of the opposition, conservative party.
	In Paris, gunmen attack a kosher restaurant; six are killed and twenty-three wounded.

10 August	Israel accepts "in principle" a proposed U.S. peace plan for Beirut, but insists that PLO forces leave before any multinational peace-keeping force enters the city; Israeli attacks on Beirut continue.

Israel accepts "in principle" a proposed U.S. peace plan for Beirut, but insists that PLO forces leave before any multinational peace-keeping force enters the city; Israeli attacks on Beirut continue.

Syria agrees to accept Palestinian forces evacuated from West Beirut.

Prime Minister Begin says that President Mitterrand's criticism of Israel's attack on Beirut led to a terrorist attack on Jews in Paris.

Israel demolishes two Arab houses in the West Bank in retaliation for an attack on a bus.

The U.S. informs the Disarmament Committee in Geneva it has evidence that the USSR uses chemical weapons in Afghanistan.

11 August

Special envoy Habib meets twice with Prime Minister Begin. Two points remain unresolved: (1) the timing of withdrawal as peace-keeping forces arrive and (2) the PLO demand that UN observers be present when the peace-keeping force arrives in Beirut.

Secretary of State Shultz assures King Hussein of Jordan of U.S. support, on the occasion of the thirtieth anniversary of the king's reign.

In Paris a car bomb is detonated at the Iraqi embassy. Responsibility is claimed by the Iraqi Islamic Action Organization.

India and Pakistan open talks at the foreign secretary level to improve relations.

12 August

Israel launches a severe, eleven-hour air raid on Beirut.

President Reagan telephones Prime Minister Begin and expresses "outrage" at this "needless destruction and bloodshed" and demands that the attack be stopped.

The Israeli cabinet orders Defense Minister Sharon not to stage any more air raids on Beirut without the prior consent of Prime Minister Begin.

The UN Security Council demands that Israel allow UN observers to monitor the cease-fires in Beirut.

13 August

U.S. officials express concern over the motives of Israeli defense minister Sharon in prolonging the bombardment of Beirut.

Soviet border troops kill two Turkish guards in Cilidir; Turkey and the USSR lodge mutual protests over border violations.

14 August

Special envoy Habib arrives in Israel with new proposals for a PLO withdrawal from Beirut.

In Israel, Defense Minister Sharon spurns calls for his resignation.

In Tehran, the trial of Sadiq Ghotbzadeh begins before a military tribunal. Charges against the former foreign minister include: (1) plotting to overthrow the present Islamic government and (2) planning to blow up Ayatollah Khomeini's residence.

15 August The Israeli cabinet approves the Habib plan for PLO evacuation from Beirut.

Iran claims damage to an Iraqi oil terminal at Fao.

Iraq warns it will attack foreign ships using Iranian oil ports.

Somalia declares a state of emergency on its border with Ethiopia.

In Corsica, the offices of Royal Air Maroc are bombed.

16 August Egypt informs the U.S. it will not accept any PLO forces from Beirut until the U.S. is committed to an overall peace settlement, including Palestinian self-determination.

Reports from Tehran indicate that about seventy Iranian officers were executed during the past three weeks for complicity with former foreign minister Ghotbzadeh, who is charged with plotting to assassinate Ayatollah Khomeini.

Egypt releases 371 people among those arrested after the assassination of Anwar Sadat.

U.S. bases in Greece are the subject of talks by Prime Minister Papandreou and the American ambassador.

Somalia reports fighting is underway between its army and Ethiopian forces inside central Somalia.

17 August Two prominent, moderate Palestinian leaders in Israel, Elias M. Freij and Rashid Shawa, say that Israel has prevented them from traveling to the U.S. to appear on television.

The United Nations Relief and Works Agency (UNRWA) reports that close to one hundred thousand Palestinians lost their homes in Lebanon.

President Mitterrand of France attacks Prime Minister Begin for charges that France is an anti-Semitic country.

18 August The government of Lebanon approves the Habib plan and decides to ask the U.S., France, and Italy to contribute troops to a multinational force.

Iraq shells Iran's oil terminal on Kharg Island.

The French cabinet bans Direct Action, a leftist group involved in three anti-Semitic incidents this month.

19 August	The Israeli cabinet approves the Habib plan for the withdrawal of Palestinian and Syrian fighters from West Beirut.
	In the UN, 120 nations vote for a Palestinian state and for sanctions against Israel; the U.S. and Israel vote against the resolution.
	Afghan insurgents raid a rally of Afghanistan's ruling party at Paghman; several hundred party members are killed or wounded, according to reports in New Delhi.
21 August	French paratroops land in Beirut as the first element of a multinational peace-keeping force.
	Palestinian detachments begin the withdrawal from Beirut.
22 August	A second contingent of PLO forces leaves Beirut by sea after Israeli warships had blocked their passage pending resolution of a dispute over the contents of twenty jeeps on board the evacuation ships.
	King Hussein welcomes 265 PLO troops to Jordan.
	President Mubarak of Egypt urges the U.S. to agree to the right of the Palestinian people to self-determination.
	At the Islamic Conference meeting of foreign ministers, the U.S. is condemned for supporting the invasion of Lebanon.
23 August	Bashir Gemayel, military leader of the Maronite Christians, is elected president of Lebanon by the Lebanese Assembly.
24 August	Fighting breaks out between Christian militiamen and Syrian units east of Beirut; Israel denies involvement.
	At a ministerial meeting of the Islamic Conference Organization meeting in Niamey, Niger, Iran's foreign minister calls for an Islamic oil embargo against the U.S.
25 August	U.S. Marines land in Beirut to take up duties as part of a multinational peace-keeping force.
	Israel begins to release many of the seven thousand persons it has detained during the occupation of Lebanon.
	Iraq reports it bombed Iranian oil facilities on Kharg Island.
	Egypt releases 244 persons who were detained after the assassination of Anwar Sadat.
26 August	Israeli defense minister Ariel Sharon, in an address before leaders of American Jewish groups in New York City, defends the invasion of Lebanon as a step toward peace; in the speech, Sharon criticizes U.S. news coverage of the situation.
	Somalia reports a major airlift of U.S. equipment in the war against Ethiopia.

27 August	Cairo refuses further talks on Palestinian autonomy (under the Camp David accords) until Israel leaves Lebanon.
	A public opinion poll in Israel shows increased popularity for Prime Minister Begin.
	A Turkish diplomat is assassinated in Ottawa.
28 August	Arab foreign ministers meet in Casablanca, Morocco, to prepare for next month's summit meeting in Fez.
	In Paris, a spokesman for the Mujahedeen-i Khalq says the Khomeini government has executed five thousand persons since March.
29 August	Israeli defense minister Ariel Sharon on CBS television indicates that a treaty with Lebanon is expected, but that Israeli troops will stay in Lebanon until all Syrian troops leave.
	King Hussein of Jordan urges a new approach to the Palestinian question.
	Babrak Karmal, president of Afghanistan, blames U.S. imperialism for provoking crises in southwest Asia.
30 August	Iraq reports it has bombed Iranian oil facilities on Kharg Island.
	Yasir Arafat, leader of the PLO, prepares to leave Beirut by ship.
31 August	As part of a new initiative toward Middle East peace, President Reagan writes to Prime Minister Begin asking for a freeze on Jewish settlements in the West Bank, where thirty thousand Jews in 104 settlements live among 1.3 million Arabs. Mr. Reagan also asks Israel not to annex Israeli-occupied areas and disavows U.S. support of an independent Palestinian state in the West Bank and Gaza.
	A Syrian photo reconnaissance plane (MIG–25) is shot down by Israeli forces over Beirut; this brings to eighty-seven the number of Syrian jet fighters downed during the Lebanon war.
	About sixteen hundred Syrian and PLO troops leave West Beirut.
1 September	President Reagan announces a major statement of U.S. policy toward Israel and the Palestinians; in a televised address, the president endorses full autonomy for Palestinians living in Israeli-occupied West Bank and Gaza, demands a cessation of Israel settlements, and calls for an undivided Jerusalem and recognition from the Arab states of Israel's right to exist.
	Foreign Minister Yitzhak Shamir of Israel says President Reagan's statements are not in accord with Camp David.

The withdrawal of Palestinian and Syrian troops from West Beirut is completed.

Colonel Qaddafi of Libya threatens to send revolutionary committees to overthrow those Arab governments that did not support the PLO in Lebanon.

Yasir Arafat leaves Beirut for Athens, Greece, where he is welcomed by Prime Minister Papandreou, who supports the PLO.

Secretary of Defense Weinberger says in Beirut that the eight hundred U.S. Marines in Beirut will be withdrawn in a few days.

The Beirut independent newspaper *al-Nahar* estimates that non-Israeli casualties in the Lebanon war amount to 17,825 dead and 30,103 wounded.

2 September   The Israeli cabinet unanimously rejects the Reagan plan for Palestinian autonomy, asserting that the proposals would lead to a Palestinian state and endanger the security of Israel.

Former U.S. president Carter says the Reagan proposals are "absolutely compatible" with the Camp David accords.

The Lebanese government security forces assume control of West Beirut.

3 September   The U.S. State Department denies the Israeli position that the U.S. violated a commitment to consult Israel before undertaking peace initiatives in the Middle East.

In Tel Aviv, the leader of the Labor party, Shimon Peres, said he plans to open a national debate on President Reagan's peace initiative.

Defense Secretary Weinberger travels to Cairo to promote the Reagan peace plan.

Western Europe reacts favorably to the Reagan peace plan.

4 September   U.S. officials reveal that Israeli defense minister Ariel Sharon refuses to share military intelligence gained in Lebanon until the Reagan government lifts sanctions against Israel, especially the ban on delivery of seventy-five F–16 airplanes.

Defense Minister Sharon of Israel says his country will not accept the Reagan peace plan.

The Egyptian government says the Reagan plan has positive aspects and could lend momentum to the peace process.

Iraq reports sinking four ships in the Gulf as part of its blockade of Iranian oil facilities.

The Ethiopian-sponsored Democratic Somali Salvation Front guerrillas claim important victories in the Ogaden region.

5 September	The Israeli government allocates $18.5 million to build three new settlements in the occupied West Bank, and approves plans to build ten new settlements; nine of the ten are to be built around the Arab city of Hebron.

Secretary of State Shultz terms the Israe'. settlement plans "not consistent with the objective of peace in the area."

The Reagan administration totally condemns the Israeli plan to build new settlements in the West Bank.

Secretary Shultz says that the resolution of the Arab-Israeli dispute must include "a totally demilitarized area" covering the West Bank.

At an Arab League conference in Fez, President Assad of Syria and the kings of Jordan, Morocco, and Saudi Arabia meet privately to discuss the Reagan peace plan.

Eight Israeli soldiers are captured by Syrian forces north of Bhamdun, Lebanon.

The leader of southern Chad, Abdelkader Kamougue, is ousted by rebel elements within his army.

6 September   Israel announces it will not resume talks on Palestinian autonomy, because the Reagan peace plan makes the talks unrealistic.

Thomas A. Dine, director of the American Israel Public Affairs Committee, a pro-Israel lobby with thirty-one thousand members, says the Reagan peace plan has many constructive points.

Defense Minister Sharon says that if Lebanon does not sign a peace treaty with Israel, then a special-status zone will be set up in southern Lebanon.

Muslim leaders in Lebanon, calling themselves the Muslim Conference, indicate willingness to open political contacts with Lebanon's president-elect, Bashir Gemayal.

The Arab League convenes in Fez, Morocco; Yasir Arafat receives a twenty-one-gun salute upon arriving, but Libya boycotts the meeting.

7 September   Special envoy Philip Habib receives the Medal of Freedom for his diplomacy in the Lebanese crisis.

8 September   The Israeli Parliament votes fifty to thirty-six to support Prime Minister Begin's rejection of the Reagan peace plan.

In Washington, the B'nai B'rith responds positively to the Reagan peace plan.

Prime Minister Papandreou alleges that Turkey and Pakistan are cooperating to build a nuclear bomb.

9 September   Secretary of State Shultz declares before the House Foreign Affairs Committee on the Middle East that the U.S. will support an Israeli-Lebanese treaty only if it is entered into freely by Lebanon.

Arab leaders meeting in Fez, Morocco, announce a plan for Middle East peace. Based on last year's eight-point Saudi plan, it tacitly recognizes Israel.

Israeli jets destroy four Syrian SAM–9 missile launchers in Lebanon.

Prime Minister Begin, in an interview made public today, says he favors parliamentary elections next May or June. He declares that "Israel provides strategic support and contributes to the national security of the United States more than the United States supports Israel."

A Turkish diplomat is assassinated in Bulgaria; two Armenian terrorist groups claim credit.

Colonel Qaddafi of Libya visits Warsaw with the aim of strengthening mutual economic ties.

10 September   Secretary of State Shultz responds favorably to the Fez peace proposals, especially paragraph 7, which implies recognition of Israel.

King Hassan II of Morocco says that seven leaders of the Arab League will begin a series of visits to Washington and European capitals to promote the Fez peace plan.

The contingent of U.S. Marines in Beirut leaves to rejoin the Sixth Fleet.

Israel rejects the Fez peace plan.

Iran agrees to supply natural gas to Turkey; a new pipeline is to be built.

11 September   President Mubarak of Egypt says the Fez peace plan has worthy goals but no mechanism for achieving them; he prefers to urge the Reagan plan.

12 September   Twenty-eight foreign teachers at al-Najah University in the West Bank refuse to sign an oath not to support the PLO.

Israeli planes destroy a Syrian missile launcher in the Bekaa Valley.

13 September   Israel launches daylong attacks on Syrian and Palestinian positions in central and eastern Lebanon; forty persons are killed.

The Vatican rejects a recent Israeli condemnation of the planned visit of Yasir Arafat to Pope John Paul II.

The Western Somali Liberation Front claims successes in the Ogaden region of southeast Ethiopia.

14 September   Bashir Gemayel, president-elect of Lebanon and leader of the Lebanese Christian Phalangist party, is killed in a bomb blast in Beirut.

King Hussein of Jordan terms the Reagan peace plan "a very constructive and a very positive move."

Former secretary of state Alexander Haig criticizes the Reagan peace plan in a speech before the United Jewish Appeal.

Soviet leader Brezhnev cables Yasir Arafat to reaffirm support for the PLO; the Beirut situation is described as a moral victory for the Palestinians.

15 September   Israeli armored forces move into West Beirut in force; the Israeli command says this is a limited action to prevent leftist militias from joining two thousand Palestinian guerrillas said to be in Beirut in the aftermath of Bashir Gemayel's death.

The U.S. expresses concern over Israel's move into West Beirut.

Egyptian foreign minister Kemal Hassan Ali accuses Israel of endangering the peace negotiations; Mr. Ali praises the Reagan peace plan and also says the Fez plan is an "important landmark" in the movement of Arab states to end the Arab-Israeli conflict.

Bashir Gemayel is buried; U.S. special envoy Morris Draper attends the funeral.

Yasir Arafat, leader of the PLO, addresses the Interparliamentary Union and, while in Rome, has an audience with Pope John Paul II.

Prime Minister Spadolini of Italy declines to meet Mr. Arafat because the European Economic Community favors mutual recognition between the PLO and Israel as a condition for a Middle East settlement.

Israeli officials increase the censorship of the Arab press in Israel.

16 September   Israeli troops secure control of West Beirut; Israel asserts it will withdraw when the Lebanese government can control the area.

The U.S. calls for an immediate pullback of Israeli troops; Israel rejects the U.S. request.

Yasir Arafat, at a news conference in Rome, asks Italy, France, and the U.S. to send back their peace-keeping forces to Beirut.

The foreign minister of Israel labels as "revolting" the Pope's meeting with Arafat.

The Egyptian attorney general's office says an undisclosed number of fundamentalist extremists have been arrested for plotting against President Mubarak.

Kuwaiti diplomats are attacked in Spain and Pakistan.

17 September   Israeli armored forces pour into West Beirut; Lebanese Christian militiamen enter Palestinian refugee camps seeking guerrillas; Phalangists, with Israeli forces guarding them, move into the Sabra and Shatila refugee camps.

Defense Minister Sharon proposes that officers of the Israeli and Lebanese armies meet to work out a plan for the gradual transfer of West Beirut areas from Israel's control to Lebanon's.

The U.S. joins a Security Council resolution condemning Israel's incursion into West Beirut.

In Paris, the car of an Israeli embassy official is bombed.

18 September   Reports are circulated of mass killings of Palestinians in refugee camps in Lebanon. Local residents report that Israeli troops sealed off the Shatila camp and then allowed Christian militiamen to enter the camp. As many as three hundred persons may have been massacred.

The Israeli Foreign Ministry denies all responsibility for the murder of Palestinians in refugee camps in Lebanon.

President Reagan calls for an immediate withdrawal of Israeli forces from West Beirut; he also says that Lebanese forces were thwarted in their attempt to gain control over Beirut by the advance of Israeli forces into the city following the assassination of Bashir Gemayel.

Soviet helicopters and MIG jets bomb the main marketplace of the Afghan town of Paghman.

19 September   Israeli officials express shock at the massacre of Palestinians in Lebanon's refugee camps; they admit knowing in advance that Phalangists intended to enter the camps to locate PLO guerrillas.

In Israel protests take place over the massacre of Palestinians in Beirut; the Labor party calls for a judicial inquiry and demands the resignations of Prime Minister Begin and Defense Minister Sharon.

The Israeli cabinet labels as "blood libel" allegations that Israel is responsible for the Beirut massacres.

The UN Security Council votes unanimously to create a fifty-member observer force to help protect Palestinians in Beirut.

Kemal Hassan Ali, foreign minister of Egypt, says he may recall Egypt's ambassador to Israel if Israel's troops are not withdrawn from Lebanon.

Italy asks the U.S. and France to join in returning an international peace-keeping force to Beirut.

20 September   The Lebanese cabinet agrees to request the return of a multinational peace-keeping force of American, French, and Italian troops.

President Reagan announces an agreement to send peace-keeping forces back to Beirut; he also reaffirms U.S. efforts to seek a solution to the Palestinian problem.

Egypt recalls its ambassador to Israel as an "expression of resentment" over the Lebanese situation.

Soviet leader Brezhnev sends a message to President Reagan urging joint action in the Security Council to curb Israel.

21 September The Begin government accedes to President Reagan's request to allow the return of a multinational peace-keeping force to Beirut.

The Israeli cabinet rejects the demand by opposition parties for a judicial inquiry into the Beirut massacres.

King Hussein of Jordan says it is time to hold talks with the PLO as called for in the Reagan peace plan.

The PLO urges the Arab League to impose sanctions against the U.S. for its responsibility in the Beirut massacres.

Amin Gemayel is elected president of Lebanon by a near-unanimous vote.

22 September In Israel's Parliament, Defense Minister Sharon says the Israeli army requested and helped plan the entry of Phalangist forces into the Palestinian refugee camps, with the understanding that no harm would befall the civilian populations of those camps.

President Mubarak of Egypt, in an address before the National Democratic party, rebukes Israel for the Beirut massacres and reiterates his support for the Reagan peace plan.

Israeli forces in West Beirut begin a phased withdrawal to be completed on 26 September.

Israeli Arabs go on a general strike to protest the Beirut massacres; violent demonstrations occur in Nazareth.

23 September In an address before the Washington Press Club, Vice President Bush says the implied recognition of Israel contained in the Fez statements of the Arab League are insufficient: full recognition of Israel is required, as is Israel's recognition of the legitimate rights of the Palestinians.

Thirty-one U.S. congressmen, all "friends of Israel," are reported to have sent a letter to Prime Minister Begin on 22 September urging a judicial inquiry into the Beirut massacres.

Amin Gemayel is sworn in as president of Lebanon; the Maronite Christians pledge to maintain ties with the Arab states.

Ayatollah Khomeini urges students to report teachers who deviate from Islamic values.

24 September The U.S. delegation to the International Atomic Energy Agency walks out after the agency voted to oust the Israelis.

Prime Minister Begin asks the chief justice of Israel's Supreme Court to inquire into Israel's involvement in the Beirut massacres.

The UN General Assembly votes to condemn the Beirut massacres and calls for an investigation; only Israel and the U.S. vote against the resolution.

King Hussein of Jordan and PLO officials begin talks on the idea of a Palestinian-Jordanian federation.

Police in Mecca, Saudi Arabia, break up a demonstration by pilgrims from Iran.

25 September The disembarkation of U.S. Marines in Beirut is delayed by the lack of an agreement on the withdrawal of Israeli troops from the airport area.

Algerian police prevent a demonstration by students who protest the Beirut massacres.

The resignations of Begin and Sharon are demanded at a rally of perhaps 350,000 persons in Tel Aviv.

Ten Russian soldiers are captured by insurgents near Kabul, Afghanistan.

26 September Prime Minister Begin's aides urge him to reverse his position and allow an independent inquiry into the Beirut massacres.

Israeli troops leave West Beirut.

Major General Amir Drori, the senior Israeli officer in Lebanon, says he had no specific information on the massacres until they were over.

King Hussein of Jordan and special envoy Philip Habib discuss the Lebanese situation.

27 September French and Italian units of the peace-keeping forces enter the sites of the Beirut massacres.

The Pakistan government extends a martial law provision for the death penalty to a wide range of "antistate" actions.

28 September Prime Minister Begin agrees to establish an independent, full-fledged judicial commission to investigate the Beirut massacres.

President Reagan says the U.S. Marines will stay in Lebanon until the Israelis and Syrians depart.

29 September The first detachment of U.S. Marines in the peace-keeping force lands in Beirut and takes up positions at the airport; the landing was delayed four days by Israel's reluctance to withdraw its troops from the area.

Elias Hobeika, chief of security and intelligence for the twelve-thousand-member force of Phalangist Christian militiamen, is implicated in the Beirut massacres.

Special envoy Habib arrives in Cairo to discuss the withdrawal of occupying troops from Lebanon.

30 September Special envoy Habib, who is touring Arab capitals, meets with the Egyptian foreign minister and assures him that an agreement on the withdrawal of foreign troops from Lebanon will be reached within weeks.

Secretary of State Shultz says at the UN General Assembly that Israel must yield territory and that the Palestinians have an "undeniable claim" to a homeland.

Iran launches a major offensive along the Iran-Iraq border near Sumar.

1 October Prime Minister Begin terms "utterly despicable" the effort to blame Israel for the Beirut massacres.

Additional U.S. Marine detachments take up positions near the Beirut airport.

2 October The Israeli military command says it is maintaining units at Baabda, site of the presidential palace of Lebanon; the U.S. position is that the Israelis should quit Beirut completely, including Baabda.

Syria says it will leave Lebanon if requested to do so by the Lebanese government and if Israel leaves also.

A bomb explodes in Tehran killing sixty and injuring seven hundred people; American mercenaries are blamed.

Iraq claims success in countering an Iranian offensive.

Iraq requests military, economic, and financial aid from all Arab states and asks them to sever political, economic, and financial relations with Iran.

Turkish authorities claim the capture of fifteen members of Rizgari, a Kurdish group engaged in guerrilla operations around Ankara.

3 October In an ambush on the Beirut-Damascus highway, six Israeli soldiers are killed and sixteen wounded.

President Mubarak of Egypt criticizes Israeli actions in an address delivered at the opening of Parliament.

Special envoy Habib meets Syrian president Assad and discusses ways to restore Lebanon's sovereignty.

Yasir Arafat appoints Muhammad Affani (known also as Abu Mu'tasim) as chief of staff of the PLO, replacing Sa'd Sayil, who was ambushed and killed the previous week.

Sudan announces it will send troops to assist Iraq against Iran.

Iraq claims to have repulsed an Iranian attack that began three days ago.

Soldiers of Ethiopia are accused by Western Somalia guerrillas of killing five hundred civilians in the Ogaden region.

India sends troops to Meerut to end three weeks of Hindu-Muslim riots.

4 October
Israeli planes attack Syrian missile sites in Lebanon; the attacks are concentrated at Dar al-Baydah.

Amin Gemayel, president of Lebanon, retains Shafik al-Wazzan in the post of prime minister.

The Security Council unanimously asks Iran and Iraq to terminate hostilities. Iraq requested the action; Iran boycotted the proceedings.

King Hussein of Jordan visits Baghdad accompanied by high Jordanian military and political officials.

Daniel Timerman, son of Jacobo Timerman, is sentenced to twenty-eight days in jail for refusing to serve in Lebanon.

5 October
Lebanese army forces search downtown West Beirut for caches of arms; more than four hundred persons are detained.

6 October
The Lebanese army continues to sweep through West Beirut; the U.S. cautions the Lebanese government not to violate the basic human rights of the Palestinians.

Iraq repels a new Iranian offensive near Sumar.

7 October
Israeli defense minister Ariel Sharon accuses the U.S. of blocking the road to peace in Lebanon, in a speech to veterans of the Irgun Zvai Leumi, a Zionist terrorist group active during the British mandate of Palestine.

Lebanese forces search for arms in West Beirut for the third day.

Prime Minister Shafik al-Wazzan of Lebanon forms a cabinet of nine men.

King Hussein of Jordan grants amnesty to hundreds of Palestinians who were jailed during the 1970 civil war.

8 October
The Lebanese army demolishes the "illegal" residences of Lebanese Shiites in the Burj al-Brajneh area of West Beirut.

Arab representatives at the UN decide to work for the expulsion of Israel.

An Israeli soldier is sentenced by a military court to three and one-half years in jail for looting a store in Lebanon.

Saudi Arabia expels sixty-nine Iranians following a riot in Medina.

Libyan leader Qaddafi threatens to assassinate any Libyan exile who works against his government.

9 October	PLO chief Yasir Arafat meets King Hussein of Jordan in Amman to discuss solutions to the Palestine problem. The Reagan peace plan is the focus of their talks.

9 October PLO chief Yasir Arafat meets King Hussein of Jordan in Amman to discuss solutions to the Palestine problem. The Reagan peace plan is the focus of their talks.

African leaders meeting in Kinshasa, Zaire with French president Mitterrand fail to resolve differences over admitting the Polisario Front to the Organization of African Unity, and over the locale of the next meeting.

A synagogue in Rome is attacked by unidentified gunmen; one child is killed and thirty-seven persons are injured.

Soviet troops in Afghanistan end a four-day assault on a rebel stronghold in Paghman and turn the area over to Afghan government troops.

10 October Israel announces that its troops will not leave Lebanon until the Lebanese government signs a security agreement; in addition, all Israeli prisoners held by Syria and the PLO must be returned to Israel, and the PLO forces must leave Lebanon first.

The information minister of Syria announces the following points: (1) Syria's present Soviet military equipment is inferior to the U.S. weapons used by Israel in Lebanon; (2) the withdrawal of PLO forces from Lebanon is a Lebanese problem: only when the Israelis leave will Syrian forces depart; (3) Syria approves the section of the Fez peace plan that gives implicit recognition to Israel; (4) Yasir Arafat, chairman of the PLO executive committee, is not authorized to speak for the PLO in talks with King Hussein of Jordan; and (5) Syria will continue to support Iran in the Iran-Iraq war.

11 October In Israel, a three-member commission of judicial inquiry, headed by Chief Justice Yitzhak Kahan, begins investigations into the Beirut massacres.

Israel announces that the invasion of Lebanon resulted in the deaths of 368 Israeli soldiers and 2,383 wounded.

King Hussein of Jordan and PLO leader Arafat fail to reach an accord on the Palestinian problem.

12 October Lebanese army units cease their searches in West Beirut.

Yasir Arafat, PLO chairman, speaking after four days of discussions in Jordan, says the Reagan plan, despite its positive aspects, is unacceptable because it does not provide for an independent Palestinian state.

Former Lebanese president Chamoun endorses the idea of a security agreement with Israel; he also advocates a larger multinational peace-keeping force.

President Mubarak of Egypt files to Sudan to sign a charter of integration that aims to coordinate the political and economic policies of the two countries.

Bülent Ecevit, former prime minister of Turkey, is acquitted of charges that he defamed Turkey in a news interview.

13 October	The Lebanese army resumes its searches of West Beirut.
	The Israeli government announces it will assist in housing Palestinians in southern Lebanon with prefabricated units supplied by charities. Israel also says it has released six hundred of the six to seven thousand Palestinians seized during the invasion of Lebanon.
	A policy dispute occurs with the PLO over the Reagan peace plan; five of fifteen PLO groups reject a plan of confederation with Jordan.
14 October	At a meeting between Israeli foreign minister Shamir and Secretary of State Shultz, a working group is set up to study means of achieving a withdrawal of foreign forces from Lebanon and securing Israel's northern border.
15 October	In Tehran, Ayatollah Ashrafi Isfahani, a close aide to Ayatollah Khomeini, is assassinated.
	The U.S. agrees to pay for the upgrading of ten Turkish airfields.
	Iraq claims successes in air and artillery attacks on Iranian positions.
16 October	Secretary Shultz declares that if Israel is denied its seat in any UN organization, the U.S. will withdraw completely.
	The U.S. government refuses to welcome the PLO member of a delegation of Arab leaders who intend to discuss the Fez peace proposals in Washington.
	Syria criticizes the concept of a federation of Palestine and Jordan.
18 October	Amin Gemayel, president of Lebanon, addresses the UN General Assembly and asks for the immediate and unconditional withdrawal of non-Lebanese forces from his country.
	Arab states urge Libya not to pursue its stated intention of expelling Israel from the UN.
	Iran claims to have captured the Kurdish village of Alvatan.
	In Ankara, Turkey, 574 suspected militant leftists are placed on trial.
19 October	The Israeli Parliament backs a tough West Bank policy in a fifty-six to fifty vote; former Labor prime minister Yitzhak Rabin urges that part of the West Bank be returned to Jordan.
	The military government of Turkey approves the final draft of a new constitution; if approved by a referendum on 7 November, General Kenan Evren will automatically be approved for a seven-year term as president.
20 October	The Israeli judicial panel investigating the Beirut massacres begins to take testimony.

A delegation of Arab leaders led by King Hassan II of Morocco arrives in Washington to discuss the Fez peace proposals.

President Mitterrand of France indicates a willingness to contribute additional French troops to the peace-keeping force in Lebanon.

The president of al-Najah University in the West Bank is deported for refusing to sign an oath disavowing connections with the PLO.

The Lebanese embassy in Rome is seriously damaged by a bomb.

21 October   The Reagan administration announces, one day prior to meeting with the Fez delegation, that the Arabs must negotiate directly with Israel.

Hissen Habré, rebel leader who captured the capital of Chad on 7 June, is sworn in as the president of Chad.

The military government of Turkey forbids all criticism of the draft constitution or of any speeches General Evren may make about it.

Oman and Southern Yemen begin talks on means to restore normal diplomatic relations.

The International Telecommunications Union votes not to expel Israel from its membership.

22 October   A delegation of Arab leaders led by King Hassan II of Morocco visits President Reagan to discuss the Fez peace proposals.

Amin Gemayel returns to Beirut after visits to the U.S., France, and Italy.

Reports in New Delhi say the Afghan insurgents attacked the Soviet embassy in Kabul this week.

Hissen Habré forms a cabinet of thirty-one members, and includes some followers of the previous government.

23 October   King Hassan II of Morocco, who is leading the six-nation Arab League delegation in Washington, says that the Arabs would recognize Israel, but only after Israel withdraws from territory gained in 1967.

A peace commission representing the Islamic Conference and headed by the foreign minister of Senegal, Mustafa Niasse, opens talks in Tehran, hoping to end the Iran-Iraq war.

24 October   The peace committee of the Islamic Conference Organization delivers a new peace plan to Ali Khamenei of Iran and Saddam Hussein of Iraq.

General Evren, head of the military government of Turkey, begins a campaign to promote the draft constitution that will be voted upon 7 November in a referendum.

25 October Israel and Lebanon agree to hold negotiations, with the U.S. as a participant, on the withdrawal of foreign troops from Lebanon.

Iran moves to oust Israel from the UN.

26 October A report by UN reveals that a trade school near Beirut was used by the PLO for military training.

Reports received in New Delhi say Afghan insurgents last week attacked Soviet and Afghan government military personnel in Kabul.

Iran announces that a special election to choose a commission to select a successor to Ayatollah Khomeini will be held on 10 December.

Iran fails in its effort to eject Israel from the UN.

Rioting among Muslim groups in Maidugur, Nigeria, leaves three hundred dead.

27 October Iraq attacks the Iranian city of Dizful with missiles, killing 21 and wounding 107 persons.

Talks begin in Athens between Greece and the U.S. on American bases on Greek territory; despite preelection promises to close the bases, Greek leader Papandreou fears a hard line would strengthen American reliance on Turkey.

Three members of the UN peace-keeping force in southern Lebanon are killed by gunmen.

28 October Egypt asks Israel to renew discussions over a strip of Sinai beach at Eilat claimed by both nations.

29 October Morris Draper, U.S. special envoy, holds meetings with Prime Minister Begin and other officials in Jerusalem in an effort to find means to effect a withdrawal of foreign troops from Lebanon; discussions deal with procedures for meetings between Israel and Lebanon.

30 October Special envoy Draper reports that both Israel and Lebanon are forming units to negotiate the withdrawal of Israeli forces from Lebanon and means to achieve Israeli security in southern Lebanon.

President Assad declares that Syrian troops will not leave Lebanon until Israel withdraws.

The Polisario Front has agreed to withdraw temporarily from the Organization of African Unity; Morocco insists on a permanent withdrawal.

31 October	Khalil al-Wazir (Abu Jihad), senior military commander of the PLO, says Israeli forces must leave Lebanon before the PLO forces in northern Lebanon depart.

Israeli military authorities state that two missiles were fired from Syria at Israeli planes over eastern Lebanon; Israel responds that this attack violates the cease-fire agreement and may delay the withdrawal of forces from Lebanon.

The Israeli cabinet, in response to an Egyptian request to renew negotiations over a strip of land at Taba (near Eilat), says this matter must be discussed as part of an effort to resolve broader issues.

Kurdish spokesmen in Paris claim that Kurds in Iran have captured the town of Bukan in western Azerbaijan.

In Cairo, the brother of Anwar Sadat is jailed on charges of business swindles.

The death toll in recent riots in Nigeria is put at 452.

1 November President Reagan agrees to expand the role of U.S. Marines in Beirut to include patrols into East Beirut.

Iran, in its third major offensive of the year, attacks Iraqi positions west of Dizful.

Israelis open a luxury hotel in Taba (near Eilat), despite Egyptian protests.

The president of Iran, Ali Khamenei, rejects efforts by a committee of the Islamic Conference Organization to mediate between Iran and Iraq.

India and Pakistan agree to form a permanent joint commission to resolve mutual problems.

2 November The prime minister of Lebanon, Shafik al-Wazzan, asks Parliament to grant him emergency powers for an eight-month period.

U.S. Marines extend their patrols to East Beirut at the request of Amin Gemayel, president of Lebanon.

Reports in New Delhi indicate that a public demonstration in Kabul by tribesmen from Pakhtia province led the government of Afghanistan to end the policy of conscripting tribal youths.

U.S. attorney general W.F. Smith visits Afghan refugees in Pakistan and says the U.S. offers "firm support."

On this or the following day, an explosion in the Salang tunnel north of Kabul, Afghanistan is believed to have killed several hundred civilians and up to seven hundred Soviet soldiers.

3 November Iran claims it retook 115 square miles in the offensive that began last Monday in the Dizful area.

4 November	U.S. Marines begin patrols in East Beirut.
	The U.S. Department of State says that the Israeli announcement that it will continue to settle the West Bank is "most unwelcome."
	Ten of the American hostages who were held by Iran file suit against the U.S. for $100 million.
5 November	A British biology teacher is deported by Israel for his refusal to sign the oath to not support the PLO.
	Ten Turkish dissidents seize a Turkish travel agency in Amsterdam.
6 November	An administration official states that President Reagan plans a new, high-level effort to remove foreign forces from Lebanon.
	Zia Khan Nassry, an Afghan-born American, is released from Iranian captivity after two and one-half years.
	Somalia will boycott the meeting on 23 November of the Organization of African Unity in Tripoli, Libya as a protest against Libyan leader Qaddafi's becoming the OAU chairman.
	Turkey votes on a new constitution; military rulers hope for an 80 percent vote of approval.
7 November	Iran's army pushes six miles into Iraq.
	King Hassan II of Morocco announces he will attend the Organization of African Unity meeting in Tripoli, Libya only if the Western Sahara issue is kept off the agenda.
8 November	Israeli prime minister Begin testifies before the commission investigating the Beirut massacres.
9 November	N.A. Veliotes, assistant secretary of state for Near Eastern and South Asian affairs, says that the U.S. is disturbed by the slow pace of negotiations on the withdrawal of troops from Lebanon.
	The Israeli Parliament votes forty-five to thirty-seven to retain civil administration in the West Bank and Gaza Strip.
	Amin Gemayel, president of Lebanon, is empowered by Parliament to rule by decree for six months.
	The U.S. State Department expresses concern over Iraq's decision to receive Abu Nidal, a Palestinian terrorist.
	Morocco and the U.S. begin joint military maneuvers.
	Iran releases U.S. citizen Zia Khan Nassry to Swiss authorities; Nassry was jailed in March 1980 on charges of espionage.
	In Turkey General Evren assumes the office of president.

10 November	Libya criticizes the current joint American and Moroccan military maneuvers.
11 November	President Reagan, in a news conference, says the Israeli settlement policy in the West Bank is "a hindrance to what we are trying to do."
	An Israeli military headquarters building in Tyre, Lebanon is destroyed by an explosion; fifteen Israelis are killed, fifteen are wounded, and fifteen non-Israelis are killed.
	Prime Minister Begin arrives in the U.S. for a ten-day visit.
	The Gulf Cooperation Council supports Iraq in its stated desire to end the war with Iran.
12 November	General Evren formally takes office as president of Turkey in accord with the new constitution that gives him a seven-year term.
13 November	Israeli authorities say eighty-nine persons died in the explosion on 11 November at the military headquarters in Tyre.
	As many as four million persons rally in Baghdad in support of the war against Iran.
	U.S. military analysts report that the USSR is constructing six airfields in southern Afghanistan; an increased Russian threat to Gulf oil fields is seen as well as a threat to the planned U.S. Rapid Deployment Force.
14 November	The death of his wife in Israel causes Prime Minister Begin to interrupt his tour of the U.S.
	Israeli authorities no longer attribute the explosion at the military headquarters building in Tyre to terrorist activity.
15 November	Lebanese president Amin Gemayel visits King Fahd of Saudi Arabia.
	Military clashes between Christian and Druze militiamen recur in Israeli-controlled central Lebanon.
16 November	The president of Iraq, Saddam Hussein, says Iraq's treaty of friendship with the USSR has not worked during the Iran war; Hussein indicates a willingness to see improved relations with the U.S.
	An eight-member delegation of the Arab League, headed by King Hussein of Jordan, visits President Mitterrand of France to explain the Fez peace proposals.
	Reports indicate that Soviet troops looted corpses of hundreds of Afghans who perished in a tunnel explosion early in November.
17 November	Two West Bank Israelis are indicted and charged in the bombings that crippled two Palestinian mayors in June 1980.

King Hussein, speaking in France at the end of a visit by an Arab League delegation, says Israel obstructs Middle East peace by building settlements in occupied Arab territories and by refusing to consider President Reagan's peace plan.

In Tehran, Iraqi dissident groups form a Supreme Council of the Islamic Revolution of Iraq to overthrow President Saddam Hussein.

Two British businessmen go on trial for smuggling arms to Libya.

18 November   Secretary of State Shultz in a news conference does not link aid to Israel with West Bank policy; he calls the settlements "not constructive at all . . . certainly not a constructive contribution to the peace process."

King Hussein of Jordan starts a two-day visit to Turkey.

19 November   Secretary of State Shultz resumes his criticism of the pledge being required by Israel of all university teachers in the West Bank not to aid the PLO.

20 November   The deputy prime minister of Iraq, Tariq Aziz, complains that the U.S. encourages its friends to sell arms to Iran; U.S. officials deny this, but do acknowledge that Israel, against American wishes, has shipped arms to Iran.

Three conservative rabbis in Massachusetts sitting as a supreme rabbinic court "excommunicate" a group of liberal Jews for supporting Palestinian causes and criticizing the invasion of Lebanon.

21 November   The Israeli army reports that the explosion in its headquarters building in Tyre was accidental.

Armed Shiites storm the town hall of Baalbak, Lebanon, to protest the government of Amin Gemayel and to break up a celebration of the thirty-ninth anniversary of independence from France.

Israel drops the requirement that foreign teachers sign a pledge not to support the PLO.

Iraqi air and naval forces attack Iranian facilities on Kharg Island.

22 November   Shiite militiamen attack a Lebanese army barracks in Baalbak, Lebanon.

Iraq claims it has pushed the Iranians back to the border.

In Tripoli, Libya, the outgoing chairman of the Organization of African Unity, Daniel Arap Moi of Kenya, initiates informal conversations with delegates to find a way to end the impasse over Chad that threatens to prevent the OAU from convening.

23 November	Secretary of State Shultz invites a visiting group of West Bank Palestinians, including two mayors deposed by Israel, to a private meeting.
	UNESCO opens a two-week special conference in Paris to plan future programs; Arab and African delegates acquiesce in accepting Israel's credentials (which were signed in Jerusalem), but the Syrian delegate denounces Israel's actions in Lebanon.
	Nigeria states it will withdraw its contingent in the UN peace-keeping force stationed in southern Lebanon.
	The Organization of African Unity does not open its Tripoli meeting: Libya objects to the seating of the pro-Western government of Chad.
24 November	The State Department reveals it has expressed official concern to Israel over Israeli measures to reduce the influence of Palestinians in the West Bank who favor Jordan or the PLO.
	The judicial commission looking into the Beirut massacres warns nine Israeli officials they may be harmed by the inquiry.
	President Mitterrand of France begins a three-day visit to Egypt.
25 November	Turkey accuses Greece of raising a baseless issue of a violation of airspace in order to prevent a scheduled meeting of their foreign ministers in Brussels.
26 November	In Damascus the PLO's Central Council denounces the Reagan peace plan for its proposal for Palestinian self-rule in association with Jordan; Reagan is also criticized for not recognizing the PLO as the sole representative of the Palestinians.
27 November	France formally agrees to supply enriched uranium to India for use in American-built reactors.
28 November	The Israeli cabinet drops its demand that talks between Israel and Lebanon be conducted at the ministerial level.
	Special envoy Habib in Cairo discusses ways to expand the Middle East peace process by bringing in additional Arab parties.
	The Arab League delegation that planned to visit London to discuss the Fez proposal cancels its visit because Britain refuses to receive the PLO representative of the delegation.
	Severe fighting is reported in the Missan province of Iraq.
29 November	Lebanon formally requests increased peace-keeping contingents from the U.S., Italy, and France.

Sporadic strikes and protests in the West Bank occur on the thirty-fifth anniversary of the partition of Palestine.

Secretary of State Shultz charges the USSR with using poison gas in Afghanistan.

The UN General Assembly demands by a vote of 114 to 21 that the USSR leave Afghanistan; Libya, Syria, and South Yemen side with the USSR.

30 November   President Mubarak of Egypt flies to India for talks with Prime Minister Gandhi on cooperation between India, Egypt, and Yugoslavia.

1 December   The State Department criticizes the Senate Appropriations Subcommittee on Foreign Operations for adding $475 million in aid for Israel.

The deputy scretary of state, Kenneth W. Dam, blames Israel for the deadlock in negotiations with Lebanon by insisting that negotiations be held in Beirut and Jerusalem.

Walid Jumblatt, Druze leader, escapes a bomb blast in Beirut that kills four and injures fifteen.

Turkish foreign minister Ilter Türkmen holds talks in Moscow to restore normal diplomatic relations.

Pakistan invites bids for building a second nuclear reactor.

2 December   A NATO communiqué issued after a three-day meeting of defense ministers gives moderate support for possible U.S. military operations in the Middle East.

The U.S. agrees to rebuild the Lebanese army to a force of forty thousand; the cost will be $85 million.

3 December   The secretary general of the UN challenges the legality of a draft resolution that would require the UN to guarantee the protection of Palestinian refugees in Israeli-held territory; the 1949 Geneva Convention assigns that responsibility to the occupying power.

About twenty-five hundred U.S. soldiers begin maneuvers in Oman.

4 December   The State Department recalls Philip Habib and Morris Draper from Lebanon for consultations on the failure to bring about negotiations on the withdrawal of foreign troops from Lebanon.

In Egypt, the trial begins for 302 persons (twenty *in absentia*) charged with conspiring to overthrow the government; most are members of al-Jihad.

5 December   President Mubarak of Egypt calls for mutual and simultaneous recognition by Israel and the PLO.

King Hussein of Jordan leads an Arab League delegation to China to seek support for the Fez peace plan.

The Israeli cabinet interprets the Reagan administration effort to reduce aid to Israel as an important shift in U.S. policy.

The state judicial commission investigating the Beirut massacres clears the Israeli-supported militia of Major Sa'd Haddad of any involvement.

Israeli defense minister Sharon leaves for a three-day trip to Honduras to discuss the sale of Israeli weapons.

Two prominent Americans, Felix G. Rohatyn and Victor H. Botbaum, sharply criticize Israeli policies at ceremonies honoring them held by the American Jewish Congress.

In Nicosia, Cyprus, a travel agency serving Arab airlines is bombed.

6 December Special envoy Habib holds talks with King Hassan II of Morocco.

President Zia ul-Haq of Pakistan arrives in Washington for talks with President Reagan on U.S. military aid, the Afghanistan situation, and American concern over Pakistan's nuclear development.

China informs the Arab League delegation it supports the Arabs against Israeli aggression, but the Arabs should recognize Israel.

A delegation from the Israeli Parliament concludes an eight-day visit to Brazil.

7 December President Zia ul-Haq of Pakistan says he seeks nuclear technology only for peaceful purposes.

Saudi Arabia is reported to agree to lending $2 billion to the French government to bolster its foreign exchange reserves.

9 December President Zia ul-Haq of Pakistan says he discerns a "hint of flexibility" in the Soviet position on its intervention in Afghanistan.

10 December Elections are held in Iran to form an eighty-three member assembly to choose a successor to Ayatollah Khomeini.

11 December The U.S., seeking to end the impasse between Lebanon and Israel on the withdrawal of foreign troops, proposes that the two sides deal indirectly with each other through envoys Habib and Draper, who will shuttle between each nation.

The deputy prime minister of Israel, David Levi, confirms there is an expansion of present settlements in the West Bank.

Fighting continues in Tripoli, Lebanon.

12 December   Defense Minister Sharon of Israel says that a U.S. proposal to have Habib and Draper travel between Beirut and Jerusalem to handle troop withdrawals is reasonable, but eventually direct Lebanese-Israeli talks must be held on security arrangements and normalization.

Fighting continues in Tripoli, Lebanon.

President Mubarak of Egypt, in a *Der Spiegel* interview, accuses Syria of blocking a solution to the Palestine problem.

Israel's foreign minister, Yitzhak Shamir, starts a twelve-day trip to Argentina and Uruguay.

Turkish president Evren begins a five-nation tour of Asia.

13 December   The foreign minister of Lebanon, in Washington for a three-day visit, seeks an increase in the multinational peace-keeping force.

Israeli officials say they are withholding military information garnered from the invasion of Lebanon from the U.S. until the U.S. accepts certain conditions on its use.

A severe earthquake strikes Yemen; major damage occurs in the area of Dhamar.

China's prime minister, Zhao Ziyang, welcomes President Evren of Turkey.

14 December   Israeli defense minister Sharon says Israel will not annex the West Bank but will retain internal and external control there for another fifty years.

The PLO and the Jordanian government, after two days of discussions, agree there will be a "special and distinctive" relationship between Jordan and a future Palestinian entity; both sides pledge to try to recover Palestinian rights.

Foreign Minister Yitzhak Shamir of Israel concludes a three-day visit to Argentina. He notes concern over the one thousand Jews who have disappeared in Argentina. Arms sales are discussed, along with the possibility of Argentine recognition of the PLO.

15 December   Special envoy Draper conveys new ideas from Washington to President Gemayel of Lebanon on means to break the deadlock on negotiations for the withdrawal of troops from Lebanon.

Syria sends two high-level officials to Tripoli, Lebanon to resolve the ten-day conflict between pro- and anti-Syrian forces.

Yitzhak Shamir, foreign minister of Israel, denies that he has negotiated the sale of weapons with Argentina.

The World Zionist Congress is reported to condemn the Begin government's policy of establishing new settlements in the occupied Arab territories; Arye Dultzin, the WZC's chairman, overrules the show of hands vote and maintains that the organization must support the government of Israel.

16 December   President Reagan sends a letter to Prime Minister Begin urging a prompt withdrawal of Israeli troops from Lebanon.

Prime Minister Begin, in an address to the World Zionist Congress, says the Reagan peace plan is a threat to the security of Israel.

Lebanon's foreign minister, Elie Salem, impresses on Secretary of State Shultz during a meeting in Washington that the continued presence of foreign troops threatens to dismember Lebanon.

The World Zionist Congress fails to reach a consensus on the Begin government's West Bank settlement policy.

The U.S. says it will sell arms to Jordan without requiring that country to join in peace talks with Israel, Egypt, and the U.S. on Palestinian self-rule.

The half brother of Anwar Sadat is indicted on various criminal charges in Cairo.

The Communist party paper *Pravda* affirms the continuation of a hard-line policy in Afghanistan.

17 December   President Chadli Benjedid of Algeria visits France. This is the first official visit to France by an Algerian head of state.

Street fighting occurs in Tripoli, Lebanon between various factions; eighteen persons are killed.

18 December   President Reagan, speaking at a news conference, says armies of occupation now in Lebanon must go.

OPEC, meeting in Vienna, faces difficult bargaining as Iran demands an increase in its production quota while others support reduced production to maintain prices.

The U.S. asserts that Iran is being supplied by North Korea.

19 December   Israel agrees to drop its demand that negotiations with Lebanon be held in Jerusalem and Beirut; Lebanon announces its willingness to begin talks immediately, with the U.S. as a partner.

Israeli authorities impose restrictions on the West Bank town of Nablus.

Pakistan's president, Zia ul-Haq, is admitted to the Walter Reed Army Medical Center.

20 December   King Hussein of Jordan begins talks in the U.S. on the possibility of joining Egypt and Israel on negotiations over Palestinian self-rule.

The Yemen government says twenty-eight hundred people died in last week's earthquake.

OPEC ends a two-day meeting in Vienna unable to agree upon oil quotas.

Chinese prime minister Zhao Ziyang visits Egypt on the start of a tour of African nations.

21 December   King Hussein of Jordan, meeting in Washington with President Reagan, says he is not ready to enter peace talks on the Middle East.

Afghan insurgents attack an airport at Jalalabad.

22 December   The Lebanese cabinet insists that all Israeli, Syrian, and Palestinian forces leave Lebanon by 15 February 1983, after which Lebanon will consider ending the state of belligerency in effect with Israel since 1948.

Moshe Arens, Israeli ambassador to the U.S., says progress is being made with Lebanon in reaching an agreement for the withdrawal of foreign troops.

The State Department reports the USSR has suffered up to fifteen thousand casualties since its invasion of Afghanistan.

23 December   Israel says that Khalde in Lebanon and Qiryat Shemona will be the sites for direct negotiations with Lebanon; the Israeli delegation will be headed by David Kimche, director of the Foreign Ministry.

The Saudi government cautions Lebanon on concluding accords with Israel before all Israeli forces leave Lebanon; the Saudis also place restrictions on the import of goods from Lebanon so as to eliminate goods of Israeli origin.

President Reagan and King Hussein of Jordan hold their second and final talks of the week; Reagan is optimistic and sees significant progress toward peace; Hussein will pursue the Reagan plan with the PLO and Arab states.

The Israeli consulate in Sydney, Australia is wrecked by a bomb blast, and a Jewish club is damaged. The Organization for the Liberation of Lebanon from Foreigners claims credit.

Egypt frees 127 Muslim militants who were detained as security risks.

24 December   Christian and Druze militiamen continue heavy artillery battles south of Beirut; during the ten weeks of this conflict, about 170 persons have been killed.

Pakistan and India sign a five-year accord that sets up a joint commission to strengthen economic and cultural ties.

Turkey releases nineteen persons, after ten weeks of detention, for defaming Turkey abroad.

25 December   Prime Minister Zhao Ziyang of China confers with Algerian President Chadli Benjedid.

26 December	It is reported that the PLO and Israel are negotiating in Austria for the release of eight Israeli prisoners captured in Lebanon.

In Cairo 235 Muslim extremists plead not guilty to charges of sedition.

Iraq claims seventy-four bombing missions on military targets and towns in Khuzistan.

27 December Yasir Arafat, head of the PLO, and Austrian chancellor Kreisky, meet for three hours on Majorca.

Prime Minister Zhao Ziyang of China arrives in Rabat, Morocco for a three-day visit.

The official *People's Daily* in Peking asks countries to give moral and material assistance to the Afghan insurgents.

28 December Lebanon and Israel open talks in Khalde, a seaside town four miles south of Beirut. The chief Lebanese negotiator, Antoine Fattal, praises the American mediation effort; U.S. special envoy Draper pledges American assistance in reaching an agreement; and David Kimche, Israel's chief negotiator, hopes to sign an agreement leading directly to a full and formal peace treaty.

In Tel Aviv, ethnic conflict erupts between Sephardic and Ashkenazic Jews after Israeli police, on 23 December, shot a citizen of Yemeni origin.

29 December U.S. and Lebanese officials discuss ways to break the impasse in Israeli-Lebanese negotiations.

Opposition is voiced in the U.S. Senate to a planned sale of helicopters to Iraq.

30 December The second session of Israeli-Lebanese negotiations takes place in Qiryat Shemona.

31 December Israeli delegates to the Lebanese-Israeli talks confer with Israeli cabinet members to find a new wording to break an impasse over language, specifically over "normalization," which Israel wants and Lebanon wishes to avoid out of regard for its ties with other Arab states.

The USSR reaffirms its position on the occupation of Afghanistan: Soviet troops will remain until foreign armed intervention is ended; until dependable guarantees exist against a resumption of hostilities; and until the Babrak Karmal government is accepted as legitimate.

Rioting by Muslims continues in Kerala State, India.

Lebanon at the Crossroads

Caesar E. Farah

The year 1982 will be remembered as a year of decision for Lebanon. It was a year of great tragedy and dislocation for hundreds of thousands of Lebanese. Lebanon witnessed in the latter half of 1982 the result of a decade of frustration, irresolution, and festering resentment among its various groups. How did the country arrive at this critical and decisive juncture in its history?

To answer this question we must examine the history of Lebanon and the country's failure to develop an identity characteristically Lebanese and capable of commanding a loyalty that would transcend all other loyalties. Some scholars believe that if Lebanon had acquired such an identity, it would not have suffered the tragedies of 1958, 1969, 1975, and now 1982 (Salem 1982, 4). By their factionalism, political divisiveness, rampant antagonisms, and inherent distrust of each other, the Lebanese have invited to a large extent the tragedies visited upon them in the last quarter century. As a former U.S. diplomat put it, "It is with the Lebanese that the problem lies. Had they not willingly acquiesced in the transformation of their country into the brothel of the Arab world, had they not sold their newspapers and their soul to the highest bidder, had they been willing to bury their fears and animosities against their fellow Lebanese, and had they been willing to give their loyalty to their state instead of to their family, foreign interference would not have been possible and they would not be in the fix they are today" (Parker 1982, 19).

In the past the peoples of other nations torn by factional and sectarian interests were able ultimately to overcome their differences by agreeing on a common ideology, but not the Lebanese. The reasons behind the people's failure to develop a bond that would carry them through a crisis is to be found in the country's traditions, the Lebanese self-perception, the country's position in regional conflicts, the American-Israeli design for the area, and the broader Arab views of Lebanon's role in the politics of the Arab world.

THE TWIN CURSE OF GEOGRAPHY AND HISTORY

Geography and history have conspired to deny the Lebanese an opportunity to develop a shared identity with which they might have overcome other disadvantages. As the late Professor Hitti observed, Lebanon is a country rich in time but poor in space; microscopic in size, but microcosmic in influence; it is at the crossroads of the world, astride the great international highway linking three continents (1967, 4), yet unable to control its own destiny. This is the legacy of a people who came together but remained, nevertheless, an "improbable nation."

The country's history is a kaleidoscope of people who have come to inhabit the land and their patterns of loyalty toward central authority. Lebanon did not acquire its present political boundaries, artificial though they might be in terms of the disparate peoples living within them, until 1920. Much of its history until then revolved around Mount Lebanon, a spur of the western range that extends from the Taurus Mountains in the north to the Arabian peninsula in the south. Though some may yearn for an origin among the Phoenicians, the historical facts point to origins in the Syrian region for most of the inhabitants of Lebanon. They had migrated to the mountain fastness of Mount Lebanon to escape the animosity of orthodox majorities, be they Christian or Muslim. This explains in part the lack of a common ancestry or a uniform historical tradition to provide the basis of a nationalism that can transcend localism and sectarianism. It also explains the absence of a common aspiration for an ideologically united political entity.

The topographical variation of the land has affected historically the attitudes of those who settled in it. On the coastal plain, the Canaanite invasion five thousand years ago led to sea-oriented commercial urban centers, especially with the founding of Tyre, Sidon, and Byblos. These developed into sophisticated trading communities. In the Bekaa Valley, east of Mount Lebanon (historical Coele Syria), villages were founded by migratory Arabs, during the Islamic era, with Shiite villages appearing in the Baalbak area and Greek Christian (both Orthodox and Catholic) villages dotting the eastern slope of Mount Lebanon, facing the Bekaa. In the fifth and sixth centuries of the Christian era Maronites fleeing Orthodox and Jacobite Christian persecution left their original homeland in northern Syria and established themselves in hamlets in the northern half of the Lebanon Range. Those who became Druzes in the eleventh century set up their villages along the southern end of that range. All sought security and escape from intolerance. They dwelt in relative isolation from each other. Their social and religious values differed, often sharply, reinforced by the dictates of geography and topography. Along the coastal and interior plains "contact, exchange, transfusion, transformation, transition became . . . the keynotes of the historical process as it unfolds itself in its lowlands . . . in its highlands conservatism, self-containment, independence, isolation and insulation became the key words to the understanding of the history" (Hitti 1967, 5).

The ways of the inhabitants were thus shaped by the constraints of environment. "The mountain impressed its rugged character upon its people. While the Nile tends to unite Egypt . . . the Lebanon, especially through its valleys and hills, tends to divide its inhabitants. City-states were the rule in Phoenicia. Self-contained nationalistic or semi-nationalistic communities have been the rule in modern times . . . groups live side by side displaying each its peculiar ethnic, social and cultural characteristics" (ibid., 7).

The vagaries of history brought Maronites and Druzes into Mount Lebanon, and Greek Christians and Sunni and Shiite Muslims into the plains; in recent times new elements have come: Assyrians (to which former president Chamoun belonged) and Armenians, both of which had fled persecution in their original lands, Iraq and Turkey, respectively. In Lebanon, the land of refugees from times immemorial, all "were allowed . . . an opportunity to live their own lives in their own ways. The minority of the plain may thrive in the mountain to become a majority, the heterodoxy to an orthodoxy. Maronites, Druzes and Shi'ites (Matāwilah) develop into nationalities or quasi-nationalities—and so they remain" (ibid., 8).

The history of Lebanon is proof of the independence fostered in mountains and vales. Even invaders were quick to perceive the prudence of permitting inhabitants autonomy over their own affairs. From Arabs to Mamluks to Turks, rulers found it more politic to bribe the inhabitants into submission than to demand loyalty from them. The fortunate few who were able to command their loyalty either by the display of overwhelming power or by political shrewdness succeeded in carving out petty dynasties for themselves. Two that come to mind are Fakhr al-Dīn al-Ma'nī II (d. 1635) and Bashīr al-Shihābī II (d. 1850). Both were able to create the rudiments of a social structure based on families, towns, and regional links in what has been described as a "sophisticated economic-political-personalistic system" (Salem 1982, 9). But bringing together these diverse entities into one political order did not lead to a coherent, independent nation. The inhabitants both then and in recent times coexisted, sometimes in tension, sometimes in peace.

Efforts to impose direct and lasting rule over Mount Lebanon in 1841 lasted only a year. Maneuvers to extend provincial control over the area from 1842 to 1845 led to two civil wars, direct intervention by foreign powers, and, following the 1860 massacres, rule by an outsider agreed upon by both the legitimate Ottoman government and the great European powers, who supervised the end of the bloody events of 1860.

Lebanon's history during these turbulent and unsettled years proved again that only men of great personal ability and charisma could command the obedience of the inhabitants and draw together the disparate groups.

TRADITION OF POLITICAL INSTABILITY

In the eighteenth century Maronites and Druzes contended with each other as Qaysis versus Yemenis; in the nineteenth century, the struggle became antifeudal. When feudal lords, both Maronite and Druze, invoked tradition and legitimacy to contain the onslaught of the Maronite clerical party and its supporters in ruling circles, the party called on Muḥammad 'Alī, governor of Egypt, for help in defeating their adversaries. In 1840 the combined forces of the Ottoman sultan and Europe's Quadruple Alliance (Great Britain, Russia, Austria, Prussia) expelled the Egyptians from Syria, of which Mount Lebanon was an appendage. The lords sought to reassert their dominance with the help of the sultan's government and British support. Maronite clerics in turn enlisted the aid of the peasantry against their lords, and the struggle culminated in three bloody encounters between Maronites and Druzes, in 1841, 1845, and 1860. When Maronite lords of Kisrawān defied clerical authority, priests and monks raised their peasantry against them in 1858.

This record of antagonism illustrates how factional ambition took on the coloring of confessionalism as sectarian delineation aroused supporters to action. The politics of gain proved more compelling than loyalty to principle and ideal. Ironically, these two powerful confessional groups were outsiders viewing domination of the country as their rightful prerogative, and both relied on foreign powers (the British and French in the past, Israelis and Americans today) to achieve their ambitions.

This tendency to turn to outsiders is rooted in Lebanon's history. The notion that political opportunities could be enhanced by alignments with foreign powers first took hold when the Maronites cooperated with the Crusaders against their fellow Syrians, who were Muslims. Distrust of neighbors continued, with Maronite clerics seeking and obtaining links with Rome, a connection that Fakhr al-Dīn exploited in the seventeenth century for political gain against his Ottoman overlords—which led ultimately to his demise.

Having espoused a creed deemed heretical by both Sunni and Shii Islam, the Druzes entrenched themselves in the mountains of south Mount Lebanon and developed a militant tradition that ensured their survival and separate identity. They abetted directly and indirectly the ambitions of war lords among the Maʿnids and Shihābs to the extent that they stood to benefit from cooperation. Thus Druzes, like Maronites, put themselves in the position of being manipulated against each other in power struggles to the detriment of intercommunal harmony in Mount Lebanon.

The dynastic struggles for political dominance (Maʿnid, 1516–1697, and Shihāb, 1697–1841) prove that central authority can assert itself only when a balance can be struck between powerful sects and confessions, or when the feuding factions can be induced to further their well-being through trade. The lure of economic gain appeared dearer to the hearts of the inhabitants than politics for its own sake. They quickly showed that the business of governing was, and remains, business.

A Lebanon oriented to the West is a tradition rooted in the Phoenician legacy. Geography, not conviction, decreed this orientation. Cut off from inland traffic because of hostile peoples to the east of Mount Lebanon, the inhabitants inevitably turned to the sea, which pointed westward, and the Western nations more often than not responded, not from any love for the Lebanese, but because of their own interests in the eastern Mediterranean. Hence, in the nineteenth century Great Britain became the protector of the Druzes, as France had been for the Maronites since the sixteenth century.

When divisions were sharpened in the post-Egyptian era, a dual administration had to be established in Mount Lebanon in order to appease mistrustful Druzes and Maronites. Even then it took months before representatives of the Quadruple Alliance (Russia, Prussia, Great Britain, and Austria) in cooperation with France and the Ottoman Sublime Porte could arrive at a working formula. Not content with the loss of administrative authority over communicants in the Druze area, the Maronite clergy and their supporters in France continued their agitation against the system until 1860.

A period of relative calm ensued, and the country appeared to settle down politically and to prosper. To Europe went much of the credit for this momentary stabilization of Mount Lebanon. But World War I finally led to one power, France, attaining its centuries-old goal: direct political control of Mount Lebanon. The Maronites were now presented with an opportunity once again to attempt domination of the country's political and administrative systems.

LEGACY OF THE NINETEENTH CENTURY

The nineteenth century witnessed intense struggles by both sides to dominate Mount Lebanon, straining the already tenuous bonds that held the various ethnosectarian groups and sociopolitical factions together. The Egyptian administration (1831–40) attempted change through centralization of authority, but no intercommunal consensus ensued. Indeed, the situation was rendered worse by Muhammad ʿAlī's favoring of Bashīr II, who in turn catered to the Maronite clergy for political support in undermining the traditional authority and privileges of his Druze antagonists. The gap of mistrust widened.

On the other hand, the country experienced increasing contacts with the West, especially France, which supported Muhammad ʿAlī's ambitious undertakings in Syria and his protégé, Amir Bashīr II, who governed the Mount as his proxy. Commerce increased, and Beirut began to flower as a leading urban center, attracting consular establishments and Christian missionaries.

No change, however, characterized the underlying premises of the prevailing social order. No concrete evidence supports the assertion that this period witnessed a transition "from medievalism to modernism" or "feudalism to democracy" (cf. Hitti 1967, 450). The veneer of modernism exhibited in the urban centers of Tripoli and Beirut in the post-Egyptian era was the product more of affectation than ideologically motivated social transformation. The loyalties of the inhabitants remained segmented and parochial, barring any efforts to create a civic or national consciousness. "Confessional, kinship and regional attachments continued to serve as viable sources of communal solidarity" (Khalaf 1979, 13), with no visible commitment of any sort to the ideal of a nation-state as a substitute for narrower loyalties (ibid., 13).

The compartmentalization of social life remained basically unchanged. With rare exceptions (Chevalier 1968, 185), particularly among the Druzes, even social mobility within the ethnosectarian groups was scarcely noticeable prior to the rise of powerful trading families in the coastal cities.

Differentiations were more discernible in the horizontal, not the vertical, structure of Lebanese society, namely, in isolated village communities separated by mountain ridges, spurs, and valleys. Relative isolation served to reinforce separateness and intensify local loyalties based on close attachments to the family and the overlord residing in the village (Polk 1963, 58).

Feuds engendered by such life styles were less the result of confessional or class differences than of partisanship and kinship ties, at least until the first few decades of the nineteenth century. The feudal (iqṭāʿ) system had allowed for some flexibility, security, and relative freedom when viewed in a broader regional perspective. It did not, however, encourage the development of transcommunal loyalties upon which a consensus could be built in the long run.

The historical events of the period attest to the course of rivalry stemming from factional political perspectives. When Aḥmad Jazzār, Ottoman governor of the vilayet (province) of Sidon (1776–1804), to which Mount Lebanon had been appended administratively, tried to hold rival chieftains in check, he could do so only by pitting them against each other, thus encouraging rather than reducing factional rivalries among feudal families, indeed often among members of the same family.

When Napoleon launched his drive on Syria from Egypt, Maronites looked to him, as they had to Saint Louis seven centuries earlier, for assistance in gaining dominance over Lebanon. Their patriarch, Yusuf Tiyyān (1796–1808), pledged his support to Napoleon (Harik 1968, 202). Amir Bashīr II took no chances, and rightly so, because Napoleon was bested by Jazzār before Acre and forced to withdraw.

Following the death of Jazzār, Bashīr suppressed the feudal chieftains of the leading Druze families: Arslāns, Janblāṭs, Abū Nakads, and ʿImāds. To appease the dominant sects he espoused the Maronite faith secretly, Islam openly, and Druzism to the Druze. After leaving Hejaz, the Shihāb family had become Druze, a few Maronites. This juggling of sectarian affiliation helped ensure them some following among the numerous mistrustful factions of Mount Lebanon.

In the eighteenth century the leading Maronite feudal families Ḥubaysh, Daḥdāḥ, and Khāzin had managed to control through appointees from their ranks the high clerical posts of the Maronites. As long as this connection lasted, clergy and feudatories could work together to protect their mutual interests. But in the nineteenth century, the graduates of the Maronite College in Rome—many were of peasant stock—began to challenge the dominance of feudal families in the upper ranks of the clergy, and began to assume the leadership in shaping new sociopolitical attitudes among the peasantry (Khalaf 1979, 40).

This was possible because priests and monks were in close contact with peasants and villagers. Their monasteries employed them; their monks educated them and printed the material they studied. From the schools they supervised came secretarial workers for administrators, notables, and princes. Indeed, scribes and financial controllers, as well as political advisers, came from the ranks of Maronite and Greek Catholic priests and monks. One could count one priest for every two hundred Maronites in Mount Lebanon. Their weight was bound to be felt everywhere (Harik 1968, 154).

Because of the dependence on the clerical institutions, it was inevitable that the clergy should come to exercise strong political influence over the Maronites and, by extension, over the rest of the country. Should their will be defied for some reason, they would not hesitate to raise their communicants against established authority, as happened in 1820, 1841, 1845, 1858, and 1860, when monk and priest armed themselves and led their communicants into battle—not unlike their actions in the 1975 civil war.

The Egyptian administration in Syria (including Mount Lebanon) introduced another tradition into the politics of the land: centralization of political authority by relying on preferential treatment. In this case, the Maronite clergy was favored because of France's support. In exchange for Maronite endorsement of Egyptian undertakings to suppress and disarm the Druzes, the Egyptians allowed the Maronites to keep their arms and took them into the administration as political advisers. Maronites were exempted from many of the public services, like conscription and the corvée, while Druzes were marched off into military service. The Egyptian era contributed much to the hardening of confessional and intersectarian jealousies and distrust.

The widening of the gap socially was matched by a similar development in economics, especially after increased contacts with Europe led to international trade stimulated by the introduction of steam navigation in the 1840s. Beirut, a city of only ten thousand inhabitants a decade earlier, grew during the Egyptian occupation to become the chief center of international trade, a position it has maintained ever since. With prosperity came a liberal lifestyle, and a new middle class did not hesitate to copy European ways. Social and cultural alienation ensued, for the traditional Muslims and Christians considered the new liberal ways an affront not only to decency but to religion as well. As Lady Hester Stanhope put it, "they cherished a feeling of vengeance against those who so openly violated their religious and moral institutions" (1846, 210).

A practice thus was established that has remained the hallmark of affected urban Lebanese society ever since: to maintain this newly acquired life style, luxury goods had to be imported. With little to export in return, it was not long before the imbalance in payments led to a serious drain of gold and silver. This was followed by general inflation, in the late 1830s and early 1840s, accompanied by a rapid rise in the cost of living, as measured in higher rents and food prices (Chevalier 1968, 210). This lopsided trade was fostered by a rising mercantile class (mostly Christian); they prospered, but the majority of the inhabitants did not.

Another development that led to imbalances in Lebanese society was improvement in public health services and facilities; this led to an increase in the population of Christians, since they were the primary beneficiaries of the improvements. Formerly Druze cities in Mount Lebanon like Dayr al-Qamar and Jezzin became populated mainly by Maronites and Greek Catholics, who constituted the artisan and merchant class. These two cities, like Zahle on the eastern slope facing the Bekaa, came to serve as centers of agitation in challenging Druze dominance even in Druze areas. Unable to match the Druzes in fighting prowess in battles urged by their clergy, Maronites and Greek Catholics began to turn to European consuls for political support and "protection," thus introducing another complication to the Lebanese scene: blatant abuse of the protégé system already strongly resented by ruling Ottoman circles, the overseers for Mount Lebanon. Inviting in the foreigner meant a challenge to Ottoman sovereign rights in Syria through unwelcome greater European interference in their domestic affairs. It also led to the granting of immunity to Maronites and Greek Catholics through the extraterritorial rights acquired by the major European powers over the centuries. Such open dependence on outside powers led to defiance of legitimate authority and only served to exacerbate tense relations between the confessional groups (millets), since the Muslim majority could now view the Christian minorities as a fifth column. Growing resentment became intense following the Crimean War, and led to outbursts against Christians, both European and native, in Jidda, northern Syria, and Mount Lebanon (1858–60).

Growing imbalances in society only served to intensify suspicion and hostile relations between the sects. Maronite disarming of Druzes in 1838 was not different in aim from Maronite-Phalange disarming of Shiites in West Beirut in 1982. In both instances only one side was disarmed. Inviting the Egyptians into the area in 1830 is no different from inviting the Israelis in 1982, since Maronite leadership on both occasions saw in the military prowess of a neighboring power an opportunity to promote its own political hegemony over Lebanon.

Thus the gap was widening socially, economically, and politically. The problems of the country were internationalized, as was its politics. Mistrust and hostility among the sects continued to grow.

Attempts to ameliorate the situation by introducing strong central government responsive to the interests of all citizens came to naught. Entrenched political interests among the feudal and clerical classes made this effort impossible. Resistance to change was made in the name of preserving autonomous privileges and rights. The dual system of administration (1842–60) was a mere palliative, as was the *wakīl* system, tailored to shield the folk from their overlords. Reforms launched by the Ottoman sultan through the imperial edicts of 1839 and 1856 did not filter down to Mount Lebanon, since the clerical chiefs of the millets were not about to give up their administrative prerogatives.

Throughout the nineteenth century, Mount Lebanon expected, and received, little reprieve from an oppressive socioeconomic system and the politics that promoted it. With insecurity widespread, citizens were reluctant to give up their arms. When systematic efforts were launched to disarm them, they managed then, as today, to conceal their arms in difficult-to-locate caches in the mountains and vales of Lebanon. In the coastal cities, councils that had been established to hear citizen complaints consolidated their authority over those who were to be checked, since they alone were familiar with the ways of serving as intermediaries between citizens and local government.

Following upheavals in Mount Lebanon, the population tended to gravitate toward the coastal cities, and among the immigrants were notables and feudal elements. They came to ally themselves with kindred sectarians, sometimes with nonsectarians—Druzes of Mount Lebanon with Muslims of the cities—creating new political alignments that were to persist until the 1980s (Hourani 1968, 62–63).

As the period of the dual administration drew to a close, it was characterized by uncertainty and insecurity due to worsening economic and social conditions. Exploitation of the peasants and heavy taxation encouraged them to abandon agriculture and to emigrate to escape improverishment (Smilianskaya 1966, 234). The ever-growing deficit of trade resulted in sharp economic and social imbalances, widening the gap between the haves and have-nots and aggravating confessional tensions.

In the Maronite districts, it was the peasantry that led the uprising against their feudal lords in the Kisrawān of 1858. Encouraged by priests and headed by a new element, "the strong man" (za'īm), the rebels rooted out feudal domination, set up their own administrative government, and gathered local authority into their own hands, thus establishing a tradition that the Phalange continued with great vigor after the 1975 civil war.

The 1860 massacres introduced another morbid tradition: large scale, senseless slaughter of the innocent accompanied by massive dislocations. In a hideous war launched by the Maronite clergy in what they termed "a war to the knife," twelve thousand of their followers and innocent Greek Christians perished in Mount Lebanon and Damascus; an additional four thousand perished as destitutes, and up to one hundred thousand were rendered homeless. Property losses exceeded £4 million. The hatred generated by this tragedy only served to deepen sectarian feelings, which manifested themselves again in Tel Zaatar, Karantina, and Damour in 1976, and in Shatila and Sabra in 1982.

REPRIEVE UNDER THE MUTAṢARRIFĪYA

Europe stepped in directly to find a solution for the Lebanon problem in 1861, as it did again with the United States in 1982, because the inhabitants so mistrusted each other that they could not arrive at a compromise government. With a large expeditionary French force on the scene, commissioners of the Quadruple Alliance, working closely with Fuʾād Pasha, Ottoman High Commissioner, devised the Réglement Définitif, which set up the administration of the Mutaṣarrifīya. Unable to agree on a governor from their midst, the feuding factions had to settle for an appointee by the sultan's government: Dāʾūd Pasha, a Greek Catholic Armenian who had served hitherto as a postal clerk in Istanbul. Under his rule the Lebanon experienced a period of unusual peace and productivity.

A twelve-page document serving as a constitution, the Réglement set up an administration headed by a *mutaṣarrif* (governor) and aided by an administrative council of twelve members elected to represent the confessional groups (thus introducing the principle of government by sectarian apportionment). The Réglement established seven districts for local administrative purposes (confined again strictly to Mount Lebanon), each headed by a deputy administrator and subdivided in turn into directorships. All offices were partly appointive and partly elective in order to ensure support from vested interests represented by notables, feudal chieftains, and ecclesiastics. Judicial authority was discharged in villages by chiefs and shaykhs in minor cases of adjudication, while priests preserved jurisdiction over personal matters.

Feudal privileges were legally abolished and citizens were assured equal rights under the law—at least on paper. The Réglement of 1861, like that of Chekib Efendi (Ottoman High Commissioner) of 1845, served notice that confessionalism was to continue as the criterion for making official appointments to government posts, ostensibly for the purpose of maintaining a balance between the sects. A system based on mistrust, not on competence, was thus perpetuated.

Unhappy with the principle of equal representation on the administrative council, Maronites agitated for a modification of the Réglement in the 1864 supplement. The changes introduced led to another tradition, namely, the proportional representation on a decreasing ratio basis: four seats for Maronites, three for Druzes, two for Greek Orthodox, and one each for Greek Catholics, Shiites, and Sunnis. Politicized confessionalism was now legally enshrined, and so it has remained.

Under the *mutaṣarrifs*, basic services were initiated and fostered. Industry received special attention. Bureaucracy underwent reform, as did the educational and judicial systems. The economy was gradually transformed from a subsistence one to a broader market system, which brought shifts in social positions. While traditional ties of fealty and primordial loyalties survived, the more exploitative features of feudalism declined. Outside the confessional system, a new aristocracy was coming into its own, nurtured by educational opportunities denied most of the inhabitants. Resourcefulness, energy, and adaptability enabled this urban aristocracy to prosper. Education thus remained restricted to those in contact with the foreign missions that promoted it, and imbalances in economy and society were far from redressed.

Disparities thus continued to underlie confessional enmity, particularly when the upper echelons among Christians and Sunnis appeared to benefit from their strategic locations in urban centers. While they acquired wealth and status, the bulk of the population continued at a subsistence level. Jealousies were aroused when public posts were passed on to family members without regard to merit. The rise of a new social group did not usually replace an outmoded or disliked one, but merely added one more element to the social order. And a complex social pattern of behavior can be quickly rendered intolerable when every new element in the social order represents a new vested interest to be served.

Disdain for duly constituted authority also stems from the nineteenth century. Under the Ottomans, heads of millets usually received their investiture from the sultan. The Maronite patriarchs, though welcoming the investiture, did not attach importance to it. They viewed themselves as promoters and defenders of a Christian autonomy in Mount Lebanon. Their influence reached down the hierarchy to priests and monks, who in turn instructed communicants on how to react when political exigencies might not favor clerical interests. And in their eagerness to protect and promote their authority, the Maronite clergy tended to oppose any movement that might threaten their concept of a Christian Lebanon. They fought Arabism, Nasserism, Syrian Nationalism, and Baʻth Socialism in recent times just as vigorously as Ottomanism and Druze hegemony a century earlier.

The tendency toward incivility in public discharge of responsibility, resorting to a bribe (*rüshvet* to the Ottomans) to obtain services that a citizen is entitled to by virtue of citizenship, corruption on the part of privilege seekers and dispensers, and the rise of a class of hangers-on—in recent years, feeding the militias of contending factions—all had their roots in the late Mutaṣarrifīya period, only to become permanent fixtures of Lebanon during the French mandate and after.

LEGACY OF THE FRENCH MANDATE

World War I ended one occupation and ushered in another, and the Lebanese were none the wiser for it. Although both Christians and Muslims suffered deprivation and martyrdom in resisting the military government of the Young Turks, this experience did not impress upon them the need for strengthening intercommunal ties and acquiring an identity of their own. Far from alleviating the sufferings occasioned by rampant confessionalism, the aftermath of World War I seemed to consecrate the institutions that fostered this disease. The Lebanese once again went about pursuing political, economic, and social opportunities on the basis of sectarian identification. More interested in furthering its own ends than in redressing imbalances, the French regime found it politic to perpetuate the status quo and to render confessionalism the basis of social relations. But by expanding the area of Mount Lebanon into what became "Le grand Liban" after 1920, France inadvertently hurt the Maronite cause, the element it had catered to since the days of Francis I. By appending to the original area the coastal and inland plains, France incorporated into the new political boundaries enough Sunnis, Shiites, and Greek Christians to render its Maronite protégés a minority element. The Muslims and Greek Christians were reluctant citizens of an expanded Lebanon, and continued to view with sympathy any nationalist movement that might reattach them to the mother country of Greater Syria. The Maronites were more resolved to preserve Lebanese separatism and ensure their political dominance.

The new Lebanon that General Goureaud ushered into being on 1 September 1920 at Syria's expense was now double its earlier size and 50 percent more populous. The apportionment of government positions according to sectarian affiliation continued. With the exception of the very first president (Dabbās), who turned out to be an Orthodox Christian, every president has been a Maronite. The premiership became the monopoly of the Sunnis; the presidency of the Chamber of Deputies, the monopoly of the Shiites. The formula was based on a "gentleman's agreement" that has been rendered sacrosanct over time under the heading of the National Pact of 1943.

To appease the other sects, the Foreign Ministry became the domain of the Greek Orthodox, and the Defense Ministry, of the Druze, until recently, when the president decided to place a Maronite in charge of this critical office. In theory the president and cabinet were responsible to the chamber, but by virtue of his power to issue laws by decree, the president gained control not only of the cabinet (including the office of the prime minister) but of the cabinet officers' activities as well.

According to the provisions of the constitution, "for the sake of justice and amity, the sects shall be equitably represented in public employment and in the composition of the Ministry" (Article 95). All Lebanese were held to be equal before the law, to enjoy civil and political rights, and to be bound equally by public obligations and duties without distinction (Article 7). The constitution further provides that every Lebanese shall have the right to hold public office with preference being shown only on the basis of merit and competence (Article 12).

The record of the Lebanese in recent decades shows the extent of their departure from the high idealism of the constitution. The document speaks of "citizens," but the inhabitants do not agree on who qualifies as a citizen. A whole generation of Palestinian Lebanese was nurtured and raised on Lebanese soil but never extended right of citizenship. Maronites came to insist that all those born abroad of Lebanese ancestry should be counted as Lebanese, even down to the third generation American, African, or Australian. The reason is in the numbers. More Maronites counted meant more government positions at home for relatives, particularly important because the overwhelming majority of early emigrants were Christian. It has been estimated that by this mode of reckoning two-thirds of Christian Lebanese are residents of other countries, indeed, third generation citizens with only vague notions of the old country.

The 1932 census, though questionable, remains the sole basis for apportionment. It shows a total citizenry of 785,543 people, of whom 392,544 were Christian, with the Maronite element accounting for 226,378 (Himadeh 1936, 408–9). The general consensus of scholars is that today the Muslims constitute a decisive majority, but the Maronite presidency has persistently resisted all demands for a new census lest the new record of the population remove the Maronite advantage.

In spite of the inequities inherent in this system it managed to survive as the basic formula for coexistence among the sects until 1958, when the system received a severe jolt. The crisis of that year was occasioned by allegations of widespread corruption in the elections held the previous year, by the insistence of President Camille Chamoun on a second term in contravention of the letter of the constitution, by his invoking assistance under the Eisenhower Doctrine when the 1943 pact clearly stipulated that Lebanon would not invoke foreign interference against Arab interests, and by fears that the newly created United Arab Republic of Syria and Egypt might seek to force Lebanon into joining.

Tension among sectarian and political groups increased sharply and riots broke out from Tyre to Tripoli, which Chamoun used as a justification for inviting in the U.S. Marines. Ten thousand landed, not to save Chamoun and Lebanon from Communism, but to make sure that Brigadier Qāsim's successful coup in Iraq did not unsettle Jordan.

Chamoun's strategy backfired. He soon found himself out of office, replaced in the next elections by Fu'ād Shihāb, commander in chief of the army. But with Shihāb's election little changed in the political process, except for an adjustment in the formula that directed six Muslims for every six Christians in government appointments. In the chamber the ratio of six to five remained, in favor of Christians.

PALESTINE IN LEBANON

The influx of large numbers of Palestinian refugees after 1948 left an indelible mark on the politics of Lebanon. Their presence in ever-increasing numbers (six hundred thousand, by recent estimates) together with the shift of PLO operations to Beirut after 1970 did much to exacerbate tensions among confessional groups.

It is interesting to note that the 1982 invasion of Lebanon by Israel was code named "Peace for Galilee," and was one of three campaigns waged by them on Palestinians of Galilee: in April-May 1948, in October 1948, and in June 1982. In 1948 the Hagannah drove the Galileans across the border into Lebanon; in 1982 the Israel Defense Forces sought to crush resistance in the very heart of Lebanon.

For thirty-four years the unwanted made do as best they could in subhuman conditions, "enclosed within walls of hostility and suspicion . . . and treated as aliens" (Jansen 1982e, 9). Their consuming passion from the start of their forcible exile into Lebanon was to return home. "Everything they did in Lebanon flowed from that fact" (ibid.). Lebanese authorities moved them north to ensure that Palestinians did not steal across the border to help themselves to their own homes and fields, now in the possession of Israelis. About one-half were settled around Sidon, the other half scattered north, to camps set up in Qar'ūn, 'Anjar, Baalbak, Tripoli, and Beirut. But though broken up as a group, "the social structures they bore with them into exile survived, reinforcing their sense of national identity in an alien environment" (ibid.).

They resisted permanent settlement in Lebanon, and that suited the Lebanese government well as neither side wanted more than a temporary stay. Although they were to have a definite rank for jobs, it turned out to be highly discriminatory; hence they chose to become as self-sufficient as possible. They founded and operated their own educational and basic service facilities, including a relatively elaborate cottage industry. They endorsed every Arab ideology that called for their return to Palestine.

The turning point in the Palestinian struggle to return home was 1967. The war of that year brought the rest of Palestine under direct Israeli control. This meant that resistance under the provisions of international law could develop as a legitimate undertaking of Palestinians forcibly dispossessed of Palestine. As a preliminary step toward organized resistance in and outside Palestine, Palestinian leaders sought to consolidate control over the camps. The Palestine Liberation Organization (PLO) began to raise and train resistance forces.

This "revolution," however, was as much socioeconomic as it was political, because it attracted to its cause many poor and downtrodden Lebanese: stateless Kurds, Druzes, Shiites, non-Maronite Christians, and lower middle-class Sunni Muslims. In December 1975, when a coalition of some of these groups was engaging the militias of the Maronites (Phalange) in the hotel district of Beirut and was about to be defeated, they called upon Palestinian allies for support. The Palestinians were thus drawn into a real revolution, that of the underprivileged Lebanese (the nationalist forces) against the privileged Maronites and upper middle-class Sunnis who silently supported the Phalange.

However reluctant a partner in the civil war, the PLO soon realized that it could not rise above the anarchy that had brought in the Syrian forces against them. Palestinian political cadres were unable to impose law and order in areas affected by combat. In the south, PLO fighters took charge of villages and towns, and created what the Lebanese called a state-within-a-state. This served to alienate many of their Shii supporters, who had come under Israeli attack by air, land, and sea.

THE CIVIL WAR: IMPACT AND AFTERMATH

The presence of large numbers of Palestinians constituted a potent force in Lebanese politics, and this threatened to deprive the Maronites of their political predominance in a country they had treated as their own. Palestinian guerrilla activities against Israel also proved disruptive of Israeli efforts to establish a stable relationship inside and outside the country. Guerrilla activities often provoked heavy retaliation, directed as much against Lebanese villagers as against Palestinian camps.

It is a thinly disguised fact that Israel seeks the waters of the Litani River. If the population in the south could be displaced through bombardments targeted at Lebanese civilians, a hitherto reluctant Lebanese government might take action against the PLO; and should it fail to do so, as reasonably anticipated in view of the army's failure to respond during sectarian feuds, then Israel would be justified in taking action, as indeed it did in 1982. Inaction by the Lebanese government not only gave Israel the pretext needed to invade in 1978 and again in 1982, but also served to arouse the indignation of the Muslim population. The nationalist-leftist coalition was driven to side with the PLO, thus adding further strain to an already weakened political system.

In 1969 the strain of internal discord led to a succession of government resignations and further increased tension among Lebanese factions (Chamie 1976/77, 175). In 1973, the Maronite-led Lebanese armed forces struck at Palestinian refugee camps in attempts to engage their fighters. This merely aroused the indignation of Palestinian supporters in Lebanon. In 1974 a showdown appeared inevitable; both sides began preparations for it by training men and enlarging their militias. They acquired heavy weapons ranging from machine guns to artillery to light armor. In 1975 the Israelis helped to ignite the war by heavy bombardment of Lebanese villages on the pretext of getting at the PLO. There were provocative incidents in the south and in Sidon, where the fishermen's strike led to the death of five soldiers. On 13 April 1975 the Phalange stopped a bus carrying Palestinians and Lebanese supporters and killed twenty-seven of them in ʿAyn al-Rummāna, a suburb of Beirut, allegedly in retaliation for the killing of a prominent Phalangist even though the assailant was not identified.

A week of violence ensued, but the Lebanese government took no action to stop the killings. The prime minister resigned in protest. President Franjieh unexpectedly appointed a military cabinet. Objections were voiced, because the officers corps was predominantly Christian Maronite with close ties to the Phalange and their militias.

The deteriorating situation prompted a number of progressive elements, both Christian and Muslim, to present a list of demands to the government. High on the list was the reform of the electoral law, in order to allow more equitable representation in government and the reduction of sectarianism as a criterion for appointment to office. They argued for greater social and economic equality for all citizens.

While the Phalange published a statement, on 24 August 1975, agreeing that such reforms were desirable, they and other supporters argued for a gradual evolution in that direction. Other Maronite organizations—National Liberal party of Camille Chamoun, Zgharta Liberation Army of Sulayman Franjieh, the Guardians of the Cedars, and the Maronite Monastic Order—supported the Phalange in this delay tactic.

The progressive forces, consisting of reform-minded Christians and Muslims, Muslim traditionalists, and Palestinians of all political positions (Syrian Nationalists, Syrian Baʿthis, Iraqi Baʿthis, October 24 Movement, Movement of the Deprived, Independent Nasserite, Popular Nasserite, Union of Popular Labor Forces, Nasserite Corrective Movement, and the Arab Socialist Union [Salibi 1976, 165; Deeb 1980, xiii–xiv for full listings]), insisted the system had become too corrupt to endure for another generation. Besides being ineffective, it was unstable and strongly biased in favor of Maronite communal interests. They wanted this bias tempered with more representation for Muslims in the Chamber of Deputies, to equal at least that of the Christians. They also argued for a more equitable balance of power between the prime minister and the president, and a larger role for the Muslims in the armed forces, particularly in the higher echelons of command hitherto monopolized by Maronites and Greek Catholics.

Lack of upward mobility in party and factional leadership contributed considerably to the imbalances of Lebanese society. For a quarter of a century men like Rashid Karami, Camille Chamoun, Kamal Jumblat, Pierre Gemayel, Sulayman Franjieh, and Raymond Edde dominated the political scene, whether they were in or out of office. Many carried on feuds with each other because of longstanding personal grudges.

No less significant are the gaps separating demographically, socially, and economically the inhabitants of Lebanon. The war that ensued was waged conveniently under the guise of "Christian versus Muslim" in order to gain the sympathy of the Christian West, but in reality it was a war between the haves and have-nots. Statistics reveal that the incomes of Christian groups (Maronite and Greek) were substantially higher on the average than those of Muslims (Shiites and lower-echelon Sunnis) (Chamie 1976/77, 179, table 2).

The educational level of Christians was also higher, and enabled them to advance in their professions. They had three times as many positions in technical and professional occupations as did the Shiites. Over 30 percent of the latter were confined to low-paying labor positions.

The higher rate of population growth among Muslims could not help but affect Lebanese politics, particularly in the distribution of government posts. Even if the 1932 census were considered an honest one, a census held today would show that the Maronites are a distinct minority of Lebanese when compared to all other sects taken as a whole.

The lack of a uniform educational system had contributed to this situation. Each community had its own schools and curricula. Numerous foreign schools (American, French, German, Italian) added to the confusion by presenting a variety of Western models. Disharmony in society was being fostered in the classroom: different educational approaches led to sharply differing perspectives on what should constitute Lebanon. All that the Ministry of Education could do was to maintain bureaucratic and procedural unification. Lebanon clearly lacked an adequate educational system based on one standard curriculum and aspiring to inculcate a strong sense of identification with the existing Lebanon, not that in the dreams of the emigrants.

Sectarians also lived in ghettos: Maronites in Zgharta, Kisrawān, and Batrūn; Sunnis in Beirut, Tripoli, and ʿAkkār; Druzes in the Shūf; Shiites in south Beirut and south Lebanon; and Greeks in Kūra and smaller enclaves in the Matn, the coastal cities, and Bekaa. The city of Beirut was a mosaic of ghettos.

Personal identification also exhibited sharp differences according to sect. The upper echelons of all sects shared one thing in common: emulation of European-American ways in language, dress, and social habits. The lower-level Maronites clung tenaciously to their conception of a Christian Lebanon, while Muslims looked to Arab coreligionists and their common Arab-Islamic heritage for identification. Shiites shared a common spiritual heritage with Iran, while Maronites remained steadfast in their conviction that they were Mediterraneans.

The government, however, rarely reflected or balanced the diverse views of the people. Maronites and Phalangists refused to allow either a new census or modification of the so-called National Pact of 1943, which was devised initially, reportedly, for the purpose of maintaining stability and harmony by balancing confessional interests (Rondot 1955, 251). Muslims accused Maronites and the president of steadily undermining the authority of the prime minister, by usurping the authority vested in the premiership. Educated elites and liberal progressives were excluded from political involvement because of the monopoly held by a handful of families: Gemayels of Matn, Khāzins of Kisrawān, Franjiehs of Zgharta, Jumblats of Shūf, Assads (Shiites) of the south, and Karamis (Sunnis) of Tripoli. Educated elites and liberal technocrats with vision and perspective tried to inject some reform into the system of taxation and education during the 1970s but failed because of the inflexibility of the political process. The central government proved deaf to public demands for political and social change.

Corruption thus continued, and agents of disruption roamed the streets at will, undermining what little cohesiveness remained. Whoever could evade taxes did so—especially businessmen and professionals. Feuds and conflicts were settled outside the legal system, often by brute force. Senseless killings became commonplace. Conflicts of interest were blatant, without any reflection: men like Chamoun could hold the post of minister of the interior and command a militia force in the civil war at the same time. There was no mechanism for translating the will of the public into legislation, or to enforce decisions legitimately arrived at by duly constituted authority. The Lebanese political system continued to be "a unique form not of governing, but of non-government" (Barakat 1979, 12–13).

It was inevitable that the strong should impose their will on the weak, and limited interest supersede the larger interest of the public. When bartering for favors failed, the whole system collapsed. The malaise was too deeply rooted in the body politic to be cured by superficial political palliatives. Loyalty could be invoked only by appeal to sectarian, not national, interest. Political community followed sectarian, not national, lines. Confessionalism, not a national ideal, motivated the communities. Parties revolved around priest and za'īm ("the strong man"), and the force necessary to defend and impose the will of the few was available in a number of paramilitary organizations: Phalange for the Maronites, Murābiṭūn for the Shiites, and the like.

Institutions developed over the years merely reinforced confessional separatism. Government was seen as another medium for gaining wealth and prestige, not as an instrument for furthering some national ideal that did not exist, except in the mystical yearning of the emigrant. As newly appointed foreign minister Elie Salem put it, "every conflict in Lebanon in recent history has given rise to confessional zealotry and has almost destroyed the delicate web which has held Lebanese society together" (1982, 4).

A laissez-faire economic policy has had an equally devastating impact on confessional equilibrium, leading over the years to open economic disorder and giving rise to rapidly increasing inflation while the government simply watched. There has never been an effective economic planning policy that might have ensured a fair share of benefits to the poorer districts of the country. South Lebanon, for example, has always been treated by the central government as marginal territory to be kept in isolation from the mainstream of development. The majority of the inhabitants were Shiites who had suffered both military blows from Israel and economic neglect from their own government; their archaic social structure, dominated by a few feudal families, had proved ineffective in eliciting legitimate help from the government. It is logical that they would strike back in the 1975 war (Sharif 1978, 9).

In ignoring pressing socioeconomic problems in the poorer areas of the south and Bekaa, the government gave the impression that its main economic purpose was to serve the interests of the entrepreneurial and commercial classes. As the gap separating the haves and have-nots continued to widen, the government pursued an ethnosectarian configuration: upper-echelon Sunnis and Christians were the enriched haves; Shiites, Palestinians, and Kurds the impoverished have-nots. The contrast could be seen in the opulence of the Hamra district of Beirut and the Karantina's squalor in East Beirut.

Differences in regional development were equally sharp. The unrestrained free enterprise system, fostered and served by organized government, ignored much needed public services. Poverty went on unameliorated (Washington Post, 27 November 1975, K21). The concentration of wealth can be seen in capital distribution: 4 percent of the population in the 1970s controlled 35 percent of all earned income; 50 percent had 20 percent of it; and 46 percent of the population secured only 30 percent of overall income.

Disparity was further manifest in the people's levels of expectation and achievement. The process began during the presidency of Bechara al-Khoury (1946–52), continued under that of Camille Chamoun (1952–58), and abated somewhat under Fu'ad Shihāb (1958–64) and Charles Helou (1964–70), when the gap was nearly bridged. But with the influx of Palestinian refugees after the 1967 Arab-Israeli war, President Sulayman Franjieh (1970–76) found it difficult to prevent a return to wider discrepancies. Rapid urbanization, modernization, and conspicuous wealth only served to strengthen the resolve of have-nots to have done with the whole system.

The situation was made worse by the influx of Arab and foreign capital, especially after 1973. Those well positioned in government and financial circles (largely Sunni Muslims and Maronite Christians) became the primary beneficiaries of sudden gains, much of which "never filtered down to the working people" (Hovespian 1981). Prosperity and apparent stability merely camouflaged bitter social resentments.

PRELUDE TO DISASTER: 1976–82

When brought under control in November 1976, the civil war had claimed up to fifty thousand lives. The army had disintegrated along sectarian lines, and the League of Arab States had authorized a peace-keeping force to help maintain security in Lebanon. The Syrians provided the bulk of this force. And while Syrian troops supported the Phalangists against the Palestinians in the last phase of the fighting, they did not involve themselves in the happenings in south Lebanon, where the PLO kept up its harassment of Israeli settlements and invited retaliation.

Lebanon was in complete disarray, both politically and socially. Numerous factions appeared, each to defend or promote its own well-being and each backed by its own armed militias. They ruled the streets of the capital in the absence of security and army units. Elias Sarkis had been elected president with the support of the Syrians, and the latter assumed the role of maintaining some order while being sniped at from all sides.

Domestic instability continued to characterize Lebanon in the aftermath of the civil war. The political balance was now tipped in favor of the Phalangists. The PLO moved its operations to the south and set up its own government in the areas it controlled in and out of Beirut, as did the Amal party, representing the Shiites and backed by the Murābiṭūn, its militia. Syrian forces were hard pressed to put out the numerous fires generated by the opposing militias.

Seeking to discourage the PLO from its forays into Israel, the Israel Defense Forces launched an invasion of south Lebanon early in March 1978 under the code name Operation Litani. The United Nations typically demanded cessation of hostilities and retreat behind borders. It authorized the dispatch of the United Nations Interim Force to south Lebanon to keep Palestinians and Israelis apart. The force took its position on 23 March 1978 in an area ten miles inside the Lebanese borders. Within a six-mile buffer zone Israel recruited former Lebanese army major Saʿd Haddad and his mercenaries to secure their border against the PLO and harass the guerrillas, now estimated at twenty thousand, entrenched in the rugged hills of the south. Haddad was armed, trained, and financed by Israel. Upon withdrawing from Lebanon in June, the Israelis handed over the zone to Haddad and his militia.

Through an understanding worked out by then secretary of state Henry Kissinger, President Assad of Syria, and Foreign Minister Allon of Israel, Israel agreed to tolerate Syrian contingents in the Arab deterrent force dispatched to Lebanon provided they stayed behind the so-called red line drawn at the Litani River in the Bekaa (Peretz 1982, 50–51). Lebanon was now being held both militarily and politically hostage by domestic factions and foreign forces.

In 1980 Bashir Gemayel, intelligent, educated, and ruthless, assumed command of the Phalange and set out to bring all Maronite militias under his control; he intensified his efforts when the alliance of Chamoun's Aḥrār (Liberal party), Franjieh's backers, and the Phalange appeared shaky, breaking up eventually over jealousies and territorial control. Launching a surprise attack, Gemayel's men brutally massacred the leadership of the Aḥrār at a bathing party to which they had been invited. The much weaker forces of Franjieh sought safety in their own district around Zgharta. The priest-led Guardians of the Cedars submitted, and Gemayel thus emerged as the unchallenged spokesman of the Maronite militias, now restyled the Lebanese Forces, with political control from East Beirut to Zgharta.

Among the diverse Druze-Muslim factions, Walid Jumblat's Druze Socialist party and the Shiites' Amal party emerged successful. Both joined with the Palestinians of West Beirut and south Lebanon. But the Amal party and the PLO soon developed differences over PLO actions that invited Israeli retaliation against Shiite villages in the south.

Traditional alliances had become blurred in the aftermath of the civil war. "Syrians fought Palestinians inside Lebanon; Lebanese Moslems and Israelis made alliances; some Christians allied themselves with Israelis in the south; others joined with Syrians in the north; Christians fought other Christians; Palestinians fought each other; and Lebanese troops had to confront all of the factions" ("The Lebanon: A Land Torn . . ." 1981, 179). Assassinations routinely led to fighting and more killings. Gemayel's men assassinated Tony Franjieh, the former president's son, because he was considered a Syrian ally. The year before, on 16 March 1977, Kamal Jumblat had been assassinated under circumstances implicating Syrian intelligence. Jumblat had been leading the demand for Franjieh's resignation before the expiration of his term and the Syrians would not endorse this, thus involving themselves in Lebanese feuds on the side of the Christians. When Franjieh bowed to pressure and authorized early elections (May 1976), the Syrians made sure their candidate, Elias Sarkis, a trained economist with no record of factional commitments, was elected president; Jumblat had supported the candidacy of Raymond Edde. The latter had been outspoken in his attack on the Syrians for their involvements in Lebanon, and finally fled to Paris for safety. President Assad branded Yasir Arafat a fool for opposing Syrian intervention and set out to crush Palestinian fighting, in September 1976.

The Syrians were in Lebanon by virtue of an agreement reached by Arab leaders at Riyadh, Saudi Arabia, on 17 and 18 October. The plan had been approved by Cairo, and called for a deterrent force of thirty thousand men to be placed under the control of President Sarkis, who had asked for a direct Arab role in the pacification of Lebanon.

While the Phalangists recognized the role of the Syrians in saving them from destruction at the hands of the Palestinians, they felt restrained by the presence of Syrian forces in Lebanon, particularly when Kissinger and U.S. ambassador Dean Brown had negotiated their presence. They became mistrustful of the United States when Franjieh let it be known that both Kissinger and Brown had recommended a solution to Maronite anxieties by encouraging their emigration to Canada, United States, and Australia (Nader 1982a, 27). To the Phalange this recommendation was tantamount to depopulating Lebanon of its Christians to make room for a Palestine state in Lebanon.

Such fears and suspicions only served to strengthen Phalangist resolve to drive the Palestinians from their midst. Since Israel shared Phalangist anxieties concerning the Palestinians, it was only a matter of time before Bashir Gemayel could be expected to enter into secret negotiations with the Israelis for an alliance that would secure them military training, equipment, and support. The die was cast. The showdown was inevitable. As one Phalangist taxi driver told this writer in April 1978, "there is one more big one [battle] ahead."

TRIGGERING THE "BIG ONE"

The facts now indicate that Israel's invasion of Lebanon in June 1982 was not simply for the purpose of destroying the Palestinian menace, though this was the pretext given the world, with some credibility. The so-called military threat of the PLO was highly exaggerated, and for a whole year prior to the invasion, Lebanon's border with Israel rarely experienced such calm.

As events toward the end of 1982 clearly reveal, Israel's main purpose for invading Lebanon was to secure "normalization of relations" with a country helplessly prostrate militarily, politically, and socially. The term "normalization" is a euphemism for political recognition, or, better, a peace treaty.

To be sure, Israeli leadership had been concerned for some time with the growing international respectability of the PLO when Israel had labored to picture it and its supporters as common terrorists entitled neither to rights nor to legitimacy. Israel sought to nip in the bud the PLO's growing political respectability and ability to command a hearing in the diplomatic capitals of the world after having been granted recognition by the United Nations, which admitted a delegation of Palestinians as observers.

There is much circumstantial evidence to show that the Israelis had a tacit understanding with certain elements in the United States for their operation in Lebanon. Certain Arab quarters led by the Saudis were also prepared to overlook such action. This would explain the near-total silence of the so-called moderate and nonmoderate Arab states on the events in Lebanon, a fact that American and European supporters and apologists for the invasion did not hesitate to bring to the attention of the public.

While pretexts for the invasion were readily available, the international climate had to be favorable to ensure that the two superpowers would not place serious obstacles in the path of Israel. One could make a case that in 1956 and 1967, the Israeli Mosaad, working closely with the CIA, managed to divert the Soviets in Eastern Europe, in the uprisings of Hungary and Czechoslovakia. In 1981 Poland became the theater of Soviet diversion in addition to the Soviet's direct involvement in Afghanistan. Egypt had been neutralized by the Camp David accords and the subsequent peace treaty with Israel. Iraq, a potent military threat, was conveniently bogged down in its war with Iran. Although enjoying a defense treaty with the Soviet Union, Syria could invoke direct military support only if its territory were invaded.

All Israel needed was a promise of no meaningful interference from the United States. It has been loudly rumored that they got this commitment in the form of a *nihil obstat* from Secretary of State Haig, who attached much significance to Israel's strategic importance in balancing Soviet influence in the Middle East.

Months before the invasion was launched, PLO leaders began to warn the world that it was coming. Haig began to criticize the Syrian role in Lebanon in harsh terms. Israel launched a steady drumbeat of raids on camps and staging areas in Lebanon to keep the Palestinian fighters off balance. Working with the Israelis, Gemayel's Phalangists initiated a campaign to bring the strategic city of Zahle, on the route to Damascus and to Haddad's area, into their orbit. The occupation of the city would give them direct land access to Israel through the southern Bekaa. But the Syrians were not about to permit this; they reacted with a heavy bombardment of Phalange positions in the hills overlooking the city when the Phalangists fired at them. When Israel flew menacingly over the area, the Syrians brought in their SAM–6 bat-

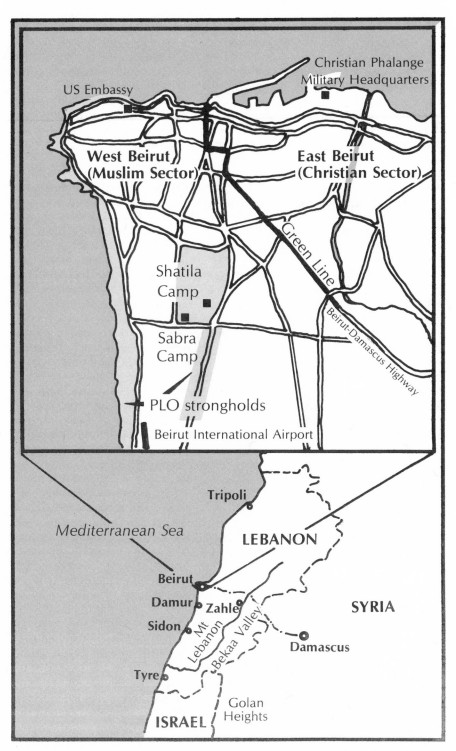

Christian Phalange
Military Headquarters

US Embassy

West Beirut
(Muslim Sector)

East Beirut
(Christian Sector)

Green Line

Shatila
Camp

Beirut-Damascus Highway

Sabra
Camp

PLO strongholds

Beirut International Airport

Tripoli

Mediterranean Sea

LEBANON

Beirut

Damur   Zahle

Sidon   SYRIA

Mt Lebanon

Bekaa Valley

Damascus

Tyre

Golan
ISRAEL   Heights

teries, thus provoking what the Israelis and the United States termed the "missile crisis."

Former prime minister Yitzhak Rabin stated in an interview that after Menachem Begin became prime minister, Maronite extremists commanded by Bashir Gemayel stepped up their efforts to involve Israel in a war with Syria through forcing the issue at Zahle (Peretz 1982, 51). Rabin clearly saw the Phalangists as the aggressors at Zahle and attached little military significance to the missiles in the Bekaa, because in his estimation "they did not change the situation very much . . . did not really interfere with Israel's mission in Lebanon" (ibid.).

The Labor alignment in Israel charged, furthermore, that Prime Minister Begin and his Likud coalition "had virtually contracted a unilateral treaty with the Christian leadership in Northern Lebanon and given it all the power to determine when, where and how the Israel Defense Forces should intervene in Lebanon" (ibid., 52).

The chain of events leading to the invasion began with a major air raid by Israeli forces on the alleged PLO headquarters in Beirut on 17 July 1981. President Reagan responded to the death of several hundred civilians by suspending for a few weeks the delivery of additional F–16 aircraft. His Arab allies were thus able to go before their angered people and refer to this gesture as proof of American disapproval of Israeli action.

Operation Peace for Galilee, the code name for the invasion, was in the planning for at least a year with little effort to disguise it from the world. PLO spokesmen offered evidence of Israeli military buildup and predicted almost to the day the launching event. Their voices elicited little response because most Arab states and policy planners in the United States were not seriously opposed to Israel's planned action in Lebanon.

Arab states generally remained silent for a number of reasons. Saudi Arabia and the Gulf states viewed most seriously the threat posed by Ayatollah Khomeini's revolution to their dynastic survival, particularly when he scarcely disguised his plans for them. They encouraged and supported financially Iraqi president Saddam Hussein's invasion of Iran, not so much to eliminate Khomeini's revolution but to cripple the vast and modern military arsenal he inherited from the shah. A huge arsenal in the hands of a revolutionary militant fired by the zeal of a crusading Islam that regarded the House of Saud as a prime target was indeed a sobering menace. Khomeini's close working relations with the PLO and Syria did not please either the Iraqis or the Saudis.

For the United States to safeguard its economic and strategic interests in the Gulf it would have to devise a strategy that could contain the potential threat of Khomeini and other revolutionary radicals among Arab factions, particularly when the influence of the Islamic Revolution seemed to be spreading. Moreover, the PLO commanded a strong following among Palestinians and sympathetic middle-class Arabs throughout the Arabian peninsula.

Time and circumstance appeared propitious for the next move, and Lebanon once again found itself caught up in the vagaries of regional and international politics. The battles of others once more were to be waged on Lebanese soil.

Foremost in Israel's quest was the normalization of relations with Lebanon, now that the Phalange enjoyed its support and confidence. Israeli leaders recognized that to keep the Phalange satisfied—they had goals of their own in Lebanon—they would have to support Phalangist plans to reduce the military capability of their primary foe, the PLO, with the ultimate goal of driving Palestinians out of Lebanon altogether should it be feasible. Bashir Gemayel saw this as a necessary first step to consolidating his hold on Lebanese politics and ensuring his election to the presidency.

Through the presidency of Bashir Gemayel Israel hoped to secure a peace treaty with Lebanon, and the United States hoped for a firmer commitment to U.S. policy objectives in the Middle East: a reduction of Soviet influence and a commensurate strengthening of American influence through implementation of the Camp David peace process with moderate states neighboring Israel.

The pattern of Israeli response to Lebanese situations since 1976 reinforces the conviction that Israel had a direct role in the destabilization of the country by making it impossible for the Lebanese government to control the domestic front. The enlistment of Major Haddad and his mercenaries in Israel's service denied the government control over its southernmost district. Further, Haddad and his men could harass the PLO by unceasing bombardment of their positions, and by forcing the PLO to retaliate could claim justification for further Israeli involvement at a time of Israel's choosing.

When Elias Sarkis was installed as president in the fall of 1976, Israel responded by expanding Haddad's territory and military forces. When the United Nations sent in a force in 1978 to help restore control in south Lebanon to the Lebanese government, Israel responded by encouraging Haddad to declare a "State of Free Lebanon" in the zone he controlled. When the UN Interim Force attempted to move in and secure the zone assigned to it, Haddad greeted them with shelling and effectively prevented them from attaining their objective.

Israel also intervened in a number of other ways to prevent stabilization, particularly by constant massive bombardment of camps and villages in the south, designed as much to undermine government authority as to retaliate for Palestinian retaliation. Begin admitted supplying the Phalange with an estimated $250 million in military hardware. This did not facilitate efforts by the central Lebanese government to rebuild the state apparatus and the army. Meanwhile, Israel "had Saad Haddad shell Lebanese civilian targets, including Sidon whenever the Lebanese government appeared to be near a political breakthrough internally and arranged for the planting of carbombs in many parts of the country in order to perpetuate the sense of crisis and paralysis" (Y. Sayigh 1982, 13).

Israel's policy of political Balkanization can be seen further in Israel's outright support for those factions that had steadily defied central authority. In addition to extending full support to Major Haddad, Israel extended support to Maronites battling Druzes in the Shūf district, even though Israeli Druzes constituted a sizable element in the Defense Forces during the Lebanon invasion. This rather unorthodox policy occasioned serious outcries from Israeli Druzes who witnessed Phalange attacks on their coreligionists in and around 'Alayh.

The fact that Druzes in Lebanon have also suffered from political divisions, with the Jumblats arrayed on one side and the Arslāns, Abū Shaqras, and others on the other, did not contribute to Druze solidarity during this critical juncture.

A similar rift could be seen among the Shiites. Many were being encouraged to break with the Amal party and join any one of the large number of semifeudal figures, like the Assads, Khalīls, 'Usayrāns, and Baydūns. As an added enticement, Israeli agents set up a new Shiite militia in south Lebanon, alongside Haddad's. It has been widely rumored that members of this militia participated along with Phalangists in the Shatila and Sabra camps massacre on 14 to 16 September.

ISRAEL IN LEBANON

On 6 June 1982 Israeli armored columns backed by air and sea forces launched an invasion of Lebanese territory. The pretexts given were (1) to stop PLO shelling of Galilee by creating a forty-kilometer (twenty-five mile) *cordon sanitaire* and (2) to eliminate once and for all the PLO threat to Israeli security. An excuse was conveniently provided by the attempted assassination of Israeli ambassador Shlomo Argov in London by what Israel insisted were agents of the PLO, although Scotland Yard, silent until after the invasion, later announced the agents were not PLO members. Some were suspicious of the manner in which the ambassador recovered after it was claimed he was mortally wounded; former president Franjieh remarked, "Begin of Israel assuredly engineered the attempted assassination of his own Ambassador . . . to use as a pretext for the invasion of Lebanon" (Nader 1982a, 27). The Israeli press has recently revealed covert operations in Beirut by Israeli agents within leftist elements of the PLO. In particular, a certain Abu Yusuf was alleged to be a leader of the "Socialist Unity Group" accused of undertaking "terrorist" acts against Israelis ("Israeli Pretended. . .", 1982). More interesting is the fact that official "Israeli statements issued before and after the British announcements indicated a lack of interest in the identity of Argov's would-be assassins" (Cockburn and Ridgeway 1982).

From 28 July 1981, when a truce was arranged by U.S. special envoy Philip Habib with Israelis and Palestinians, until 9 May 1982, United Nations reports from south Lebanon show that not a single PLO rocket or shell was fired from Lebanese territory. But during that same period, reports list 2,125 airspace violations and 652 encroachments in territorial waters by Israeli craft. This is in addition to the constant firing on PLO positions by Israel's proxy, Major Sa'd Haddad.

No sooner did Israeli armor eliminate pockets of resistance in south Lebanon than they began the race toward Beirut. A new pretext was given this time: to drive all PLO terrorists from Beirut. The Syrians put up a token resistance, and suffered far fewer losses than alleged in the Western press. But the world was given a different version, namely, that Israelis had shot down over a hundred Syrian planes and destroyed eighteen missile batteries in addition to wiping out hundreds of tanks. Even television coverage of the battle scene did not show any proof of this, giving credibility to skeptics who have alleged on numerous occasions that a tacit understanding underlay Syria's role in this grand game of charade.

The invasion was preceded by an aerial bombardment of the Beirut area on 4 June, followed by heavy artillery fire and more air strikes on the fifth, including on Damur. On the evening of 5 June, the United Nations Security Council adopted a unanimous resolution calling for a cease-fire by 6:00 A.M. Middle Eastern time on 6 June. Long accustomed to ignoring such resolutions, the Israelis responded with a full-scale attack.

By the night of 12 June indiscriminate shelling by land, sea, and air had resulted in forty thousand casualties, among them fifteen thousand known dead (the figures were released by the hospital of the American University of Beirut). Over one hundred thousand were rendered homeless. The centers of Tyre and Sidon were reduced to rubble. Thousands of Lebanese and Palestinians were arrested summarily and led away to detention camps inside Israel.

The war in Lebanon was heralded as an attempt to rescue Christians from Muslim terror. As a noted expert pointed out, "Of course Israel benefits by calling the conflict Muslim versus Christian-Jew because many Westerners will automatically side with the latter" (Peretz 1982, 52).

There is little doubt that the Phalange had made this their strategy shortly after 1976, when its agents in the Western hemisphere launched the World Union of Lebanese and, in the United States, the American Lebanese League. These groups were founded for the purpose of convincing Americans that the struggle in Lebanon was one of Christian versus Muslim, with the Palestinians and Syrians depicted as agents of the Soviet Union and thus responsible for Lebanon's problems. *Lebanon News*, founded in 1977, focused on the alleged crimes of Palestinians and Syrians in Lebanon, recounted on a day-to-day basis. "Bashir Gemayel has stressed this theme . . . repeatedly called attention to the 'plight of Christians in this part of the world' " (Peretz 1982, 52 citing John Yemma in the *Christian Science Monitor*, 30 April 1982).

This strategy, abetted by Israeli organizations in America and designed ostensibly to draw attention to Lebanon's sufferings, amounted to a thinly disguised attempt to gain American support for the Maronite Phalange cause. Bashir Gemayel himself had visited the U.S. to gain official U.S. support for Phalangist strategy and endorsement of plans being coordinated secretly between himself and top Israeli leaders.

THE POSITION OF THE UNITED STATES

Soon after the invasion was underway, the American Israel Public Affairs Committee (Israel's official lobby in Washington) sent representatives to Capitol Hill to justify Israel's actions. As former senator James Abourezk explains, their "success can be measured by the near total silence of our legislators on the matter. Conservatives, who were once heard loudly protesting the Soviet invasion of Afghanistan, as well as liberals, who recently were shouting slogans about Vietnam and El Salvador, all seem to have lost their voices. Meanwhile, the Reagan administration would not take concrete action to stop the killing in Lebanon and, in fact, even vetoed a UN resolution aimed at restraining Israel" (1982).

The relative indifference of American legislators might be attributed in part to a campaign of disinformation engaged in by the press, which for decades has been notoriously pro-Israel. Both the *Washington Post* and *New*

York Times published editorials justifying the invasion. And when Israel's bombing of Lebanese cities took a heavy toll in life, the importance of the wounded and dead received little attention from the press, although the television coverage did attempt to show the suffering of the innocent. Attention focused, rather, on Christians joining with Israeli forces, or Christians cheering Israeli army units. The fact that the majority of Lebanese were repulsed by the invasion and its consequences received little attention (Hooglund 1982, no. 10).

Even official U.S. government policy showed clear signs of ambivalence (if we were to take it on face value). While the United States voted for UN Resolution 508, calling on all parties to cease hostilities, and on 6 June for Resolution 509, demanding that "Israel withdraw all its military forces forthwith and unconditionally to the internationally recognized boundaries of Lebanon" (passed fifteen to zero in the Security Council), on 8 June it cast the lone veto to prevent the condemnation of Israel for noncompliance with either resolution. Two days later Foreign Minister Saud al-Faisal met with President Reagan in Bonn and told reporters afteward, "What we are expecting from the U.S. is a clear sign of its position as regards the unprovoked and premeditated aggression on the part of Israel." On that same day, 10 June, Edwin Meese III, Reagan's adviser, announced that the president was not considering sanctions against Israel to compel compliance with proclaimed U.S. policy.

Later, Alan Romberg of the U.S. Department of State declared that the United States was not working on an immediate withdrawal of Israeli forces on the grounds that "the issue of not having Lebanon be a launching pad for attacks against Israel is linked to Israeli withdrawal." On that same day, the department issued a statement saying that "one thing is clear. A return to the previous conditions in Lebanon cannot be allowed. Conditions must be created that will permit the restoration of the full sovereignty, unity and territorial integrity of Lebanon on the one hand, and the protection of Israel's security on the other." The United States was now actively engaged in the affairs of Lebanon, and on 12 June the Department of State admitted that it had helped arrange a cease-fire in Beirut (one of many to be broken).

Criticism of the U.S. role in Lebanon was absent in official Arab circles, except for muted pro forma statements. Mindful, however, of the impact of silence on Saudi Arabia's position in the Arab world, Foreign Minister Saud al-Faisal said officially that "Israel's invasion of Lebanon creates the view that the United States is at least ineffective in checking the Israeli aggression." No milder a statement could have been employed, and it confirmed suspicions in and out of the Arab world that Arab governments were not overly exercised by Israel's invasion of Lebanon.

On 21 June, following a personal meeting with Prime Minister Begin, President Reagan openly declared that "we agree that Israel must not be subjected to violence from the north." By now it was quite clear that Arab governments, the United States, and Israel showed more agreement than disagreement in their respective positions.

The bombardment of Beirut intensified in the next several weeks and took a heavier toll in civilian lives. The United States nevertheless remained content, as did most Arab governments, with making ineffectual protests and disclaimers. When the devastating impact of the U.S.-supplied cluster bombs revealed the cruel maiming of children and other civilians on television screens around the world, the United States responded by proclaiming on 28 July the suspension of cluster bomb shipments to Israel. In so doing President Reagan still made it clear he did not hold Israel accountable when he stated, "I must remind you . . . it's also been two way." (*Washington Report*, June and July 1982).

With President Reagan issuing qualified statements in response to rising indignation around the world, the United Nations Security Council again voted unamimously for a cease-fire in Beirut and for the dispatch of observers to monitor the situation, but to no avail. When Israel followed up on 4 August with a twenty-four-hour bombardment of West Beirut, Reagan simply "expressed to the government of Israel the absolute necessity of reestablishing and maintaining a strict cease-fire" (ibid.) No firm measures were proclaimed, or even considered.

Other governments continued their posturing for public opinion at home and abroad. It was announced that King Fahd of Saudi Arabia did indeed telephone President Reagan on 5 August to express the need for the United States "to exercise a more potent role" in restraining Israel. And when the Soviet Union finally bestirred itself publicly for the first time to call on UN members to cease supplying arms to Israel in the face of its continual ignoring of UN decisions, the United States responded by vetoing the resolution introduced to that effect on the grounds that "it calls for sanctions . . . which will not contribute to our goals of achieving a peaceful settlement."

Victimized beyond endurance, the majority of the Lebanese saw the necessity for all foreign troops to withdraw from Lebanon in order to enable their government to reestablish a strong central authority. The government announced on 18 August that with the mediation of the United States it was able to reach agreement with the PLO for its evacuation from Beirut. Israel announced it would agree, but made some reservations. The president of Lebanon requested on the following day that the United States, France, and Italy send troops to oversee the evacuation of PLO fighters.

This announcement did little to assuage what critics at home termed the humiliation of the United States by Israel beginning on 4 July, when Israel chose to ignore requests that Israel Defense Forces in Lebanon restore water and electricity and allow the delivery of essential medication and food supplies to the people of West Beirut. Israel responded by further intensifying the bombardment of the besieged inhabitants. The United States took no measures to disclaim what many by then believed to be true, namely, that an agreed-upon strategy was being implemented through Israel while government officials in Washington hoped to excuse inaction by repeating the assertion that firm measures would only strengthen Begin's defiance.

PLO EVACUATION AND ELECTIONS

Following assurances in writing from the United States that the civilians left behind in the camps of Beirut would be protected, Yasir Arafat and his fighters agreed to evacuate Beirut. This was done under the supervision of the multinational force requested by President Sarkis. The evacuation began on

22 August and was completed by 1 September. Lebanese army units were deployed in West Beirut to enforce security and disarm illegal militias. The Shiites were disarmed, but not the Phalange. Bashir Gemayel, candidate for president, was now indisputably the strongest man. His enemies were either gone or disarmed. Realistically, Lebanese factions opposing Gemayel had no choice but to support his candidacy, the first proclaimed. No one dared challenge it. Moreover, he enjoyed the support of both Israel and the United States. All that his opponents could hope for was that the office of the presidency might render him responsible to and cognizant of the welfare of all Lebanese.

U.S. defense secretary Caspar Weinberger visited Beirut and conferred on 1 September with the outgoing and incoming Lebanese presidents, proclaiming afterward that the United States endorsed the withdrawal of all foreign troops from Lebanon. Outgoing foreign minister Fu'ād Butros praised U.S. efforts and President Reagan's newly announced Middle East peace plan favoring a Palestinian-Jordanian confederation. The United States realized that Lebanon would never be fully stabilized until a solution for the Palestinian problem was found, allowing nearly half a million Palestinians to leave Lebanon or find permanent settlement somewhere acceptable to them.

The Islamic group led by former prime minister Saeb Salam offered to cooperate with the president-elect, provided he did not attempt to lead Lebanon into a formal peace treaty with Israel as Prime Minister Begin expected from Bashir in return for his support over the past several years. A voice of reason and moderation throughout the bombardment of Beirut, Salam emphasized the need for a complete withdrawal of Israeli forces from Lebanon if mistrustful Lebanese were to be reconciled to their government.

Withdrawal meant also that Syrians and Palestinians would evacuate their forces from north and east Lebanon. Supporters of the Syrians in the Tripoli area would not endorse this plan. Fighting broke out between the faction demanding withdrawal, a Sunni Muslim extremist group styling itself "the warriors of God," and their opponents, predominantly pro-Syrian 'Alawite immigrants. As 1982 drew to an end, over one hundred had been killed in the fighting.

The Syrians insisted that they were in Lebanon at the official request of the president and would leave only if the invitation were withdrawn and the Arab League in turn requested the withdrawal. Meeting in Fez to design a peace plan to counter President Reagan's proposal, spokesmen of the league offered to accept a plan for Syrian military withdrawal provided Israel withdrew its forces first.

Not wishing to be caught in an untenable situation, the United States announced withdrawal of its twelve hundred marines on 10 September, two weeks earlier than planned, after President Reagan announced his satisfaction that the mission of the marines was fully accomplished. Four days later, on 14 September, the president-elect, Bashir Gemayel, was assassinated by a certain Habib Chartouni, a Maronite Phalangist who acted allegedly on instructions from an agent of an unnamed foreign intelligence service (*Lebanon News*, October 1982, 2).

The assassination was the signal needed by Israel to occupy West Beirut, since its commanders were not able to induce Lebanese security forces to move into the camps and seek out the two thousand PLO guerrillas supposedly still there. Israeli forces moved into West Beirut on 16 September, two days after the assassination, and on that same night, a detachment of Phalange and south Lebanon Shiites, assembled and trained by the Mosaad, was deployed first at the airport immediately south of the camps. There they were supplied with armor and bulldozers and allowed to move into the camps already surrounded by Israeli units, where under the observation of Israeli officers there ensued one of the most brutal, coldblooded massacres of modern times. It has been estimated that up to twelve hundred people, mostly women, children, the old and infirm, were gunned down or axed to death from 16 to 18 September. Later it was reported that no guerrillas were found in the camps (Interview on ABC TV "Closeup," 7 January 1983). Israeli chief of staff Eytan denied that units of the Defense Forces were near the camp, even though television cameras showed them on top of buildings overlooking the camps and Israeli soldiers themselves admitted they were inside the camps at the time, alerting to no avail their superiors.

THE MASSACRES AND ISRAEL

While Sharon, Begin, Shamir, and other high-ranking Israeli officers sought to disassociate themselves from the terrible happenings in the Shatila and Sabra camps, the Knesset was not prepared to accept their claims on face value.

Although all parties involved denied responsibility, reports to the *Washington Post* appeared to implicate three Phalangist leaders: Efrem, Edde, and Hobeika, the latter a close associate of the late Bashir Gemayel and his chief of intelligence with apparently close working ties to both the Israeli Mosaad and the CIA. Reports reproduced around the country by most newspapers on 26 September seem to puzzle over the same question that journalist Loren Jenkins had raised: "What happened to turn the Gemayal plan from a sweep through the camps in search of armed Palestinians and men of military age into a murderous rampage . . . is still not clear" (*Washington Post*, 26 September 1982).

The Israeli newspaper *Ha'aretz* published a report by Zeef Shiff on 28 October that stated on good authority that "an authorized investigation carried out after the massacre in the refugee camps has shown that this was not a spontaneous act of vengeance for the murder of Bashir Gemayel, but a premeditated attack which was designed to cause a mass flight of Palestinians from Beirut and from the whole of Lebanon." The report went on to add, "It is now known that for several weeks the Falangists had been talking among themselves about the need to expel the Palestinians from the whole of Lebanon. They had said that this process would have to start in Beirut."

It has been generally conceded that Israeli commanders had warned that the Phalange might "run amok" given their threats and proclivities. These warnings were reportedly conveyed by the deputy prime minister David Levi and General Eytan to the Israeli cabinet. During heated debates, Defense Minister Sharon admitted that he gave permission for the Phalange to enter the camps in spite of warnings from his Beirut commanders. During the investigation that ensued, forty-five Israeli officers admitted to knowing what was going on in the camps when the massacres were being staged (interview on ABC TV "Closeup," 7 January 1983). Detractors accused Sharon of choosing to ignore individual warnings from Israeli soldiers, even congratulating the Phalange for their work in the camps (Jansen 1982b, 6).

THE MASSACRE AND THE LEBANESE GOVERNMENT

Outcries of indignation and anger aroused 400,000 Israelis to demonstrate openly in the streets of Tel Aviv angrily demanding resignations and an open investigation of the massacre, compelling Begin's government to cave in to the pressure and authorize the investigation by an independent commission. But in Beirut the silence of Lebanese Phalangists only served to confirm suspicions of their complicity. Strongly denying any responsibility, the Phalangist leaders held a perfunctory "investigation" and quickly absolved themselves. The government was helpless even to contemplate an investigation let alone conduct one. Arab governments shed ample tears, but were content to let the incident pass into memory. Yasir Arafat bitterly accused the multinational force of withdrawing before the proper time, contrary to U.S. assurances.

In the midst of the carnage, the Phalange nominated Amin Gemayel, brother of Bashir, for the presidency. Amin had established a good rapport with Muslim groups and thus his election was quickly expedited. He took the oath of office on 23 September and declared that he would do all within his power to reconcile the Lebanese and help heal his country's wounds. To lend credence to Gemayel's insistence on the reinforcement of domestic security measures, President Reagan authorized the return of U.S. Marines. They and their French and Italian counterparts arrived in Beirut on 27 September.

Amin Gemayel's first order of business was to put together a government. He asked Prime Minister al-Wazzān to help form one. After consultation and intense negotiations with eleven parliamentary groups, the new cabinet was announced on 7 October. A ray of hope was held forth in that all were well-educated "technocrats" with no connection to discredited feudal and other self-serving groups.

While the government was being installed, the Lebanese army continued its careful search for illegal residents and arm caches in West Beirut, detaining those who had no proper residence permits and confiscating large quantities of ammunition hidden by militias. King Hassan II of Morocco offered to deploy twenty thousand troops to help Lebanon regain control over its territory. The U.S. deputy secretary of state Frank Carlucci arrived on a one-day visit to review military needs with the president and commander of the Lebanese army, as well as the chief of staff. The United States agreed to assist in the reconstruction and rearming of the Lebanese army.

AMIN GEMAYEL'S INITIATIVES

No sooner did he assume office than President Gemayel embarked on an international tour to plead the cause of Lebanon for peace and stability based on the withdrawal of all foreign troops from its soil. He made the United States his first stop, arriving in New York on 17 October in the company of his new foreign minister, Elie Salem, who had been dean of the faculty of arts and sciences at the American University of Beirut when appointed. Addressing the UN General Assembly on 18 October, Gemayel proclaimed that he brought a "message of confidence from a nation active in a daring adventure of peace and reconstruction." In his message he emphasized, "We have had enough—enough of bloodshed, enough of destruction, enough of dislocation and despair." He expressed the desire of his war-torn country to live in peace with its neighbors, calling for strong relations with Syria "in the context of independence and mutual respect."

Meeting afterward with the Security Council, Gemayel won approval of the United Nations to extend the mandate of the Interim Force in south Lebanon until 19 January 1983. In Washington, Gemayel pleaded for help to reconstruct Lebanon economically and militarily and for continued U.S. political support while Lebanon recovered. In a meeting with President Reagan, Gemayel expressed the gratitude of the Lebanese to him for his and America's "courageous and decisive efforts to help bring an end to the suffering of my country."

President Gemayel had come to the United States at the invitation of President Reagan, the first such visit by an incumbent president. He came away assured that twelve hundred marines would help patrol operations, and not merely guard the airport. He apparently gained approval for a plan to reconstruct and retrain the Lebanese army under U.S. tutelage. There was reference to supplying this army with communications gear, armored personnel carriers, howitzers, and tanks. Reagan also promised to consider seriously increasing the size of the multinational peace-keeping force. The United States agreed to play the role of the mediator to help secure the withdrawal of all foreign forces from Lebanon.

Much urgency was attached to the withdrawal of such forces, since both Reagan and Gemayel were fully aware that the longer it took for these forces to leave, the greater the likelihood of renewed fighting, not only among Lebanese factions—as in Tripoli and the Shūf—but possibly among the foreign forces stationed in Lebanon.

After leaving the United States, Gemayel stopped in France and Italy to urge those governments to increase the size of their units in the multinational force. President François Mitterrand of France and Foreign Minister Claude Cheysson held talks with him on 20 and 21 October in Paris, as did Defense Minister Charles Hernu. Mitterrand promised to supply "any sort of aid that is wanted by Lebanon for reconstruction." Walid Jumblat, successor to his father Kamal as leader of the Druzes and Socialist faction in Lebanon, was present at a press conference in a show of unity held in Paris on 20 October to emphasize the trend towards reconciliation.

In Italy, Gemayel had a long audience with Pope John Paul II in the Vatican, and afterward with President Sandro Pertini and Prime Minister Giovanni Spadolini. Foreign Minister Salem conferred with his Italian counterpart, Emilio Colombo. Before making any commitment of support, the Italian high officials asked for and received assurances from Gemayel and Salem that the Palestinians left behind in Lebanon would be given full protection under the law.

Shortly after returning to Lebanon, President Gemayel embarked upon a journey to Morocco, where on 1 November he conferred with King Hassan II on the Arab peace plan arrived at during the meeting of the Arab

League in Fez. His majesty renewed his offer of troops to boost the multinational force in Lebanon.

In Saudi Arabia on 14 November Gemayel exchanged medals with King Fahd and asked him for further aid, after expressing his gratitude for the Saudi role (undefined) during the invasion and afterward. The Lebanese delegation conferred on every level with its Saudi counterpart, expressing the common theme that Lebanon would not be a theater of violence and terrorism. Lebanese independence and sovereignty were stressed, as was the need to help in the reconstruction of the country financially and politically. In addition, Gemayel asked Fahd's support in securing the withdrawal of Syrian and Israeli forces from Lebanon. During a press conference later, Information Minister Yamani characterized the discussions as "successful" (without reference to particulars), adding that "Saudi Arabia would deploy [sic] all its efforts to liberate Lebanon."

Despite the rhetoric, the bleak reality facing the Lebanese, Saudis, and Americans was the continued presence of Israel's military forces in Lebanon without any commitment or assurance by the end of the year that they intended to withdraw in the near future. Indeed, with Israelis shouting anger and defiance at their leaders over their role in Lebanon, it became all the more urgent for Begin and Sharon to come away from Lebanon with some positive results in return for the heavy investment in men and materiel. This meant much hard bargaining with the Lebanese and Americans. They pushed hard for concessions that would normalize relations in fact, if not in name. And as the year drew to a close, representatives on both sides agreed to meet alternately at Khalde, near the Beirut airport, and Qiryat Shemona, inside Israel, to agree on an agenda for discussions that would lead to Israeli withdrawal. Morris Draper headed the U.S. team of mediators, while special envoy Habib was held in reserve, to appear when President Reagan saw fit to stress his views.

Lebanese and American sources revealed that the Israelis were bargaining specifically for open borders, joint patrols in the south, early warning stations on Lebanese soil, the free movement of tourists and trade, mutual bureaus to coordinate relations, Israeli positions in the Shūf district, access to the coast, and the right of Israel to control Lebanon's territorial waters and air traffic (Lebanon News, December 1982, 2).

To accept such demands was tantamount to compromising Lebanese sovereignty, making a mockery out of its independence and self-respect as a nation. But as Israelis reminded observers: Lebanon was not an independent state; indeed, not a state at all in the full political sense.

POSTINVASION DILEMMA

The principal dilemma confronting Lebanon at the end of 1982 was how to regain lost sovereign rights and self-respect by ridding itself of the invader and other non-Lebanese troops in the country. But more important than this is the other question many were asking: Can there evolve a truly united and politically viable Lebanon from the ashes of the most recent carnage? What indeed lies ahead for this politically, religiously, socially, and economically shattered country?

Israel's conditions for negotiations are bound to make them long and tortuous. The United States quite clearly is not prepared to exercise the kind of economic and military pressure that would make Begin yield. Reagan had said in advance that no sanctions would be applied to Israel.

With much optimism Reagan had declared in September that he expected all foreign troops to be withdrawn from Lebanon by the end of December. Gemayel came to realize that Lebanon would not be able to take charge of its destiny until it could put together an army of between sixty and one hundred thousand men. In the interim he hoped for a sizable increase in the multinational force, to thirty thousand men. This request was formally made to the three participating powers on 29 November, but with no promise of a favorable response.

Meanwhile, Israel proceeded with its objectives, expressed by Foreign Minister Shamir to the Knesset's Foreign and Defense Committee on 6 December: Israel seeks to establish peaceful relations (with Lebanon) as a prelude to a peace treaty. For that reason he was insisting on a high-level negotiation team on both sides. Both Lebanon and the United States recognized that to pursue such an objective at this time would obviate Gemayel's own commitment to a strong, reunified, and truly independent Lebanese state, since the majority of Lebanese (Muslims of all denominations) and most Arab states would not concur in such concessions as demanded by Israel, and Lebanon would be faced with isolation when it needed most the help of these states. Lebanon could not afford to find itself isolated and boycotted as Egypt did following its peace treaty with Israel.

Yet while many recognized that "an imposed normalisation with Israel would jeopardize both Lebanon's internal cohesion and its Arab position . . . hard core Phalangists made little effort to conceal their desire for closer ties with Israel, as two minorities clinging together in a hostile Muslim sea" (Muir 1982b, 4). Etienne Saqr (alias Abu Arz), leader of the hard-line Guardians of the Cedars Maronite minority, expressed openly his group's gratitude to Israel at a press conference in Jerusalem and did not deny involvement in the massacres at the Shatila and Sabra camps; he viewed them rather as "dealing with our enemies as we see fit" (Muir 1982b).

Fadi Efrem, another hard-line Phalangist and commander of the still-armed Lebanese Forces, declared at a Phalange rally on 28 November that Lebanon should join the peace process and develop cultural and special ties with other minorities in the Middle East, that is, Israel.

U.S. objectives in the Middle East and the role Lebanon plays therein cannot be ignored in assessing the country's prospects in the aftermath of the war. Upon taking office President Reagan declared open war on "terrorism" and wasted no time in provoking Colonel Qaddafi of Libya in the Gulf of Sidra incident, which resulted in U.S. carrier planes shooting down two Libyan planes over Libyan territorial waters. The lesson was not lost on Libya's ruler, and he has remained relatively quiet through 1982. Libya's support of Syria and Iran (all three have been backed by the Soviet Union) did not endear any one of them to the United States. The Ayatollah Khomeini's threats to dispose of the enemies of Islam, which include all the rulers of Arabia and their dynastic families, constituted a threat to America's strategic and economic interests in the Gulf. The House of Saud's survival is linked to the United States on every level. Urging Iraq into war with Iran in order to destroy its military capability and arouse Iranians to depose the Ayatollah has backfired.

To Khomeini the Palestinian cause is an Islamic cause. He has supported it openly from the moment he assumed power in Iran. Indeed, it was in deference to PLO pleadings that he agreed to release some of the hostages first taken in the seizure of the U.S. embassy in Tehran. The United States, on the other hand, also had an unexpected ally in Iraq, a country ostensibly in the Soviet camp. That the Ayatollah is viewed as the Gulf countries' serious enemy can be judged by the billions of dollars they have invested in Iraq's war with Iran.

If the United States is to secure its line of communication with the Gulf in order to mobilize the Rapid Deployment Force quickly in times of emergency, it becomes necessary to stabilize the eastern Mediterranean littoral. To do so it would have to dislodge strong pro-Soviet elements, namely, the PLO from Beirut, and stabilize a Lebanon that has promised through its radical rightist elements, the Phalange, to ally itself firmly with the United States. Should this objective be accomplished, the United States would have a solid alliance ranging from the northeast corner of the Mediterranean south and westward to the borders of Libya. Jordan is treated as a moderate supporter, which leaves only Syria, isolated and surrounded by strong, hostile neighbors. It would only be a matter of time before Syria would be pried loose from the Soviet grip, particularly when its ʿAlawite minority leadership has demonstrated firm resolve only when the matter of its survival was at stake.

Viewed in this context, one can understand Gemayel's close rapport with the United States and the so-called moderate Arab states. As a military analyst put it, "it is striking how the US has stepped in as de facto protector of Lebanon in the wake of the Israeli invasion, with a view to Lebanon playing a central role in US plans to stabilise the Middle East as a whole" (Glubb 1982, 5). Some sources claim that the late Bashir Gemayel had envisaged a "strategic alliance" with the United States, offering in time of crisis the port of Jounieh to the Rapid Deployment Force.

It would be a disservice to dismiss summarily the notion of complicity in the whole strategy leading to the invasion. As Professor Binder stated, "many observers are willing to believe that there was some complicity, coordination, or tacit understanding between the Israelis and the top echelon in the Haig State Department. The general idea was to force the withdrawal of the Syrian troops from Lebanon, to disarm the Palestinians and destroy the military infrastructure of the PLO, to support the Sarkis government with foreign forces, and to provide for the rebuilding of a Lebanese armed force by a newly elected, liberal, and pro-western government" (1982, 15).

The potential threat of an Iranian-Syrian alliance should Iran succeed in its war against Iraq must have weighed heavily on planners' minds. Hence, the recourse was to "deadly force in order to coerce the transformation of a chronically provocative situation . . . [the] result of American shortsightedness in failing to pursue a political solution to the Lebanese situation for six long years, and it is the result of Israeli short-sightedness in failing to allow the PLO to stew in its own juice in West Beirut" (ibid., 16). Seen in this context, the United States can be adjudged to have acted precipitously in "seeking to resolve the Lebanese crisis by means of instrumentalities which are not now in existence but which are to be fashioned in the course of the resolution itself" (ibid., 17).

But whatever the consideration, the United States did move quickly to consolidate its political gains by capitalizing on "new opportunities," particularly those following the assassination of Bashir Gemayel and the massacre of the camps. The first concern of the United States was the speedy buildup of the Lebanese army and equipping it with light, medium, and heavy tanks, as well as F–5 aircraft and Hawk antiaircraft missiles. Plans also called for an increase in the army from the 18,000 men before the civil war to 60,000 men by late 1983 and eventually to between 120,000 and 150,000 by 1987 (Glubb 1982, 5).

While Lebanon is to be aligned firmly with the West, the alignment would not be through openly declared instruments, but rather through an unwritten "gentleman's agreement," in order not to alienate non-Phalangist Lebanese. By such an arrangement, the United States would be allowed temporary use of facilities in emergencies without giving the appearance of a long-term military presence. For "while the US military mission is envisaged as permanent, it is certain to keep a low profile and confine itself to advising and training the Lebanese army" (ibid.).

The most important gain for the United States is Lebanon's potential role in American plans to stabilize the Middle East as a whole. Gemayel's policies "are aligned in regional terms with the majority of conservative Western-aligned Arab states, including an Egypt accepted back into Arab ranks despite its peace treaty with Israel" (ibid., 6). This would help ensure a predominantly pro-Western Arab orientation and safeguard oil and strategic interests. The Soviets would be satisfied to hold onto Iran and Afghanistan as a sphere of immediate interest while abandoning all Arab countries (save Syria and South Yemen) to American influence. Israel's security also would be served with a settlement of the Palestine problem. This, in a sense, is a primary consideration in Reagan's peace plan of 1 September. "Before the Israeli invasion," declared Glubb, "Lebanon was a focus of revolutionary activity from many parts of the world. The fact that it is no longer so, and is now being converted into a state with a firm central government that can be a partner in US plans to stabilise the Middle East, should be acknowledged as an important US strategic gain" (ibid.).

PROSPECTS AND PROMISES

If plans are to develop as envisioned, the question still remains: what shape will a reconstructed Lebanon take? The central issue is not the reconstruction of the army and central authority but of reaching a common consensus that can draw together the factions whose feuds tore Lebanon apart in the past. Ghassan Tuéni, a brilliant technocrat with strong intellectual perceptions, serving both as editor of Lebanon's independent newspaper al-Nahar and as the country's ambassador to the United Nations, strongly cautions against a return to the status quo ante. He calls for a nation of all Lebanese "brought together in a new social as well as political contract." To that end he advocates the restructuring of Lebanon's democratic institutions to integrate a traditionally pluralistic society into a unity that resists conquest and destabilization.

A strong Lebanon requires the reconstruction of the vital infrastructure of public services, the reconstitution of the middle class as the backbone of the country, and both organic and structural reform to reunite legitimacy and authority in the central government and to eliminate the numerous "statelets" that had usurped this prerogative. In other words, what is needed is a new "national pact" to replace the one that brought ruin to Lebanon, to be forged not by maneuvering factions and feudal entities but by regional representatives. Tuéni advocates the election of the president by universal suffrage, not by Parliament, in order to break the monopoly of the ruling elites; the creation of a second chamber representing the corporations, to counterbalance confessional representation; and the establishment of *competence*, not religion, as the criterion for public service. He believes strongly that Lebanon can best achieve its goals only by remaining neutral in foreign affairs. Neutrality to him, however, does not preclude close working relations with sister Arab countries, in view of the material and moral support reconstruction will require of them. "Peace in Lebanon is not only an elementary right of the Lebanese but a necessity for regional and international security" (1982, 95–99).

Over a year before the invasion, in speculating on the prospects of Lebanon, then academician (now foreign minister) Elie Salem saw four options for his country: 1) continuation of the status quo, 2) partition, 3) dismemberment by its neighbors, and 4) rebuilding a united, independent sovereign Lebanon along new lines (1981, 8). The first option would infect neighbors like a disease, leading to further radicalization and anomic political action in the region, particularly in countries with mixed societies; partition could lead to separate Christian and Muslim states, thus putting an end to Christian-Muslim symbiosis, with a leftist state emerging ideologically from the Muslim side and bringing the Soviets to the borders of Israel, thus becoming a vehicle for superpower conflict, leading to further fragmentation: an 'Alawite state in Syria, Shiite in Iraq. Dismemberment would lead to the loss of the south to Israel, the north and Bekaa to Syria, and a PLO ministate around Beirut and in the south.

Salem dismisses these options in favor of rebuilding, because in his view "Lebanon has the essential elements of a stable political system. . . . The internal aspect of the conflict is not very serious and could be resolved without too much difficulty" (ibid.). To support this contention he draws on Lebanon's history under the emirate and Mutaṣarrifīya, even defending the confessional structure as one producing a political culture with a strong secular orientation that "has worked relatively well." This political structure, he asserts, is based on compromise, conciliation, consensus, and the avoidance of ideological issues.

Herein lies the secret of reconstruction for Salem: each confession remains true to its values; the new Lebanon will respect one and all provided they do not assault the values of another. Cultural or religious identification need not affect one's loyalty to the state.

A precondition for Lebanon's reunification is a clear national identity (Salem 1982, 4). This identity, he insists, must be forged from history and society as it now exists. He blames Lebanese intellectuals for missed opportunities and for their profuse "pamphleteering and journalistic attempts . . . allowing Lebanon to aimlessly stumble into its future, while they, like Don Quixote, pursued ethereal and vacuous phantoms that shone brilliantly and inconsequentially at distant horizons" (ibid., 4–5). Lebanon thus failed to achieve, when it might have, an integrated, harmonious, and unified political order. The challenge still before the Lebanese is how to use basic persisting ingredients "to create a viable and strong political community that can accommodate diversity of views without violence, and that can sustain change without calling to question its very existence" (ibid., 10).

Salem outlined concrete preliminary steps for the political and societal integration of the Lebanese at a conference sponsored by the American Enterprise Institute on 1 May 1981 in Washington. At that time he still deferred to the principle of sectarianism in high offices but insisted on rendering the presidency more responsive to political demands and developmental needs. He advocated the powers of the prime minister be constitutionally defined; representation in Parliament be made on an equal basis for Muslims and Christians; the principle of concurrent majorities be observed as a safeguard against majority rule on fundamental issues; rights and duties of citizens be clearly defined; a national education system be designed to reinforce socioeconomic responsibilities; decentralization be carried out within the context of safeguarding fundamental rights of individuals and confessions; extensive reform at all levels of government and bureaucracy, to render political behavior responsible; and, finally, a strong army and strong internal security force to serve as the arm of the new political consensus.

No doubt such reasonable suggestions helped secure a cabinet post for Salem a year and a half later. The U.S. government was singled out by him for the role it has come to play at this time: to help Lebanon come to grips with its own problems. Indeed, he had urged the United States to put Lebanon on the list of its foreign policy priorities; provide sustained support for it; collaborate with Saudi Arabia in resolving the Arab dimension of the Lebanese crisis; persuade the Israelis not to put obstacles in the Lebanese path; provide quantitative and qualitative support to the Lebanese army and security forces so that they may become the unchallenged military force in the country; and provide selective economic support (1981, 8). Judging from the U.S. response over a year later, one might conclude that it had responded well to Salem's suggestions.

In June 1982, Israel precipitated the action that paved the way for direct U.S. involvement, lending further credence to suspicions voiced by experts that a *modus operandi* had been agreed on well in advance of the invasion. There is little room for doubt that the U.S. was maneuvered into this position by former Secretary of State Haig. He had advocated for some time Israeli collaboration in forcing the issue in Lebanon. It had been a foregone conclusion that of the great powers, only the U.S. was poised to play the role of mediator-conciliator in Lebanon. As Foreign Minister Salem declared in Washington in December 1982, "I think America is in a position to deliver on anything America feels strongly about in the Lebanon-Israeli situation and nobody's going to convince me otherwise" (Lee 1982, 3).

Now that the United States has indeed assumed a direct role in the affairs of Lebanon, and in the process of untangling them, it must move quickly (1) to normalize the internal and external problems hampering stabilization and (2) to work closely with other Arab states to bring about a permanent solution to the Palestinian problem to ensure regional stability and protect thereby its own interests in the Arab world. The United States has to deliver in Lebanon and not appear to endorse Israeli intransigence on both fronts. If Israel succeeds in drawing out negotiations over troop pullouts from Lebanon, the United States will find it increasingly difficult to regain credibility, and the advantages accruing to America from the present opportunity will be lost. If the United States expects the Saudis to continue their containment of radical elements in the Arab world, then it has to attempt to contain Israel expansionism "by using its leverage with Israel" (Seelye 1982, 23).

As the year 1982 drew to an end, Israel continued to justify the assertions by American experts that "it will haggle over every inch of Lebanon in order to bog down American diplomacy and stall progress on the wider US peace initiative" (Muir, 1982a, 4). The Syrians appeared no less in a hurry to leave, biding their time while the Soviets restocked their military arsenal and installed advanced SAM–5 missiles able to reach deep into Israeli skies. The question raised by some skeptics is whether they are both encouraging each other not to withdraw, confirming the Lebanese people's worst fears "that instead of moving swiftly into a period of balanced withdrawal," they could become "stuck indefinitely with balanced occupation" (ibid., 4).

Salem informed Washington in December that unless foreign forces withdrew within a four-week period, Lebanon could face another war. The situation was deteriorating as casualties in Tripoli and the Shūf mounted, with the Syrians backing the Baʿth ʿAlawites and the Israelis the Phalangists in the fighting still continuing at year's end. The deteriorating situation thus justified the decision by both Syrians and Israelis to not withdraw.

Both Gemayel and Reagan have an image to bolster in Lebanon. The former needs to pacify the Shūf before he can do anything else, since the district commands the Beirut and adjoining coastal area with its airport and strategic Beirut-Damascus highway. It has been said that "who holds the Chouf dominates Beirut and who dominates Beirut rules Lebanon" (Jansen 1982a, 3). Reagan on the other hand must restore a tarnished image, namely, that of "Israel's partner in . . . the Lebanon slaughter," as a *New York Times* editorial phrased it (Ajami 1982, 99). However one views it, the invasion, if not a product of complicity, did at the very minimum "put on display the disarray of America's Middle East policy" (ibid.). What is now at stake is "American capacity to behave justly, to rein in Begin and draw a line for him, to see its way past geopolitical abstractions and its obsession with Soviet power, into an honest and serious encounter with the things that ail a region of great importance to the United States" (ibid., 109).

Foreign Minister Salem also has a problem on his hands: how to win the race with time; for without the quick withdrawal of foreign forces from Lebanon, the country "will be positioned at a new angle and I cannot say where it will end." He foresaw a new war "far more destructive, far more regional, far more international in its implications than the war of 1975" (Weinraub, 1982).

CONCLUSIONS

At the end of 1982 Lebanon stood dangerously on the edge of the precipice. A formidable challenge awaited the Lebanese and a seemingly insurmountable obstacle their newly elected president: how to end the fighting and secure the withdrawal of all foreign forces, in the first instance; and how to devise a working political formula acceptable to a multitude of deeply mistrustful factions, in the second.

While Lebanon stood at the crossroads, the question remained: will the country succeed in transcending the limitations of geography and tradition to forge a truly distinct identity of its own? To take even the first step in that direction, the government must become master in its own house in order to instill the inhabitants with confidence and inspire them to come together in a challenging adventure of rebuilding. This entails making those necessary institutional changes that would enshrine the rule of justice and give all citizens the right to equal social and economic betterment. This in turn necessitates granting all Lebanese an active political role in selecting their representatives on the basis of merit and competence, not confessional affiliation.

One can only hope that the Lebanese will rise to the occasion and meet the challenges boldly, for one unmistakable fact characterizes their history: an uncanny ability to turn disaster into a positive benefit. There are enough optimists who maintain they will do it again.

REFERENCES AND ADDITIONAL READINGS

Abourezk, James. 1982. "The Double Standard on Lebanon." *Chicago Tribune*, 23 June.

Ajami, Fouad. 1982. "The Shadows of Hell." *Foreign Policy*, no. 48 (Fall): 94–110.

American University of Beirut. Department of Political Studies. 1960. *The Lebanese Constitution*. Beirut: Khayat.

Barakat, Halim. 1977. *Lebanon in Strife: Student Preludes to the Civil War*. Austin: University of Texas Press.

———. 1979. "The Social Contest." In *Lebanon in Crisis*, edited by P. Edward Haley and Lewis W. Snider. Syracuse: Syracuse University Press.

Bashir, Iskandar E. 1977. *Civil Service Reform in Lebanon*. Beirut: American University Press.

Binder, Leonard. 1982. "Operation Bootstrap: The Logic of American Strategy in Lebanon." *Middle East Insight* 2, no. 4: 11–17.

———. 1966. *Politics in Lebanon*. New York: John Wiley and Sons.

Bloom, James J. 1982. "From the Litani to Beirut: A Brief Strategic Assessment of Israel's Operations in Lebanon." *Middle East Insight* 2, no. 4: 37–45.

Chamie, Joseph. 1976/77. "The Lebanese Civil War: An Investigation into the Causes." *World Affairs* 139, no. 3 (Winter): 171–88.

Chevalier, Dominique. 1968. "Western Development and Eastern Crisis in the Mid-Nineteenth Century: Syria Confronted with the European Economy." In *The Beginning of Modernization in the Middle East*, edited by William Polk and Richard Chambers, 205–22. Chicago: University of Chicago Press.

Cockburn, Alexander, and James Ridgeway. 1982. "War in Lebanon." *Village Voice*, 22 June.

Deeb, Marius. 1980. *The Lebanese Civil War*. New York: Praeger Publishers.

Entelis, John P. 1974. *Pluralism and Party Transformation in Lebanon, Al-Katā'ib, 1936–1970*. Leiden: E.J. Brill.

Fisher, W.B. 1972. "Lebanon: An Ecumenical Refuge." In *Population of the Middle East and North Africa*, edited by J. Clarke & W.B. Fisher, 143–60. New York: Africana Publishing Co.

Glubb, Faris. 1982. "Lebanon and the US: Gentleman's Agreement." *Middle East International*, no. 189 (10 December): 5–6.

Gordon, David C. 1982. "The Crisis in Lebanon: Structure and Contingency." *Middle East Insight* 2, no. 4: 24–26.

Hagopian, Elaine, and Samih Farsoun. 1978. *South Lebanon*. Detroit: AAUG Inc.

Haley, Edward P., and Lewis W. Snider. 1979. *Lebanon in Crisis: Participants and Issues*. Syracuse: Syracuse University Press.

Harik, Iliya F. 1968. *Politics and Change in a Traditional Society: Lebanon 1711–1845*. Princeton: Princeton University Press.

Himadeh, Said. 1936. *The Economic Organization of Syria and Lebanon*. Beirut: Khayat.

Hitti, Philip K. 1967. *Lebanon in History*. New York and London: St. Martin's Press.

Hooglund, Eric. 1982. *US Press Coverage of the Israeli Invasion of Lebanon*. Washington, D.C.: ADC Research Institute.

Hourani, Albert H. 1954. *Syria and Lebanon: A Political Essay*. London: Oxford University Press.

———. 1968. "Ottoman Reforms and the Politics of Notables." In *The Beginning of Modernization in Middle East*, edited by William Polk and Richard Chambers, 41–68. Chicago: University of Chicago Press.

Hovsepian, Nubar. 1981. "The Lebanon Quagmire." *Nation*, 6 June.

Hudson, Michael. 1968. *The Precarious Republic: Modernization in Lebanon*. New York: Random House.

"Israeli Pretended to be Lebanese Leftist Leader." 1982. *Ha'aretz*, 9 September.

Jansen, G.H. 1982a. "American Credibility Is Now on the Line." *Middle East International*, no. 190 (23 December): 3–4.

_____. 1982b. "Conflicting Evidence." *Middle East International*, no. 187 (12 November): 6–7.

_____. 1982c. "Lebanon: Quenching the Chouf." *Middle East International*, no. 190 (23 December): 6–7.

_____. 1982d. "Lebanon's Fatal Flaw." *Middle East International*, no. 185 (15 October): 15–16.

_____. 1982e. "Thirty-four Years in Lebanon." *Middle East International*, no. 187 (12 November): 9–10.

Khairallah, Shereen. 1979. *Lebanon*. World Bibliographical Series. Oxford: CLIO Press.

Khalaf, Samir. 1979. *Persistence and Change in Nineteenth-Century Lebanon: A Sociological Essay*. Beirut: American University Press.

Khalidi, Walid. 1979. *Conflict and Violence in Lebanon: Confrontation in the Middle East*. Cambridge, Mass.: Harvard University Press.

"Lebanon Invasion: The Record." *Washington Report on Middle East Affairs* 1, no. 6 (28 June): 3–5.

Lee, William. 1982. "American Credibility Is Now on the Line." *Middle East International*, no. 190 (23 December): 3–4.

Meo, Leila M.T. 1965. *Lebanon, Improbable Nation: A Study in Political Development*. Bloomington: Indiana University Press.

Moughrabi, Fouad, and Naseer Aruri. 1977. *Lebanon: Crisis and Challenge in the Arab World*. AAUG Special Report, no. 1. Detroit: AAUG Inc.

Muir, Jim. 1982a. "Daunting Tasks Face Gemayel and Habib." *Middle East International*, no. 188 (26 November): 3–4.

_____. 1982b. "Lebanon: Challenge to Gemayel." *Middle East International*, no. 189 (10 December): 4–5.

_____. 1982c. "Lebanon, Target: The Reagan Plan." *Middle East International*, no. 184 (1 October): 4–6.

Nader, George. 1982a. "An Exclusive Interview with Suleiman Franjieh." *Middle East Insight* 2, no. 4: 27–29.

_____. 1982b. "Exclusive Interview with Yitzhak Rabin." *Middle East Insight* 2, no. 4: 30–32.

Orfalea, Greg. 1982. "United States: Words But No Deeds." *Middle East International*, no. 184 (1 October): 7–8.

Parker, Richard. 1982. "The Crisis in Lebanon: Whose Fault Is It?" *Middle East Insight* 2, no. 4: 18–20.

Peretz, Don. 1982. "The Media in the United States on Lebanon: Reporting Lebanon the 'Christian' Way." *Middle East Insight* 2, no. 4: 46–52.

Polk, William R. 1963. *The Opening of South Lebanon*. Cambridge, Mass.: Harvard University Press.

Qubain, Fahim I. 1961. *Crisis in Lebanon*. Washington, D.C.: Middle East Institute.

Rondot, Pierre. 1955. *Les Chrétiens d'Orient*. Paris: Peyronnet.

Safa, Elie. 1960. *L'Émigration Libanaise*. Beirut: University of St. Joseph Press.

Salem, Elie A. 1981. "Prospects for a New Lebanon." *Campus* [AUB Newsletter] (Spring): 6–8.

———. 1982. "Lebanon: The Forging of a National Identity." *Middle East Insight* 2, no. 4: 4–10.

Saliba, Maurice. 1979. *Index Libanicus*. Antelyas (Lebanon).

Salibi, Kamal. 1965. *The Modern History of Lebanon*. London: Widenfeld and Nicholson.

———. 1976. *Crossroads to Civil War: Lebanon, 1958–1976*. Delmar, N.Y.: Caravan Books.

Sayigh, Rosemary. 1982. "The Massacre in West Beirut and Its Aftermath: A Premeditated Act?" *Middle East International*, no. 184 (1 October): 2–4.

Sayigh, Yezid. 1982. "Dividing and Ruling in Lebanon." *Middle East International*, no. 184 (1 October): 13–14.

Seelye, Talcott W. 1982. "Implications of the Israeli Invasion of Lebanon." *Middle East Insight* 2, no. 4: 21–23.

Sharif, Hasan. 1978. "South Lebanon: Its History and Geopolitics." In *South Lebanon*. See Hagopian and Farsoun 1978.

"Siege of Beirut: Horror for Lebanon." *Washington Report on Middle East Affairs* 1, no. 8 (23 August): 2–3.

Smilianskaya, I.M. 1966. "From Subsistance to Market Economy, 1850's." In *The Economic History of The Middle East*, edited by Charles Issawi, 226–47. Princeton: Princeton University Press.

Stanhope, Lady Hester. 1846. *Memoires of the Lady Hester Stanhope*. Vol. 1. 2d ed. London: Henry Colburn.

Suleiman, Michael W. 1967. *Political Parties in Lebanon: The Challenge of a Fragmented Political Culture*. Ithaca: Cornell University Press.

"The Lebanon: A Land Torn by War, A Nation in Name Only." 1981. In *The Middle East*, 177–83. 5th ed. Washington, D.C.: Congressional Quarterly.

"The Lebanon Labyrinth." *Washington Report on Middle East Affairs* 1, no. 14 (15 November): 2–3.

Tuéni, Ghassan. 1982. "Lebanon: A New Republic?" *Foreign Affairs*, 60, no. 3 (Fall): 84–99.

United States. Department of State. 1979. "U.S. Policy on Lebanon." Revised August 1979. *Current Policy*, no. 84.

Weinraub, Bernard. 1982. "Report to the *New York Times* Service: The Lebanon." *International Herald Tribune*, 14 December.

Zagorin, Adam. 1982. "A House Divided." *Foreign Policy*, no. 48 (Fall): 111–21.

The Reagan Peace Initiative

Donna Robinson Divine

It is as difficult to describe President Reagan's proposals for resolving the Arab-Israeli dispute as it is to explain them. President Reagan's 1 September 1982 statement on the Middle East was not a simple catechism of political principles. It was the product of particular political circumstances and a general foreign policy perspective that the president shares with his senior advisers in the Departments of State and Defense and in the National Security Council. While the proposals were consistent with views of the Arab-Israeli dispute formulated during previous administrations, they also sprang from the dynamics of the current bureaucratic process. The antecedents of President Reagan's policy on the Middle East are manifold and deep, necessarily implying a course of action that is both new and old. This essay will address the Reagan proposals in light of the forces—political, foreign, domestic, ideological, and bureaucratic—producing them. We shall begin by presenting those elements of the policy that are significantly new.

For the first time during his presidency, Reagan acknowledged the kinship of the Arab-Israeli dispute to other strategic and economic interests of the United States.

> The Lebanon War, tragic as it was, has left us with a new opportunity for Middle East peace. We must seize it now and bring peace to this troubled area so vital to world stability. . . . But the opportunities for peace in the Middle East do not begin and end in Lebanon. As we help Lebanon rebuild, we must also move to resolve the root causes of conflict between Arabs and Israelis. (Reagan 1982)

Shifting rather substantially from statements issued during his campaign, President Reagan isolated the homeless condition of the Palestinian Arabs as fundamental to the dispute. Observing that "the military losses of the PLO have not diminished the yearning of the Palestinian people for a just solution of their claims," he formulated the crucial issue as one of reconciling

"Israel's legitimate security concerns with the legitimate rights of the Palestinians." And departing from his own earlier silence concerning the form an ultimate settlement should take, President Reagan asserted that Israel should not remain in control of the lands occupied on the West Bank and the Gaza Strip during the 1967 war.

> We base our approach squarely on the principle that the Arab-Israeli conflict should be resolved through negotiations involving an exchange of territory for peace. . . . Self-government by the Palestinians of the West Bank and Gaza in association with Jordan offers the best chance for a durable, just and lasting peace. (Reagan 1982)

In spite of President Reagan's implied claim of originality, the policy he announced was unique primarily in terms of its detail denoting, in the president's words, "America's position on the key issues." This particular policy departure, so clearly intended by President Reagan, can only be explained by virtue of the widespread perception among officials of the administration that the Israeli invasion of Lebanon on 6 June 1982 had brought in its wake a military and political transformation in the Middle East that warranted renewed American attention and involvement. We must begin, then, by examining the ways in which this military action influenced American foreign policy.

FOREIGN POLITICS: THE INVASION

The Israeli invasion of Lebanon began with the stated goal of securing Israel's northern border, thus arguably entailing military action in a twenty-five-mile zone of Lebanese territory. Following swift and decisive assumption of control over this zone, the Israeli military continued its march north, engaged Palestinian fighters, and finally, besieged the city of Beirut in an effort to destroy the military power of the Palestine Liberation Organization (PLO). In pursuit of the PLO, the expanded confrontation not only rearranged control over Lebanon but also redistributed power in the entire Middle East. Besides eliminating the Palestinian militias from their land-based strongholds in south Lebanon and cutting their access to the port of Sidon, the Israeli military also destroyed the batteries of Syrian missiles in the Bekaa Valley, curtailing the scope of Syrian political and military influence in Lebanon and presumably in the entire Middle East. President Reagan's closest advisers—among them then secretary of state Alexander Haig—saw in the early stages of this war a basis for hope in the power of the Israeli military to stabilize Lebanon. The positive American assessments became more qualified as the armed struggle Israel carried into Lebanon widened its course and aimed at removing the PLO armies from Beirut and southern Lebanon. The more comprehensive the military and political confrontation undertaken by the Israelis became, the more deeply engaged American interests appeared to be in the outcome of the fighting.

The question of where to accommodate the Palestinian fighters stimulated American foreign policy makers to consider the problem of where to find a home, if not a homeland, for the entire Palestinian refugee population. Simply put, the assumptions about Palestinian refugees toward which policy makers gravitate are at considerable variance with conventional notions of American national interest. American policy makers take for granted that America is served well by politically and socially stable societies in which leadership is transferred without violence and no commitment to socialism rigidly guides economic policy. In this respect, Israel is an attractive American ally in the Middle East. By contrast, the Palestinians seem threatening.

On the question of the Palestinians, it is assumed that a people whose political orientations were born in national disappointment and nurtured and radicalized in continued political subordination will carry opposition and revolution to any land in which they reside. It is a corollary of this conventional foreign policy wisdom that the national self-interest of the United States requires that it prevent the emergence of migrant populations who, ill-absorbed and oppressed by their social and political environments, perceive no political choice but revolution to meet their immediate needs and to fulfill their collective goals.

The Palestinians, as refugees, are also presumed to threaten American interests in the Arab oil-producing countries. Their possible resettlement in these economically attractive but politically fragile areas raises questions about their effects on countries that supply oil for the entire Western world. Most recently, the migration of Palestinian refugees has been deterred simultaneously by the PLO's capacity to provide security and employment, above all in Lebanon, and by the restrictions imposed by the Arab oil-producing states afraid of the problems that could arise from additional Palestinian residents. As long as Palestinians could live with the hope of returning to their homeland as the center of their individual and communal lives, and also work to establish grounds for that return, they did not constitute an acute problem for other Arab countries. No less an authority than Michael C. Hudson has called the PLO's achievements in Lebanon impressive, and it is not unreasonable to postulate that the prolonged civil war in Lebanon made gains of this magnitude possible.

> Its military establishment numbered over 30,000 fighters, well equipped with light and medium weaponry including long-range artillery. . . . The PLO had developed an economic organization, Samed, that was estimated to have grossed $40 million in 1981 through its light industries and businesses. A social welfare department provided health care, education and financial assistance to the families of killed fighters. The Palestine Red Crescent Organization operated many hospitals and clinics, mainly in Lebanon. (Hudson 1983, 5)

Without the economic security and political protection afforded by the PLO, the pressure on Arab oil-producing states to accept more Palestinians is bound to increase. Also intensifying the pressure are the development programs undertaken by these countries, which often require linguistically skilled labor—teachers, clerks, secretaries. Describing the force of economic development on Arab immigration policies, Nazli Choucri has observed that labor needs vary with the level and scope of development, and that market rather than political conditions determine the ethnic origins of a labor force (Choucri 1982). No matter what restrictions are placed on the movement of Palestinian immigrants, many Arab countries may be forced to capitulate to a process of economic development whose consequences could lead to political collapse.

President Reagan's advisers saw in the further dispersal of greater numbers of Palestinian refugees to Arab lands such marked revolutionary potential that they feared allies of strategic importance to the United States might be overthrown. Israel's insistence on the explusion of Palestinian fighters from Beirut required the dismantling of the Palestinian economic and political structures, and, accordingly, the locus of the Palestinian problem had to shift. Notwithstanding the sympathetic attention in the Arab press to the suffering of the Palestinians and to their serious material losses, other Arab countries recognized that the removal of Palestinians from Beirut could intensify the potential for disruption in their own societies. The fragmentation of power in Lebanon may have impeded the unification of the country, but it afforded Palestinians the opportunity to create there the nucleus of a government and an economy. In this sense, Lebanese disunity increased stability in the countries of the Persian Gulf. For that reason, the Israeli determination to destroy the PLO signaled the end of an old balance of regional power and highlighted the beginning of a new predicament for American strategic and economic interests.

DOMESTIC POLITICS: GENERAL PERSPECTIVE

While American policy makers sought to limit the political and military changes induced by the Israeli invasion, paradoxically it was American policy that facilitated assertive Israeli military actions. "The American people overwhelmingly elected Reagan because they believed he would be able to deal effectively with the domestic economy and establish a more influential and decisive foreign policy" (Sisco 1981, 28). President Reagan's major foreign policy premise has been to assume that the Soviet Union is engaged in a relentless pursuit of power and influence. Administration officials regard the Soviet threat as eclipsing all other threats and dangers whatever their roots. To establish links with countries of the Middle East whose governments were considered potential targets of Soviet aggression was the foreign policy of the Reagan administration. Denials from leaders of many of these countries that the Soviet Union constituted a special threat or a threat greater than that of other regional adversaries did nothing to alter this premise.

> President Reagan won his office in part because he convinced the electorate that the Soviets had hoodwinked all Administrations of the last decade. He proposed to reverse the unfavorable trend of U.S.-Soviet power relations and, quite simply, to "stand up to the Russians." . . . Despite various adjustments and adaptations, both the domestic and foreign policies of the Reagan Administration, like the

Reagan campaign, continue to display the characteristics of an ideological crusade. (Bialer and Afferica 1982/83, 251)

By using the supply of advanced weapons to fortify relations with countries like Saudi Arabia, the Reagan administration proposed to turn countries of strategic importance to the United States into credible regional deterrents to Soviet expansion. The most well-publicized expression of this policy came when the Reagan administration gained approval for the sale of the Airborne Warning and Control System (AWACS) to Saudi Arabia. Administration officials proposed to make Saudi Arabia the political and military center of regional stability (Binder 1982).

The danger in the American obsession with securing strategic superiority over the Soviet Union lay in its granting the opportunity to military and political elites on both sides of the Arab-Israeli dispute to seek ceaselessly to improve their own regional strategic advantages. Recognizing that to proffer advanced military equipment to Saudi Arabia would antagonize Israel, whose strategic superiority would be compromised, the administration decided to render a quid pro quo service to the Israelis by maintaining silence on Israeli settlements on the West Bank and on any retaliatory raids initiated against Palestinian fighters in southern Lebanon (Perlmutter 1982b).

In 1981, mutually adversary postures in Lebanon spiraled into military confrontations between Christian Phalangists and Syrians, Israelis and Palestinians, all accompanied by material and human devastation. Such military activities undermined the relatively controlled level of violence in Lebanon and brought American involvement through the intervention of a special presidential adviser on the Middle East, Philip Habib, sent to stop the carnage and arrange a truce. The violence did eventually abate, but the truce Habib concluded was designated at the outset by Israel as unsatisfactory, because it simply called on, but did not force, the Syrians to remove their ground-to-air missiles from Lebanese territory. Just as each position of strategic inferiority for Syrians, Christian Phalangists, or Palestinians provoked compensatory military actions, so the military circumstances frozen by the truce of 1981 proved but an incentive to future military action for the Israelis. Though challenged in word and deed by Arabs and Israelis, the Reagan administration continued to insist on its reading of Middle East politics, namely, that moderate regimes would not take immoderate actions and that local disputes would not affect global and crucial United States interests.

Measured against the ruling foreign policy principle of the Reagan administration, the war in Lebanon provided evidence of Soviet losses and American gains. The low visibility of Soviet activity and the vulnerability of Soviet weaponry vis-à-vis U.S. weapons deployed by the Israelis seemed to support the proposition that America's purposes could be served by Israeli military victories. The view of the Soviets as beleaguered in Afghanistan and embarrassed in the Iraq-Iran war reinforced the administration's foreign policy perspective, with its almost exclusive focus on the Soviet threat. For all the attention brought to bear on the Middle East, the president's advisers provided no genuine pluralism in matters of global politics, and United States involvement in Lebanon was still seen as a counter to possible Soviet expansion.

DOMESTIC POLITICS: ELECTORAL REWARDS

President Reagan's world view was not the only factor that tended to erode the saliency of the Arab-Israeli dispute in American politics; political self-interest also encouraged Reagan to keep his distance from this political mine field. If Ronald Reagan drew any lessons from Jimmy Carter's failure to secure reelection, it was that Carter's political career had been damaged by attending to Middle East politics. Even when Jimmy Carter brought about the Camp David accords and a peace treaty between Egypt and Israel, his preoccupation with Arab-Israeli issues secured no palpable electoral benefits. Although the Reagan administration formally confirmed its commitment to the Camp David peace process, it subsequently took no steps toward active involvement. It appointed no high-level person to conduct Egyptian-Israeli autonomy talks on the fate of the West Bank and Gaza Strip. Nor did the administration create a mechanism for expanding the negotiations.

The Israeli pursuit of Palestinian fighters to the outskirts of Beirut in early July, however, precipitated a formal review of the administration's policy on the Arab-Israeli conflict. The review came amidst increasing official unease with the numbers of civilian casualties and with the possibility that the Israeli military might actually enter Beirut. In addition, Saudi Arabia and Syria both tried to convince United States policy makers to stop the war and to prevent the Israeli army from invading Beirut. Among the president's closest advisers, discord grew in late June over the issue of whether continued, unfettered Israeli military action in Lebanon served American strategic interests in the Middle East. The resignation of secretary of state Alexander Haig on 25 June 1982 brought to mind the unspoken reservations of administration officials about American policy on the war in Lebanon.

If only to distinguish United States from Israeli policies with respect to Lebanon, the president's speech "intended to reinvigorate Camp David negotiations by attracting additional participants through a clear indication of the positions they could expect of the United States." (Kreczko 1982/83, 141). Haig's successor, George Shultz, pointedly stressed during his July confirmation hearings the centrality of the Palestinian problem for Middle East stability, thereby suggesting that a personnel change would surely induce a shift in the substance and orientation of America's Middle East policy. But American policy in the aftermath of the reassessment demonstrates how difficult it is to widen foreign policy beyond the basic principles of those who create it.

Stirred by fears that Israeli military action would bring increased instability rather than stability to Lebanon and hence present an opportunity for Soviet expansion, President Reagan authorized the stationing of American troops in Beirut as part of a multinational force. The European and American troops did stop the Israeli advance on Palestinians in Beirut and facilitated the dispersal of the Palestinian fighters from the city. Although the troops were ostensibly sent only until Lebanese military and political authority could be reconstituted, the administration's policy still seems to be guided by the notion that the Israeli invasion can be used to restore Lebanese sovereignty with little material or political cost to the United States. Given Lebanon's history of civil wars, the American troops may find their service in Lebanon prolonged, complicated, and, ultimately, costly. Because Reagan perceives the Lebanese situation through the prism of global politics, he may find himself beset by the very problems that consumed his predecessor.

IDEOLOGY: POLICY ANALYSIS

Neither differences in perspective nor the idiosyncrasies of domestic politics have completely severed links between present and past American Middle East policies. American policy makers take for granted that the peace process between Arabs and Israelis must be comprehensive in order not to trigger more oppositions and political instability. For example, former secretary of state Henry Kissinger engaged in step-by-step diplomacy with Egypt, Syria, and Israel that was designed to avoid coming to any terms upon which other Arab states could consolidate their opposition (Quandt 1977). And President Carter's foreign policy advisers had difficulty believing that Sadat's mission to Jerusalem could advance the cause of regional peace without imperiling the stability of moderate Arab states supportive of United States interests in the area.

No policy designed to expand American influence in the Middle East has ever omitted the supply of military equipment. Partly because of the strategic location of the Middle East with respect to the Soviet Union, American policy makers have long desired alliances that, in the right circumstances, could accommodate American military needs. American military and strategic interests in the Middle East still serve as points of reference for almost all official political judgments.

Hence, the policy discourse is not entirely controlled by events or by changing domestic political circumstances. Rather, policy issues contribute a vocabulary so fully assimilated into the process of analysis that concepts, to an extent, control the perception of reality. On the Arab-Israeli conflict, it is virtually impossible to describe an American policy, let alone create one, outside of two accepted premises: first, that the conflict is simultaneously over Israeli security concerns and the nationalist aspirations of the Palestinian people, and second, that Arab respect for the United States depends, largely, on the Arab perception that the United States can influence Israeli military and political activities.

The credibility of these premises derives from the circumstances of past Arab-Israeli wars, when it has generally been conceded that Israel's survival was threatened (June 1967), or when U.S. intervention halted the violence (October 1973) but did not end the hostilities. No administration since 1967 has gone beyond these premises and developed an active Middle East policy that considers more than Arab-Israeli wars and confrontations.

American policy makers are generally tempted to create policies for short-term reasons and only in crises. Such actions—new force positioning or new weapons and supplies—tend to be consistent with the perception of crisis but difficult to reverse or control once the emergency has lifted.

The tendency is to react only to Middle East crises, and that is damaging to the effectiveness of American policy. Policy decisions are often obsolete at the time they are issued, since they derive from outdated notions about political conditions in the area. For example, both Carter and Reagan generated an array of measures to press Israel for territorial concessions, based on a knowledge of the political behavior and orientations of the Israel Labor party, defeated in the elections of May 1977. Not only were the leaders of this party—Yitzhak Rabin, Shimon Peres, Abba Eban—out of office, but, more importantly, their political views neither shaped nor guided the leadership with which Carter and Reagan had to contend. Significantly, the rhetoric of crisis can only find a suitable organizational response on the highest levels of government, demanding the preoccupation of the president or the secretary of state. Further, attention can only be mobilized at this level for relatively brief periods of time without impoverishing policy making in other areas, domestic and foreign. Practical political considerations, then, have held America's Middle East policies to very short-term standards.

BUREAUCRACY: THE POLICY PROCESS

In examining current American policy on the Arab-Israeli dispute, it is also important to remember that the process by which policies have been formed is a legacy of past experiences even though current political conditions constitute very different challenges for the United States. Divergent points of view of individuals and institutions in matters affecting the Arab-Israeli dispute are, as elsewhere, the product not only of dissimilar preconceptions and perceptions but also of differing roles and responsibilities. These divergences are often strong and deep, for they are rooted in differences over basic values of concern for Americans: American support for democratic governments, American dependence upon secure supplies of oil. Our economic well-being and our collective notion of who we are sets the tone and content of Middle East policy debates. No clear institutional demarcation has existed for the formation of America's Middle East policies. Responsibility for fashioning a Middle East policy has been taken partly by the Department of State, partly by the White House and National Security Council staff, and partly by various high-level negotiators, whose reports of events on the scene have exerted substantial influence. Hence, the goals elevated by United States policy makers in their responses to particular Arab-Israeli crises place no long-term, binding obligations on American officials in their conduct of affairs in the region.

Further, it has often been remarked that each department has brought its own institutional bias to bear on the dispute. What has mattered most to the Department of State is population and natural resources. American influence could not be enhanced in the Middle East, State Department experts have contended, except through a close association with the Arab world. Our relations with Israel, therefore, should not be allowed to compromise association with the Arab world. Countering this tendency has been the disposition of the chief executive to favor close ties with Israel because of electoral concerns or cultural affinities.

But in the crisis-oriented environment in which policies have been formed, differences between the State Department and the White House staff have tended to dissolve. Not only have key policy makers served in both institutions, but the perception of crisis tends to ease the strains of divergent opinions and encourage consensus (Quandt 1977).

In the days immediately before President Reagan's speech
. . . and for several weeks after it, Secretary of State George
P. Shultz held almost daily discussions on strategy with his
own aides and those at the White House. Officials with
knowledge of these discussions described them as harmonious, with little sharp disagreement, a process of consensus-
building. Broad conversations on Middle East policy were
mixed with making daily decisions on the crisis in Lebanon. (Gelb 1982)

Because Middle East policy making often takes the form of a crisis
response, the institutionally bred differences among officials recede, and it is
generally conceded that policies should be subject to central direction at the
highest levels of government. This kind of organizational consolidation can
obtain for only brief periods. Given the number of different bureaucracies involved in implementing policies in the Middle East, emergency organizational consolidation produces its own policy anomalies, most noticeably,
increased disharmony between long- and short-term American interests.

Formed in the medium of American bureaucracy, then, however
evenhanded and balanced, the Reagan peace proposals are trapped in dishar-
monies between short- and long-term goals. President Reagan's declaration
that Israeli settlements constitute a serious obstacle to peace has not deterred
the Israeli government from continuing to build them. Neither has it led to
American measures to impede their expansion. It appears as either an abdi-
cation of responsibility or an admission of political weakness to call for a halt
to Israeli settlements when the call, as such, appears to have no bearing on
political actions either in the United States or in Israel. Arab leaders, like
King Hussein of Jordan, are disposed to judge the peace proposals not only
by principles they endorse but also by the concrete policies they contain.
Whereas the Reagan proposals are based upon the assumption that the United
States and moderate Arab regimes, like that in Jordan, now share common
purposes, there is little evidence to indicate that American economic, military, or political policies have actually originated in these purposes. Given
the historical realities of American policies, the promise of American support
cannot provide a strong enough basis for Arab leaders to negotiate the return
of all territories conquered by Israel in the 1967 war. From the Arab stand-
point, so long as the Reagan proposals generate no policy momentum, what
little profit they would bring in terms of land or peace would also threaten
the particular political conditions so-called moderate Arab regimes wish to
defend.

Consequently, President Reagan's proposals have heightened rather
than dampened other anomalies of American foreign policy on the Arab-
Israeli dispute. American diplomatic strategy currently upholds the standard
of the legitimate rights of the Palestinian people while it enjoins the creation
of an independent Palestinian state. American diplomacy credits the principle of territorial security even as it insists on extinguishing Israeli control
over the territories deemed vital by present leaders to their state's integrity.
With the straightforward Arab demands for Palestinian sovereignty and the
commitment of current Israeli leaders to the right to possess the territories in

dispute, United States diplomacy appears, at the very least, indifferent to political reality.

REACTIONS: ARAB AND ISRAELI

In his speech, the president brought into view an American position opposed to the stated aims of Arab and Israeli political leaders. Not unexpectedly, these leaders pronounced the initiative unacceptable to one extent or another. The very fact of a presidential speech on the subject, however, raised expectations, once again, not only that the United States possessed arguments whose logic can compel the disputants to enter negotiations, but, more importantly, that the United States possessed the power to force Arabs and Israelis to end their historic conflict.

What are the possibilities for a successful conclusion to the Arab-Israeli dispute in the Reagan peace initiative? Since one purpose of the initiative was to add Arab state participants to the Camp David peace process, we must consider whether the initiative enhanced prospects for expanded negotiations. The Reagan administration consulted with political leaders in Jordan and Saudi Arabia before launching the initiative in an attempt to convince regimes deemed moderate and politically significant to negotiate their political disputes with Israel. In response, the leaders of these and other Arab states have pronounced the initiative to be in some respects positive. But participants in the twelfth Arab summit convened by the Arab League, at Fez, Morocco, on 8 September 1982 (including Jordan and Saudi Arabia), rejected the initiative and issued a peace statement, on 9 September, that was faithful to traditional Arab demands.

1. The withdrawal of Israel from all Arab territories occupied in 1967 including Arab Al Qods (East Jerusalem).

2. The dismantling of settlements established by Israel on the Arab territories after 1967.

3. The guarantee of freedom of worship and practice of religious rites for all religions in the holy shrines.

4. The reaffirmation of the Palestinian people's right to self-determination and the exercise of its imprescriptible and inalienable national rights under the leadership of the Palestine Liberation Organization, its sole and legitimate representative, and the indemnification of all those who desire to return.

5. Placing the West Bank and Gaza Strip under the control of the United Nations for a transitory period not exceeding a few months.

6. The establishment of an independent Palestinian state with Al Qods as its capital.

7. The Security Council guarantees peace among all states of the region including the independent Palestinian state.

8. The Security Council guarantees the respect of these principles. (*American-Arab Affairs*, no. 2 (Fall 1982): 155)

Significantly, the summit meeting did authorize its own representatives to explore the Arab-Israeli issue with political leaders of countries holding membership in the Security Council.

Arab states generally recognize that the alternative to the United States proposals is *de facto* Israeli annexation of the West Bank. But even though the Reagan initiative offered more than the perceived alternative, it did not contain enough ideological credibility for regimes in Jordan or Saudi Arabia to mobilize their own political resources fully and unequivocally in its behalf. The same Arab states, which recognize that the time is ripe for United States pressure on Israel to withdraw from the West Bank also understand that pressure, politically sustainable by an American administration, may prove insufficient to the task, given Israel's present awesome military power. After all, the United States was able to halt but not finally end the Israeli invasion of Lebanon. Leaders of all Arab states believe that only American pressure can lead to the fulfillment of Arab objectives, but they see in the current balance of regional power in the Middle East possibilities for Israeli intransigence, at least in the short term. And given the short-term perspectives of American Middle East policy, these very same Arab leaders have little reason to believe in a long-term, consistent United States policy designed to force major Israeli territorial concessions.

In attempting to put aside policy barriers that were once considered insuperable, Yasir Arafat and Jordan's King Hussein engaged in prolonged discussions in October, indicating the deference of at least part of the Arab world to the Reagan proposal. The logic of the Reagan administration's policy is based on one key underlying assumption: that Jordan's King Hussein will negotiate the return of West Bank territories in order to prevent their full absorption into Israel. The origins of this logic are not difficult to find. They lie in the expansion of Israel's West Bank settlements, the increased building activity in the area, and the numbers of West Bank Jewish immigrants and Arab emigrants. In an ironic twist, Israeli minister of defense Ariel Sharon has noted that demographically Jordan already is a true Palestinian state, lacking presumably only a true Palestinian political head of state. This logic has, however, proved unpersuasive for the following reasons. Since the loss of the West Bank territories to Israel, King Hussein's political position has grown stronger, not weaker. In a serious confrontation with Palestinian guerrillas in September 1970, the king and his military forces emerged with a military victory and political security. Since the civil war intensified in Lebanon during the middle 1970s, Jordan's capital, Amman, has enjoyed added prosperity. King Hussein recognizes that his government and army may not possess the capacities to control a West Bank Palestinian population significantly changed in political outlook and economic orientation as a result of the Israeli occupation.

In his search for a mandate to legitimize participation in negotiations over the future disposition of the West Bank and Gaza Strip territories, King Hussein turned, appropriately, to PLO chairman Yasir Arafat. The military defeat of the PLO and the subsequent exodus of PLO leaders and fighters from

Beirut appear to strengthen the American view that Palestinians must immediately begin a peaceful dialogue with the Israelis. But in Palestinian political circles, these same circumstances have also spawned a view that supports continuing the violence. The war in Lebanon had a devastating impact on the PLO, but it is important to remember that the devastation of the PLO leadership was not so much new in kind as new in degree. Palestinians and the impressive array of institutions they had established in Lebanon were subjected to a dispersal, but not for the first time. The ideological differences of the several political movements within the PLO intensified but were in no way dramatically altered. In Michael C. Hudson's words, "the Fatah-dominated PLO leadership seemed to come through the summer of 1982 with increased legitimacy and no major internal challenge" (Hudson 1983, 34). Under the chairman, Yasir Arafat, the PLO leadership had always operated on the basis of a narrow consensus that foreclosed substantial deviations from traditional political principles.

On the Arab political side, the fear of having to acquiesce forever in Israeli occupation of Arab lands beckons Arab leaders to start negotiating the disposition of these lands. But the call cannot be casually accepted when it is tied to negotiations whose very terms preclude the possibility of attaining long-stated Arab goals. The knowledge that to act under such circumstances may easily be read as acting in bad faith overrides all other considerations and tends to keep Arab leaders from the negotiating table.

In the name of adhering to the Camp David accords, Israeli prime minister Menachem Begin immediately denounced the Reagan initiative. Begin has turned his belief in Israel's historic right to claim the West Bank into a premise of the Camp David accords. The American insistence that the West Bank be properly associated with Jordan cancels, in Prime Minister Begin's view, both the five-year transitional period stipulated at Camp David and the role of the United States as an "honest broker" between Arabs and Israelis. Moreover, the similarity of the Reagan plan to the policy of the Israel Labor party to return West Bank territories to Jordan subjects the plan to the stigma of association with the largest political party competing with Begin's own Likud. On grounds of self-interest, Prime Minister Begin, then, must oppose the plan.

Still, Israeli reaction to the Reagan initiative is not covered entirely by the pronouncements of the nation's political leaders. "When Ariel Sharon, Israel's defense minister, led his troops into Lebanon," one astute observer of Israeli society has written, "he opened a season of anguish for Jews" (Wieseltier 1983, 64). The Reagan initiative helped turn that anguish into a fierce debate in Israel about the wisdom of holding the West Bank territories. Most Israelis may believe the military pursuit of the PLO to be just, but there is growing doubt about its wisdom. Over four hundred and fifty Israelis have been killed in Lebanon, with no clear prospect for a rapid withdrawal that would produce concrete political achievements. Lebanon has not yet been pushed to achieving political stability or to consolidating its own military power. But new elections in Israel bringing the Labor party into office would not necessarily alter Israel's policy to agree with the American position. Although the issue of territorial compromise has become the focus of serious discussion in Israel, there is no major political party for which this issue serves, unconditionally, as the center of debate. It is very difficult to find in the contemporary Israeli political scene forces that will end Israeli occupation of the West Bank and Gaza Strip. Apparently, none of the region's political leaders finds either the current situation or the particular proposals set forth by President Reagan persuasive enough to warrant altering their traditional positions.

The major purpose of this analysis has been to highlight the ways in which general foreign policy attitudes, particular perceptions of the Arab-Israeli dispute, and organizational politics intersect to stimulate public policy. In spite of the need for long-term planning to produce "a more tractable political situation" (Lustick 1980/81, 33), a characteristic of American public policy has been its short-term orientation. American policy makers have attended so often to emergencies resulting from the Arab-Israeli dispute that they have quite naturally perceived the issues solely in these terms. Guided by a crisis response generally designed to fulfill American national interests, the Reagan peace initiative has been served, but not entirely well, by its historical policy-making precedents. Concerned with the urgency of bringing peace to the Middle East now—a goal that may be immediately unachievable—the Reagan administration has not yet provided for what may be achievable: policies that will create an environment in which the winning of peace need not occasion or excuse another war.

REFERENCES AND ADDITIONAL READINGS

Baccus, William I. 1974. *Foreign Policy and the Bureaucratic Process.* Princeton: Princeton University Press.

Bialer, Seweryn, and Joan Afferica. 1982/83. "Reagan and Russia." *Foreign Affairs* 61, no. 2 (Winter): 251–71.

Binder, Leonard. 1982. "United States Policy in the Middle East: Toward a Pax Saudiana." *Current History* 81, no. 471 (January): 1–4.

———. 1983. "United States Policy in the Middle East: Exploiting New Opportunities." *Current History* 82, no. 480 (January): 1–4.

Bolling, Landrum R. 1982. "A Realistic Middle East Policy." *Orbis* 26, no. 1 (Spring): 5–11.

Bruzonsky, Mark A. 1981. "America's Palestinian Predicament." *International Security* 6, no. 1 (Summer): 93–110.

Buheiry, Marwan R. 1978. "The Saunders Document." *Journal of Palestine Studies* 8, no. 1 (Autumn): 28–40.

Choucri, Nazli. 1982. "The Arab World in the 1980s: Macro-Politics and Economic Change." *Journal of Arab Affairs* 1, no. 2: 167–87.

Destler, I.M. 1981. "Congress as Boss?" *Foreign Policy*, no. 42 (Spring): 167–80.

Garfinkle, Adam M. 1982a. "Jordan and Arab Polarization." *Current History* 81, no. 471 (January): 22–25.

_____.1982b. "United States-Israeli Relations: The Wolf This Time?" *Orbis* 26, no. 1 (Spring): 11–19.

Gelb, Leslie H. 1982. "United States Sees Opportunities and Risks in Mideast after War in Lebanon." *New York Times*, 31 October 1982.

Halperin, Morton H. 1974. *Bureaucratic Politics and Foreign Policy*. Washington, D.C.: The Brookings Institution.

Harrison, Michael M. 1981. "Reagan's World." *Foreign Policy*, no. 43 (Summer): 3–16.

Hoffmann, Stanley. 1981. "Requiem." *Foreign Policy*, no. 42 (Spring): 3–26.

Hudson, Michael C. 1982. "The United States Decline in the Middle East." *Orbis* 26, no. 1 (Spring): 19–26.

_____. 1983. "The Palestinians after Lebanon." *Current History* 82, no. 480 (January): 5–9, 34.

Jerusalem Post. Various issues.

Kaplowitz, Noel. 1982. "The Search for Peace in the Middle East." *International Security* 7, no. 1 (Summer): 181–207.

Kerr, Malcolm H., and El Sayed Yassin, eds. 1982. *Rich and Poor States in the Middle East: Egypt and the New Arab Order*. Boulder, Colo.: Westview Press.

Kreczko, Alan J. 1982/83. "Support Reagan's Initiative." *Foreign Policy*, no. 49 (Winter): 140–53.

Lustick, Ian S. 1980/81. "Kill the Autonomy Talks." *Foreign Policy*, no. 41 (Winter): 21–43.

_____. 1982/83. "Israeli Politics and American Foreign Policy." *Foreign Affairs* 61, no. 2 (Winter): 379–99.

Miller, Linda B. 1978. "America and the Palestinians: In Search of a Policy." In *The Palestinians and the Middle East Conflict*, edited by Gabriel Ben-Dor, 281–90. Ramat Gan, Israel: Turtledove.

Newsom, David. 1981. "America Engulfed." *Foreign Policy*, no. 43 (Summer): 17–32.

New York Times. Various issues.

Perlmutter, Amos. 1982a. "Begin's Rhetoric and Sharon's Tactics." *Foreign Affairs* 61, no. 1 (Fall): 67–84.

_____. 1982b. "Reagan's Middle East Policy." *Orbis* 26, no. 1 (Spring): 26–30.

Pipes, Daniel. 1982. "Increasing Security in the Persian Gulf." *Orbis* 26, no. 1 (Spring): 30–35.

Quandt, William B. 1977. *Decade of Decisions: American Policy toward the Arab-Israeli Conflict 1967–1976*. Berkeley: University of California Press.

_____. 1981. "Riyadh between the Superpowers." *Foreign Policy*, no. 44 (Fall): 37–56.

Rabinovich, Itamar, and Haim Shaked, eds. 1978. *From June to October: The Middle East between 1967 and 1973*. New Brunswick: Transaction Books.

Reagan, Ronald. 1982. Address on 1 September 1982. *American-Arab Affairs*, no. 2 (Fall): 149–54.

Reilly, James A. 1982. "Israel in Lebanon, 1975–82." *MERIP Reports*, no. 108/109 (September/October): 14–20.

Ross, Dennis. 1981. "Considering Soviet Threats to the Persian Gulf." *International Security* 6, no. 2 (Fall): 159–80.

Rubin, Barry. 1981. *The Arab States and the Palestine Conflict*. Syracuse: Syracuse University Press.

Safran, Nadav. 1978. *Israel the Embattled Ally*. Cambridge, Mass.: Harvard University Press.

Sayegh, Fayez A. 1979. "The Camp David Agreement and the Palestine Problem." *Journal of Palestine Studies* 8, no. 2 (Winter): 3–54.

Shaked, Haim, and Itamar Rabinovich, eds. 1980. *The Middle East and the United States: Perceptions and Policies*. New Brunswick: Transaction Books.

Shultz, George. 1982. "Statement before the United States House of Representatives Committee on Foreign Affairs on 9 September 1982." *American-Arab Affairs*, no. 2 (Fall): 156–60.

Sisco, Joseph J. 1981. "Selective Engagement." *Foreign Policy* no. 42 (Spring): 27–42.

Thompson, W. Scott. 1982. "The Persian Gulf and the Correlation of Forces." *International Security* 7, no. 1 (Summer): 157–80.

Tillman, Seth P. 1982. *The United States in the Middle East*. Bloomington: Indiana University Press.

Vlahos, Michael, and Geoffrey Kemp. 1981. "The Changing Strategic Tapestry in the Middle East." In *Middle East Contemporary Survey*, edited by Colin Legum, Haim Shaked, and Daniel Dishon, 33–44. New York: Holmes and Meier.

Wieseltier, Leon. 1983. "Have Conscience, Will Travel." *Harper's*, 266, no. 1592 (January): 64–68.

Wright, Claudia. 1982. "Shadow on Sand: Strategy and Deception in Reagan's Policy toward the Arabs." *Journal of Palestine Studies* 11, no. 3 (Spring): 3–36.

Yorke, Valerie. 1979. "Palestinian Self-Determination and Israel's Security." *Journal of Palestine Studies* 8, no. 3 (Spring): 3–25.

The Internationalization of the Conflict in Western Sahara

Robert A. Mortimer

The admission of the Saharan Arab Democratic Republic (SADR) to a conference of the Organization of African Unity (OAU) in February 1982 was a diplomatic bombshell exploding in a treacherous mine field. To King Hassan II of Morocco, the seating of the SADR was an act of "juridical brigandage." For Algiers, it merely accorded the Saharawi government in exile its "legitimate place" in African affairs (*Le Monde*, 25 February 1982). Whatever its legal status, the February decision shattered the Implementation Committee that the OAU had established in 1981 to negotiate a settlement of the war in Western Sahara. Indeed, the explosion burst asunder the OAU itself, opening a breach that had not been repaired by the end of 1982. That this conflict among Arab peoples and governments has become a major issue for the Pan-African organization is but one intriguing facet of the complex struggle over this arid, inhospitable stretch of desert territory.

The dispute over Western Sahara has raged since 1975, when Morocco and Mauritania annexed the territory of what had been Spanish Sahara. What had appeared a decolonization issue suddenly erupted into a crisis between Morocco and Mauritania on the one hand and Algeria and the nationalist Polisario Front on the other. The former pair argued that they were reintegrating parts of their historic territory colonized for ninety years by Spain. The latter pair maintained that the population of the erstwhile Spanish colony—the camel-herding Reguibat, the Ma El Ainin, the Ouled Delim, and other essentially nomadic peoples—was entitled to self-determination. Algeria provided sanctuary to the resistance movement, whose guerrilla fighters have prevented the Moroccan army from securing the territory against their raids. Both sides have mounted major diplomatic campaigns alongside their military operations. In February 1982 the diplomatic hostilities became as dangerous as the hit-and-run desert warfare—at least insofar as the OAU was concerned.

In order to understand the most recent developments in this smoldering conflict, we must review its causes and identify its stakes for Algeria and Morocco (Mauritania having been knocked from the field in 1978). Numerous other actors including Libya, the United States, and France have had to deal with the repercussions of this Maghrebi struggle. However little known Western Sahara may be, this war at the western extremity of the Arab world has become part of an intricate strategic calculus. This article examines how a regional conflict has taken on implications of continental and global political significance.

BACKGROUND TO THE CONFLICT

King Hassan II is the heir of a dynasty that has ruled Morocco since the seventeenth century. Throughout the western reaches of the Sahara, nomadic Muslim peoples paid fealty to the Moroccan sultan during the nineteenth century before the imposition of French and Spanish colonial claims. Moroccan nationalists, and most notably Allal al-Fassi of the Istiqlal party, remember these past glories with national pride—not to say irredentist longing. (al-Fassi defined Greater Morocco as extending to Timbuktu and the Senegal River, thereby incorporating southwestern Algeria, part of Mali, and all of Mauritania.) The historical record of religious allegiance to the Moroccan throne is the basis of the government's contemporary claim to Western Sahara.

Spain took possession of part of the territory in 1884, delimiting its claims progressively in a series of agreements with France. In practice, Spain limited its occupation to the littoral, a rich fishing area south of the Canary Islands, while the Saharan clansmen roamed uninhibitedly across the hinterland. The administrative structure was rudimentary, but it served to demarcate a juridical entity apart from the French administration all around it. To Morocco this merely meant a different colonial occupant of a chunk of its precolonial Saharan domains, but for others it implied an eventual right to self-determination.

Two factors, the superficial character of Spanish rule and the disparate nature of the nomadic clans that lived there, explain the relative tardiness of any coherent anticolonial movement. Indeed, the pressure for decolonization in the mid-1960s came primarily from the neighboring states sponsoring self-determination resolutions in the United Nations General Assembly. Spurred by this encouragement, Saharawi organizations began to appear in the late 1960s and claimed responsibility for demonstrations against Spanish rule in June 1970. No organization gained any genuine popular footing, however, until 1972–73, when Saharawi students educated in Rabat began to line up support for the movement that was formally constituted as the Polisario Front (Popular Front for the Liberation of Saguia el Hamra and Rio de Oro) in May 1973. Although Polisario needed external backing to challenge the Spanish forces, "the strength of the Polisario Front has been due to its concentration on the one objective deeply rooted in Western Saharan traditions, that of total independence from foreign controls" (Thompson and Adloff 1980, 135).

The paradox of Saharawi nationalism lies in a spirit of independence that so transcended the structures of colonial authority as to virtually ignore them. The population of Western Sahara is composed of a number of qabael [qabā'il], autonomous clans organized in loose confederations, of which the largest is the Reguibat. Their pastoral lives were relatively little touched by the sparse administrative network of the Spanish authorities (let alone any earlier Moroccan sultanic authority). The Reguibat were prominent in the resistance to French colonial authority when it was extended into the outreaches of the Sahara to Tindouf as late as 1934; indeed it was France that insisted that Spain extend its occupation into the interior in order to assist in the pacification of the Reguibat and other smaller clans (Hodges 1982a). Only in the late 1960s did the continental wave of decolonization directly implicate these desert peoples in a more modern style of politics.

Algeria was a force in injecting liberation movement politics into Western Sahara. Decolonization has been a major theme of Algerian diplomacy far and wide. There was nothing exceptional in its application of the principle to an adjacent territory (however modest the border strip between them). The matter was rendered delicate, however, by Moroccan claims, which Algeria hesitated to challenge directly. The early 1970s were in fact a period of rapprochement between Algeria and Morocco during which they resolved the border tensions that had provoked the 1963 Algero-Moroccan war. In June 1972 the two states signed a treaty that demarcated the border to Algeria's satisfaction including renunciation of Moroccan claims to Tindouf, later to become the principal Saharawi refugee site. According to I. William Zartman, Morocco won one point in the negotiations over the treaty: "Algerian support for Moroccan claims over the one remaining piece of the irredenta, the Spanish Sahara" (Zartman 1979, 132).

Whatever understanding the Moroccans may have had of Algerian intentions, the Algerians took an interest in Saharawis committed to independence. They supported a short-lived organization called Morehob for a time in 1973, rebuffing the earliest overtures of the nascent Polisario. By 1974, however, after Polisario's initial attack against Spanish garrisons, Algeria shifted its attention to that movement. By no means did Algeria create Polisario; it paid heed to the Polisario fighters once they had shown their mettle in hit-and-run operations against the colonial occupier. Clearly Algeria had a geopolitical interest in an independent state south of Morocco. However cordial or strained Algerian-Moroccan relations may be at any moment, Algeria must be reluctant to see a potential rival extend its power deep into the Sahara. The presence of a buffer state in the region, separating Morocco from Mauritania and permitting a potential corridor from Algeria to the Atlantic, constitutes a more attractive regional environment from the perspective of Algiers. Geopolitics suffices to explain Algeria's unfailing support for the principle of self-determination in Western Sahara.

Morocco has argued that Algeria temporarily acquiesced in its plan to recover its Saharan "province." The Moroccans cite a speech by President Houari Boumediene at a closed session of the 1974 Arab summit meeting in which he is said to have accepted a joint Moroccan-Mauritanian partition of the territory. The public record indicates, however, that Algeria consistently articulated its position in terms of self-determination. It is reasonable to believe that Algeria cultivated a measure of ambiguity on its commitments because it was confident that Spain would eventually have to organize a referendum, the outcome of which would be a vote for independence.

Algeria may also have calculated that Moroccan-Mauritanian rivalry would neutralize their competing claims and provide further pressure for an electoral consultation on the fate of the territory. Mauritania's shift from a policy of contesting Moroccan claims to a policy of partition was thus a significant turning point in the evolution of the conflict. Mauritania was itself from 1960 to 1969 the object of Moroccan irredentism on much the same grounds as Western Sahara. The Mauritanian leader Mokhtar Ould Daddah countered Moroccan nonrecognition policy by asserting the existence of a "Mauritanian personality" based upon a common Moorish culture that encompassed some of the peoples living in Spanish Sahara. Just as some Saharawis went to Rabat for higher education, others became students in Nouakchott and Nouadhibou. Yet others became workers in the Zouerate iron mines located near the Western Saharan border. Family and cultural ties did exist across the colonial borders, but Mauritania scarcely had the means to impose any new Moorish order upon the disputed territory. Its own claims were in large measure a response to its Moroccan problem.

During the 1960s Mauritania enlisted the support of Algeria as a counterweight to Morocco. Ould Daddah became a frequent visitor to Algiers, and the Algerians gave both technical assistance and diplomatic support to Mauritania. Boumediene helped to fashion the eventual rapprochement by which Morocco renounced its claims and established diplomatic relations with Mauritania. The saliency of the Spanish Saharan issue appeared relatively low for Ould Daddah until 1974, when Portuguese decolonization and the failing health of Spanish dictator Francisco Franco increased the pressure upon Spain for change in the status of the colony. The Mauritanian leader found the Moroccan offer of partition his best option. No doubt he has pondered the wisdom of that decision since his overthrow in 1978, largely attributable to the internal costs of the Mauritanian war against Polisario.

When Spain abruptly announced in 1974 that it would conduct a referendum in the territory, King Hassan adroitly submitted the question of precolonial sovereignty to the International Court of Justice. The move forestalled direct Spanish action and gave Morocco time to plot its own strategy; Hassan may well have been confident of his legal case, but he did not rest upon that alone. Algeria formally approved the submission to the ICJ, but restated its own view that the opinion of the population directly involved will always constitute the primordial and determinative element of any settlement. Just how far Algeria was prepared to press its case remained unclear until July 1975 when Boumediene dispatched Mohamed Bedjaoui to The Hague to argue on behalf of self-determination. (Bedjaoui, who has served as Algeria's ambassador to France and to the United Nations, was elected to a seat on the ICJ in 1982.) The decision publicly to contest the Moroccan case dissipated any remaining uncertainty regarding Algerian determination to press for some kind of referendum. Concurrently, Algeria stepped up its aid to Polisario.

The court announced its decision in October. It held that the evidence "does not establish any tie of territorial sovereignty" between Western Sahara and Morocco. The evidence did "provide indications that a legal tie of allegiance had existed . . . between the Sultan and some, but only some, of the nomadic peoples of the territory." Its findings regarding Mauritanian claims were similar. The court concluded that these legal ties did not dilute the applicability of the "principle of self-determination through the free and genuine expression of the will of the peoples of the Territory" (cited in Hodges 1982a).

King Hassan was not in the least deterred by this apparent legal setback. On the contrary, he announced that the ICJ opinion confirmed the Moroccan thesis of sovereignty and called upon the Moroccan people peacefully to enter and liberate the territory. This was the remarkable Green March, a stunning display of popular support for the annexation policy in which hundreds of thousands of Moroccans armed only with flags and the Qurʾān crossed the frontier, daring the Spanish authorities to open fire upon them (in fact Moroccan troops also entered under the cover of the march). Spain buckled under this show of fervor, and negotiated a tripartite agreement with Morocco and Mauritania known as the Madrid accords. Spain agreed to establish "an intermediate administration in the territory with the participation of Morocco and Mauritania and the collaboration of the Djema (local assembly)," to which it would transfer power definitively by 28 February 1976 (from the text of the accords as cited in Schulman 1979, 123). After the signing of this agreement, Moroccan and Mauritanian troops occupied the territory.

Polisario was hardly capable of resisting this onslaught, but it was able to organize a large-scale exodus of the population. The Polisario leadership also induced a majority of the members of the Djemaa [Jamāʿah] (a consultative body weighted in favor of older, traditionalist elements of the population) to sign a proclamation dissolving the assembly and proclaiming that the Polisario Front was the sole legitimate representative of the Saharan people. The occupying powers later managed to convene a rump session of the Djemaa (attended by approximately half its membership) in accordance with provisions in the Madrid accords; at this meeting a vote in favor of integration into Morocco and Mauritania was passed, but virtually no one has considered this a legitimate exercise of self-determination. Rather, the flight from the territory of large numbers of Saharawis and the ensuing armed resistance of the Polisario Front indicated that the conflict was entering a new phase of military and diplomatic struggle.

WAR AND DIPLOMACY

Although they have needed external support and sanctuary, the Saharawis have waged their own war of national liberation. Algeria, of course, has been Polisario's major ally, providing both material support and access to other governments. Aside from a brief military engagement near Amgala in January 1976, however, Algerian forces have left the fighting to the Saharawis, who decided almost immediately to carry the war directly into Mauritania and southern Morocco. As early as June 1976, Polisario forces successfully crossed Mauritania to raid Nouakchott. They carried out several attacks around Zouerate, where they managed to capture several French nationals. From guerrilla harassment, the situation in Mauritania escalated to grave military and economic insecurity as Polisario constantly threatened the Zouerate-Nouadhibou railroad line. Moroccan reinforcements were sent into the country, a dubious benefit so far as the Mauritanian high command was concerned. The war against the Saharawis did not enjoy the same popular support in Mauritania that it had in Morocco. These circumstances prompted the military to depose Ould Daddah in July 1978, in effect removing Mauritania from the battlefield. Morocco successfully moved its forces into Dakhla in the former Mauritanian sector and declared its annexation as well.

Since then Polisario has faced a tougher and more determined adversary. Morocco has steadily increased its contingents in the Sahara to over 40,000 soldiers. Moreover, most of the rest of the army of about 180,000 men—up from 70,000 in 1975—is stationed in southern Morocco or along the eastern border. Government security expenditures exceed $1 billion, about one-third of the national budget and even more when military-related spending under the separate investment budget is considered. Budget deficits, state borrowing, and a debt service obligation of 35 percent of export earnings are the result (figures from Hodges 1982c, 6). This massive commitment has permitted Morocco to control the northwest sector of the territory, around which it has erected a huge fortification—a sand wall variant of the electronic battlefield. The Moroccans also hold an enclave around Dakhla, but the rest of the territory is unsecured, essentially abandoned to the Polisario guerrillas.

The war has been bitterly contested. From 1975 to 1978, Polisario gradually escalated its operations from hit-and-run raids against isolated outposts and convoys to full-scale attacks on the FAR (Forces Armées Royales) positions in Saharan towns. In 1979, the Saharawis attacked the town of Tantan, some fifty miles into Moroccan territory. This attack obliged the Moroccan armed forces to adopt a new offensive strategy through the creation of a mobile strike unit named the Ohoud Division. In the spring of 1980 Morocco launched the Ohoud offensive under the direct command of chief of staff Ahmed Dlimi, with the declared objective of absolute control of the hinterland by the end of the year. The campaign failed to neutralize the Polisario forces, now armed with increasingly sophisticated equipment.

Morocco disputes the contention that it controls only a small portion of the former Spanish colony. Foreign Minister Mohammed Boucetta insisted in the spring of 1982 that "we control and have our people throughout the territory of Western Sahara. . . . I can confirm to you that we are in military control and that our administration operates through every part of the territory" (Boucetta 1982, 13). Yet the testimony of numerous journalists who have traversed the region with the guerrillas renders this claim dubious. The announcement in May 1982 that the fortified wall was being hastily extended from Bu Craa to Boujdour on the Atlantic coast appeared to confirm that Morocco had reverted to a strategy of defending the "useful triangle" in the northwest (Le Monde, 9–10 May 1982).

The area enclosed by the wall runs south from Ras el-Khanfra to Smara, a city of religious significance, and then arches westward to Bu Craa, site of the phosphate mines that constitute Western Sahara's greatest economic resource. The new extension protects the modest port of Boujdour, the only settlement of any size that had remained outside the fortified area. The capital city of al-Ayun and the conveyor belt from the mines to the sea lie inside the triangle. The wall itself is no mere pile of sand but a sophisticated barrier equipped with radar, electronic sensors, and other detection devices mainly supplied by the American corporation Westinghouse. Clearly Morocco had dug in to defend this hunk of the Saharan "provinces."

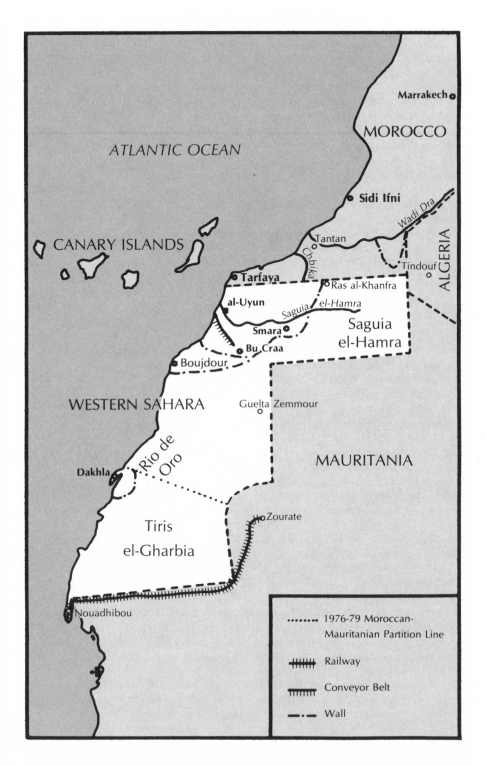

MARRAKECH ○

MOROCCO

ATLANTIC OCEAN

Sidi Ifni ●

CANARY ISLANDS

Tantan

Wadi Dra

Chbika

Tindouf ○

ALGERIA

Tarfaya ●

Ras al-Khanfra ○

al-Uyun ●

Saguia el-Hamra

Saguia
el-Hamra

Smara ●

Bu Craa ●

Boujdour ●

WESTERN SAHARA

Guelta Zemmour ○

Rio de Oro

MAURITANIA

Dakhla ●

Tiris
el-Gharbia

Zourate ○

Nouadhibou ●

········· 1976-79 Moroccan-
Mauritanian Partition Line

╪╪╪╪╪ Railway

╥╥╥╥╥ Conveyor Belt

─ ∙ ─ ∙ Wall

Yet there is no evidence that the Saharawis have wearied of their cause. Rather, they have responded to Morocco's military expenditures by seeking more advanced equipment for their own use. They have acquired ground-to-air missiles, heavier transport equipment, and perhaps some tanks. One must assume that they will get the long-range ground-to-ground missiles that would be necessary to launch an attack against the wall. The Moroccans state that some of these arms are now passing through the Mauritanian port of Nouadhibou. Algeria and Libya are the main sources of these arms, and more than any other factor continued Algerian support of the Saharawi resistance is critical to the fortunes of Polisario.

The war does constitute a drain on Algerian resources also, although to a lesser extent than is true of Morocco. The Algerian government has maintained its commitment to self-determination through two administrations. Colonel Chadli Benjedid, who became president in February 1979 after the death of Boumediene, has not altered his predecessor's policy in any substantial way. Algeria has viewed the struggle for Western Sahara through the lens of its own historical experience. The strategy of the Algerian Front of National Liberation and its Provisional Government was to wage a two-pronged campaign, military and diplomatic. The military effort was essentially to tie down and embarrass the colonial occupier; the diplomatic campaign exploited that political embarrassment. In addition to its material support to the refugees and the guerrillas, Algeria has sponsored an unremitting diplomatic campaign on behalf of the SADR's claim to independence.

Hassan's Green March and extraction of the Madrid accords from Spain caught Algeria unawares on the diplomatic front. Since then Algeria has been working to undo the Moroccan fait accompli. In every available international arena, the Algerians have pressed the principle of the Saharawi right to self-determination, and have encouraged other governments to meet the Polisario leaders and to recognize the SADR. Algeria has elicited favorable resolutions at nonaligned and United Nations forums, but it has focused its diplomatic campaign on the Organization of African Unity. As early as 1976, the Algerians won a resolution that called for an Extraordinary Summit to reexamine the issues concerning Western Sahara. As Morocco, however, had no intention of attending such a meeting, it proved impossible in practice to convene. The pattern was repeated after the 1977 regular annual meeting. This time Algeria succeeded in pressuring President Omar Bongo of Gabon to issue invitations to such a summit, but nothing came of the initiative. Since the summit tactic was ineffectual, the 1978 meeting voted to set up an Ad Hoc Committee on Western Sahara. The committee, comprising the heads of state of Nigeria, Mali, Tanzania, Guinea, and Sudan, met with all parties over the course of the ensuing year and finally submitted a report to the 1979 summit that called for a cease-fire and a referendum. Upon approval of this recommendation, the Moroccan delegation walked out of the conference; the resolution proved unimplementable.

While opinion of the OAU majority was shifting in this direction, more and more individual African states were formally recognizing the SADR. By mid-1980, twenty-three states, or almost half of the OAU's total membership of fifty states, had recognized the government in exile. The prospect of SADR admission to the Pan-African organization began to loom as a real possibility that would constitute a significant diplomatic blow to Morocco's interests. When the annual summit convened in Freetown in July 1980, three more states (Chad, Mali, and newly independent Zimbabwe) declared their support for entry of the SADR into the OAU. In these circumstances Morocco was obliged to stay and mount a diplomatic counterattack.

The 1980 summit thus witnessed an acrimonious debate and a Moroccan power play. Prime Minister Maati Bouabid first raised a procedural question. The OAU charter, he argued, provides only for the admission of sovereign, independent states; as the SADR did not meet these requirements, the charter would have to be amended, a change that required a two-thirds majority. Morocco's real argument, however, was that it could enlist several African allies in a walkout movement that would cripple the OAU. Among the states ready to join Morocco in protest were several important francophone moderates (Senegal, Ivory Coast, Guinea, Cameroun, Zaire) and several Arab supporters (Egypt, Sudan, Somalia, Tunisia). Morocco had long been cultivating these states (by actions such as its aid to Zaire during the Shaba province outbursts of 1977 and 1978 and its approval of President Anwar Sadat's diplomacy) in order to counterbalance Algeria's pro-Polisario diplomacy.

The Moroccan threat to splinter the organization was a sufficient deterrent to Algeria, which was reluctant at that moment to bear the onus of provoking such a split. So far as Algeria was concerned, the Freetown proceedings in themselves raised the pressure upon Morocco and opened the possibility for further negotiation. The proponents of SADR admission agreed to defer or "put into abeyance" this question and once again referred the entire matter to the Ad Hoc Committee. The final resolution welcomed "Morocco's willingness to engage in discussions with all parties and participate in the work of the committee" (Novicki 1980, 40). Morocco thus warded off an act of legitimization of the Polisario cause and gained time to shore up its deteriorating political position.

Efforts to achieve a negotiated settlement did occur after the Freetown summit, as indeed various initiatives had predated that conference. Not much is known in detail about these talks, which have been held discreetly beyond public view. Subsequent leaks and rumors have merely verified their existence and confirmed the obvious—that Morocco and Polisario have not been able to agree upon any partition or other compromise arrangement that might somehow allow both sides to save face and avert total capitulation. The mere rumor of such talks produced criticism of the government in the Moroccan press. This reaction illustrates the narrow margin of room available to the king. Indeed Hassan initially used the Saharan issue to stabilize his own domestic political situation, which was shaky after two attempted coups in the early 1970s. The very legitimacy of the monarchy may be at stake so far as he is concerned.

For Polisario the stakes are also high: control of an independent state endowed with significant mineral resources. The guerrillas and the refugees have made sacrifices and they have become more politicized in the process. Having successfully "internationalized" the conflict—just as the Algerians did during their war with France—and stymied the Moroccan army, they have grounds on which to expect rewards. They have earned their own bargaining power, and Algeria cannot impose a settlement; Polisario objections are said to have been the stumbling block in some of the futile secret talks arranged between Algeria and Morocco.

Compromise is perhaps easiest for Algeria to envisage. Benjedid no doubt would like to be free of the costs of the conflict. So long as some kind of Saharawi entity is established, Algeria will have acquitted itself of obligations both to principle and interest. It cannot abandon Polisario nor sell it out egregiously, but it can presumably get by with less than a total defeat of Morocco. Algeria's basic objective has been to force Morocco to the bargaining table and it has seen the OAU as the most promising instrument to achieve that end. Having eased the pressure a bit at Freetown, Algeria allowed Morocco some time to digest the new situation before tightening the screws again.

The engagement of the OAU, in contrast with the negligible role of the Arab League, is worthy of comment. One must recall that the OAU charter designates self-determination in the framework of colonial boundaries as one of its founding principles. The respect of colonial borders undermines secessionist movements and irredentist claims in a universe of fragile nations. The principles are tailor-made to fit the Algerian position. At the same time, the Arab world has been reluctant to become embroiled in the battle, an abstention that basically supports the status quo. Arab states have refrained from recognizing the SADR (aside from Algeria, only South Yemen in 1978, and Syria and Libya in 1980). In January 1978 Boumediene made a major effort to rally support in the Middle East during a journey to ten Arab countries. Other issues were on the agenda at the time, notably Sadat's trip to Jerusalem, and Boumediene appears to have sought to link the Saharawi cause to the Palestinian cause. The ploy did not work, Hassan having successfully lined up the monarchies and the sheikdoms behind his appeal to sultanic allegiance. Since then Algeria has preferred to press its advantage in the OAU, while Morocco, which likes to consider the case closed, has not raised the issue in the Arab League. Saudi financial support, it is worthwhile to add, has been of considerable importance to Rabat.

Arabs and Africans are not the only parties affected by the conflict. The major powers have had to make decisions about the extent of their aid to the belligerents. France, for example, became briefly involved militarily on behalf of Mauritania in 1977. The Soviet Union has sold weapons to Algeria and Libya that have found their way into Polisario hands. The United States has had to respond to Morocco's pleas for arms. The Carter administration agonized over arms sales, especially following the fall of the shah of Iran, and finally agreed to provide helicopters and other equipment with the understanding that the king, having strengthened his military position, would seriously pursue a negotiated settlement. Through 1980, nonetheless, the major powers all sought to maintain an officially neutral stance on the substance of the diplomatic issue so as to preserve their ties with both Morocco and Algeria. By the end of 1980, it was clear that Morocco was most in need of new external support to bolster a deteriorating position. It found that support in the Reagan administration.

TRIALS AND TRIBULATIONS OF THE OAU

Two factors have distinguished the years 1981 and 1982: Morocco's new confidence in the American connection and the crisis in the OAU. What first appeared to be an OAU-sponsored breakthrough turned out to be an OAU breakdown. Meanwhile global strategic calculations in Washington transformed Hassan from a friend in need into an indispensable ally of the United States.

During the first six months of 1981 all the pressure seemed to be building up on Morocco. The economic costs were becoming more and more painful, and troop morale was flagging. Popular fervor for the protracted war began to wane as more families suffered losses at the front. Mauritania had not only abandoned the war but was permitting Polisario to install base camps on its territory. Libya pursued an erratic policy that fluctuated between peace initiatives and arms deliveries, but on balance was becoming more influential within Polisario ranks, an unpalatable outcome for Morocco. In mid-June riots over food prices and unemployment in the war-bled economy erupted in Casablanca. Hassan felt obliged to diffuse the pressure by a conciliatory gesture at the 1981 OAU summit.

The king personally led the Moroccan delegation to the Nairobi conference. He announced that Morocco was prepared to permit a "controlled referendum" in the former colony. The offer was perceived as a major concession by Morocco and a great opportunity for the OAU to settle the dispute peacefully. Hassan's dramatic about-face captured the headlines at Nairobi, but knowledgeable observers understood that the gesture obscured a myriad of practical difficulties that would plague the OAU over the following months.

Indeed, even at Nairobi considerable debate was necessary to define the terms that would govern the referendum process. The principal issues involved a cease-fire and the withdrawal of Moroccan forces. Morocco wanted the former but not the latter. Polisario saw the latter as a precondition for a fair vote and was reluctant to grant a cease-fire without that condition. Furthermore, the very nature of the "controlled referendum" was open to different interpretations, and Morocco was unwilling to recognize Polisario as a party to the process of consultation. The Nairobi summit resolved these uncertainties in classic fashion: it set up a committee. The Implementation Committee was an expanded version of the earlier Ad Hoc Committee, Kenya and Sierra Leone being added to the original five members. The heads of state entrusted the new committee with a substantial mandate: "to meet before the end of August 1981 in order to work out in collaboration with the parties to the conflict the procedures and all other details regarding installation of a cease-fire as well as the organisation and holding of a referendum" (*Le Monde*, 30 June 1981).

In deference to Morocco, the OAU resolution did not explicitly designate "the parties to the conflict." It appeared to fix a cease-fire as a prerequisite, but said nothing about withdrawal of the Moroccan army. The heads of state voted down an Algerian-sponsored amendment to require withdrawal of the Moroccan troops and administration during the electoral campaign. The only concession made to Polisario was explicitly to use the expression "self-determination referendum," which Hassan had not used. It soon became apparent that Hassan did not consider Morocco bound by the notion of self-determination. Upon his return to Rabat, he declared:

> In truth I have never refused a referendum but solely self-determination, which places sovereignty in question. This referendum will be only an act of confirmation, because the Moroccan people [of the Sahara] will not go back on their past oaths of allegiance. (*Le Monde*, 4 July 1981)

The king added that so far as he was concerned, the parties to the conflict were Morocco, Algeria, and Mauritania—not Polisario, "which has never existed for the African community." In these circumstances, it was evident that the Implementation Committee had its work cut out for it. Polisario expressed its skepticism about Moroccan intentions. Algeria, having failed in its attempt to tighten the committee's terms of reference, nevertheless cautiously welcomed the new OAU framework as "the first step in the search for peace" (*New York Times*, 27 June 1981).

The divergent conceptions of Morocco and Polisario were but the most obvious obstacles facing the Implementation Committee. Perhaps the knottiest issue of all is the question of who will be entitled to vote in the eventual plebiscite. Who, in other words, should be counted as a Saharawi, especially now that very large numbers of the population are living outside the boundaries of the former Spanish colony? There exists a 1974 Spanish census, but Polisario insists that it is far from complete. Already at the time of that census, many members of the Western Saharan qabael were not resident in the colony. Conversely, there are many "mainland" Moroccans now living in the territory as well as Saharawis who might have settled temporarily in southern Morocco prior to the annexation. Who is to determine who the eligible voters are? Can the UN (upon which the 1981 resolution calls for assistance in policing a cease-fire and administering the referendum) or the OAU make such decisions? That hardly seems feasible without the involvement of representatives of the qabael themselves, which in turn implies participation by Polisario.

No less perplexing than the issue of eligibility is the matter of electoral campaigning. Polisario questions the authenticity of any consultation carried out in the presence of the Moroccan authorities, while Hassan has stated that "foreign publicists" and "troublemakers who are against us" cannot be tolerated on Moroccan territory (that is, in Western Sahara). The gulf between the two parties' notions of what would constitute a fair election was very great. Polisario confirmed this early in July by publishing its own list of demands, including complete Moroccan withdrawal, return of Saharawis to their villages of origin, establishment of a provisional international administration, and direct talks between Morocco and the nationalist Front (Lewis 1981, 413). All that was achieved at Nairobi, therefore, was a framework for negotiations that might begin to bridge the gap.

The Implementation Committee duly set about its task in August, summoning Hassan, Benjedid, President Khouna Ould Heydalla of Mauritania, but also Mohamed Abdelaziz, the secretary general of Polisario. Having heard these parties separately, the committee established some guidelines for the plebiscitary process, rejecting the Moroccan proposal that the poll be limited to those on the 1974 census roll and directing that the refugees in Tindouf be enfranchised. Although the committee itself dealt directly with Polisario, it respected Moroccan sensibilities by referring only to the "parties concerned" when it renewed its call for a cease-fire, which the committee offered to help negotiate. Hostilities had subsided considerably since the summit, but Polisario made no formal commitment in the absence of Moroccan willingness to negotiate directly. For the committee, a cease-fire was a practical necessity to any further implementation; for Morocco, a cease-fire was a respite for its army and administration in its Saharan province; for Polisario, a cease-fire was part of a quid pro quo: it would accept the cease-fire only for a guarantee of an equal role in the referendum process. As Morocco was not willing to grant this, the implementation process could make no headway.

Polisario shrewdly recognized that its next military operation would have to be convincing. They chose as their target the town Guelta Zemmour, one of Morocco's last strongholds outside the "useful triangle." On 13 October, the guerrillas launched a spectacular attack against the outpost, which they succeeded in occupying for several days. They captured some two hundred prisoners and abundant weaponry before withdrawing from the post (which Morocco shortly chose to abandon after this demonstration of its vulnerability). In the course of the engagement, Polisario downed several Moroccan aircraft as well. This was the aspect of the confrontation that King Hassan astutely chose to emphasize.

He declared that the attacking force employed Soviet-built SAM–6 missiles that no African army, let alone Polisario, had the personnel to operate. Implying that Soviet (or Cuban) advisers must have been implicated in the Guelta Zemmour battle, Hassan added, "If the enemies of Africa have decided to use Soviet missiles installed by non-Africans in Moroccan territory [Western Sahara], that means that they are ready to do worse yet in other regions of Africa" (Le Monde, 15 October 1981). Hassan also charged that Polisario had introduced unprecedented armored vehicles into their offensive. All these assertions were flatly contradicted by Moroccan prisoners interrogated by journalists near the front (Le Monde, 28 October 1981). The real issue here, however, is not who used what. The tenor of the king's remarks suggests that they were addressed in fact to Washington, and that Hassan was making a bid for increased U.S. support. His pleas did not go unheard.

Before examining the American policy response, the impact of the Guelta Zemmour operation upon the OAU mediation effort must be considered. The attack placed the Implementation Committee in a dilemma, for it demonstrated irrefutably that the Polisario Front was a force to be reckoned with in any realistic assessment of military capabilities in the disputed territory. The committee was stalemated in the absence of a cease-fire, and a cease-fire was impossible in the absence of Moroccan recognition of its adversaries. Polisario's African supporters renewed their pressure upon the Implementation Committee (three of whose members—Tanzania, Mali, and Sierra Leone—had recognized the SADR) to name the unnameable, that is, officially designate the Polisario Front as one of the parties to the conflict.

The Implementation Committee thus convened for its second session on Saturday, 6 February 1982, in Nairobi. Over that weekend, the foreign ministers of the states constituting the committee drew up a document for approval by their heads of state. As one OAU secretariat official put it, the document "called a cat a cat": it identified Polisario as a party to the conflict. Dismayed by this prospect, Morocco reacted vigorously, enlisting notably its ally, President Ahmed Sekou Toure of Guinea, in denouncing the proposal. In the end, the heads of state gave in to Moroccan objections and refrained once again from stating "what everyone knows," as Kenyan president and committee chairman Daniel T. Arap Moi himself acknowledged. The Moroccan press exalted Morocco's "three nos": no recognition of Polisario; no direct negotiations with it; and no withdrawal of its military or administrative personnel during the referendum period (Le Monde, 12 February 1982).

The Implementation Committee recognized that it was at an impasse. It felt obliged to retain Moroccan cooperation. Yet Rabat's insistence that it could deal only with Algeria—Polisario being solely a band of Algerian mercenaries—thwarted the committee's quest for a cease-fire. The committee decided to send President Moi on a diplomatic shuttle mission to try to mediate a solution. Morocco appeared to have shifted the pressure back onto Algeria, but Algiers had run out of patience with the Implementation Committee. The Algerians now moved to mobilize the OAU majority and create a new diplomatic environment.

The admission of the SADR to the OAU was a genuine coup de théâtre. The secretary general of the OAU, Edem Kodjo, explained that he issued credentials to the Polisario delegation because the SADR had been duly recognized by a majority of the OAU's member states. Yet this situation had of course existed since July 1980. Since then there had been a tacit understanding not to press the matter in order to allow the special committees to pursue a diplomatic settlement (although Kodjo asserted that he had periodically been harassed to seat the SADR). This diplomatic consensus deteriorated after the February session of the Implementation Committee, and according to Kodjo, "Polisario and its supporters returned to the charge" (Kodjo 1982). Arguing that he had no juridical grounds on which to resist their demand, Kodjo made an administrative decision to admit the SADR to the Council of Ministers' meeting scheduled for 22 February.

No doubt Kodjo recognized that his decision was of the highest political significance, yet he neglected to inform Morocco or Kenya of his action. Perhaps he hoped to force a dramatic confrontation that might unblock the impasse. Perhaps he acquiesced in a diplomatic stunt designed to embarrass Morocco. Perhaps he believed that the exercise would be pointless unless Morocco and its allies were present to register the tremor. Whatever Kodjo's reasoning, the startling entrance of the Saharawi delegation into the conference hall on the afternoon of 22 February proved to be more drama than the OAU could bear. Within hours the organization was reeling under the impact of a severe political crisis.

The admission maneuver split the OAU into predictable camps. Morocco rallied its supporters to execute the long-threatened walkout: Ivory Coast, Senegal, Zaire, Cameroun, Guinea, Central African Republic, Niger, Djibouti, and Gambia took the rostrum on the following afternoon to protest the "irregularities" that they perceived in the form or the substance of the admission decision. Finally, eighteen governments joined Morocco in boycotting the session, enough to reduce the quorum of two-thirds necessary to conduct business. The Moroccan camp was composed essentially of political moderates—mainly francophone states—while the bulk of those backing the Algeria-Polisario position were the African radicals. A handful of important states, like Nigeria, Kenya, and Egypt, that had not recognized the SADR did not join the walkout, and attempted to reconstitute some common ground. For all practical purposes, however, the OAU had become a hostage to the war in Western Sahara.

Although Edem Kodjo did not specifically name the states that pressured him, one must assume that Algeria set the process in motion. Why did Algeria drop its restraint on this matter in February 1982? One can presume that the Algerians were dismayed at the Implementation Committee's refusal to press harder for direct Morocco-Polisario talks. Having placed the matter in the committee's hands for over seven months, Algeria now questioned the efficacy of that instrument. Moreover, the Algerians were sensitive to the renewed American interest in aiding Morocco. One must assume that the Algerian decision to raise the diplomatic stakes and jeopardize the OAU was influenced by the new Reagan administration policy.

After Guelta Zemmour, the United States had dispatched a large military delegation to Morocco. The head of the delegation, assistant secretary of defense Francis J. West, flew to Western Sahara to inspect the Moroccan security installations and announced that the American government was considering new forms of assistance. A few weeks later secretary of defense Caspar Weinberger arrived in Rabat to meet the king. Early in February 1982 he was followed by secretary of state Alexander Haig, who characterized Polisario as a pawn of Libya and the Soviet Union. This parade of dignitaries could only unsettle the Algerian leaders. Fearful that the United States was signing on to the Moroccan cause, Algeria decided to sharpen the line of cleavage across Africa. The risk of splitting the OAU now became diplomatically acceptable in the face of the growing American involvement in a continental dispute.

The repercussions of the admission decision were felt over the rest of the year. In the month following the ministerial council meeting, two OAU-sponsored conferences had to be abandoned because of a boycott by one or the other side (Senegal refused to admit a Polisario delegation, prompting one bloc to withdraw, while Zimbabwe seated the SADR and lost the moderates). Kenya, as the presiding state, called together the OAU bureau, which issued a call to both sides to attend the next regularly scheduled summit in Tripoli in August. The plea was in vain as Morocco's supporters held out against attendance. Despite sustained diplomatic efforts and a variety of compromise proposals, twenty states staunchly refused to participate; for lack of a quorum, the Tripoli summit could not be held. A second try in November failed again in a somewhat different set of circumstances. What became apparent over the summer was that the Western Saharan question was snarled in a larger set of African issues and global calculations.

These issues revolved around the host country. The practice in OAU affairs is to confer the acting "presidency" of the organization upon the chief of state of the country in which the annual summit is held, a prospect that discomfited the American government insofar as Muammar Qaddafi was concerned. The SADR admission question provided an opportunity to sabotage a Libyan presidency. American ambassadors were instructed to lobby African moderates to stay away from Tripoli. The ostensible grounds were disagreement over the admissibility of the SADR; at the same time, encouraging a boycott carried the bonus of a rebuff to Qaddafi. The tactic worked perfectly, to Moroccan and American satisfaction, not to mention a number of African governments wary of Libyan policy in Chad and elsewhere. With a little help from its friends, Morocco succeeded in immobilizing the OAU.

Algeria and Polisario might have gained some diplomatic leverage from a divided and hobbled OAU, but they had little to gain from an inert OAU. Moreover, the majority of those who did not boycott Tripoli sought to avert a total rupture. Thus, Algeria persuaded Polisario to change its tactics as efforts were undertaken to salvage the annual summit by reconvening in November. At the end of October, the SADR announced that it would "abstain voluntarily and temporarily" from the projected second try. A crisis resolution committee proposed that in return for this abstention, Morocco should attend the meeting and concur in the organization of a referendum before the 1983 summit. This proposal constituted an attempt in effect to undo the February admission and resume the Implementation Committee's mandate. Morocco responded that it would attend the meeting only if the issue of Western Sahara was excluded from the agenda.

Although Morocco did not receive formal assurance of this, it was present when preparatory meetings began in Tripoli in mid-November. The Polisario spokespeople remained discreetly in the wings, but this time the issue of Chad moved to the center of the stage, and reproduced the same alignments. The Chad question bore a distant resemblance to the Western Saharan question: desert peoples aided by Libya fighting to change the status quo. The details, of course, were different—a long civil war between rival factions, Libyan intervention and withdrawal, the defeat of the Libyan-backed faction by Hissen Habré in June 1982, and most recently a resumption of active Libyan aid to Goukouni Oueddei in October 1982—but the Habré faction had essentially the same foreign support as Morocco. The issue in November was who would represent Chad. The OAU secretariat had issued an invitation to the Habré government in power in Ndjamena. This embarrassed the Libyans, who sought to pressure the Habré delegation "voluntarily" (like Polisario) to suspend its participation. When this proposal was formally tabled, Morocco protested and left the preparatory meeting, once again followed by Senegal, Gambia, Ivory Coast, Niger, Zaire, and Togo. The preparatory meeting then deteriorated and the quorum again slipped away. Once more Qaddafi lost "his" summit, this time with considerable help from his own machinations.

What had happened by the end of 1982, therefore, was the entanglement of the Western Saharan dispute in a welter of conflicts within and beyond Africa. In February, Algeria and Polisario had been willing to endanger the OAU mediation process, which in any case they found ineffectual. They may well have believed that they could bring around the thirty-four governments necessary to keep the OAU operational even in a fractured state. The discreet intervention of the American government contributed to their failure to achieve this. In taking the risk of splitting the OAU into rival blocs, they also accepted the prospect of an extended war of attrition in Western Sahara.

Algeria very likely believes that Polisario can outlast Morocco in guerrilla warfare. The costs to Algeria of backing the guerrillas are not so great as the costs of resisting them are to Morocco. The unknown in this equation, however, is the new American connection.

THE AMERICAN SEARCH FOR FRIENDS

One of the Reagan administration's first acts, well before the attack on Guelta Zemmour galvanized it into further action, was to announce arms deliveries to Morocco. The announcement came only a few days after the successful conclusion of the Algerian-mediated negotiations for the release of American citizens held hostage in Iran. However maladroit the timing appeared to be, the delivery was a perfect indicator of the new administration's intentions. In March, deputy assistant secretary of state Morris Draper told a congressional committee that "we intend to carry out a relationship that assures Morocco that it will be able to count on the United States as a steadfast and reliable friend" (U.S. Congress 1981, 4). Furthermore, Draper continued, America's traditional friends would not be subjected to conditions regarding the use of U.S. weapons. For the new administration, shoring up friends in need was deemed a high priority.

The reasoning of the Reagan administration was not, of course, purely sentimental. As Draper put it, "Morocco is important to broad American interests and occupies a pivotal strategic area" (ibid., 3). The United States has had military bases and communications facilities in Morocco in the past. The last of these facilities was closed only in 1978. Since then, American planning for the Rapid Deployment Force has once again highlighted the attractiveness of Moroccan territory as a transit point en route to the Middle East and the Persian Gulf. In light of Morocco's strategic value, President Reagan was prepared to give it "special support and consideration" (ibid., 14).

One form of consideration was to drop the Carter administration's linkage between arms support and negotiations. Draper indicated that the new administration, while encouraging Morocco to explore a negotiated settlement, would not "make decisions on military equipment sales explicitly conditional on unilateral Moroccan attempts to show progress toward a peaceful negotiated settlement" (ibid., 5). Another form of consideration was evidenced by the string of high-ranking officials from the White House and Pentagon who arrived in Rabat to discuss mutual security matters through the spring and summer of 1981. The king was confident that he had an attentive audience when he sounded the alarm after the battle of Guelta Zemmour.

The American government feared that a defeat or humiliation of the Moroccan forces in the Sahara might spell the end of the king as well. Landing rights for the Rapid Deployment Force could well be jeopardized if Hassan were to fall. The succession of politico-military contacts already mentioned produced a classic deal. The United States agreed to new military training and supply arrangements, while Hassan agreed to accord transit facilities to the RDF. The agreement, proposed by Secretary Haig during his February visit and further negotiated during Hassan's visit to Washington in May, was formally signed at the end of May 1982. Its full terms were not made public, but they involve access to two airfields, on one of which the United States will spend $20 million to upgrade.

Morocco entered into the agreement, Foreign Minister Boucetta declared, because it was a matter of defending its "territorial integrity" (Hodges 1982b). The deal was justified to Moroccan public opinion, in other words, by implicit reference to the war in Western Sahara. The increased U.S. support came first in the form of a training team dispatched to instruct Moroccan pilots in missile avoidance techniques. Second, a commando force was sent to train Moroccans in more aggressive seek-and-destroy tactics. The two governments set up a joint military commission and the American government requested authorization to increase the number of Moroccan officers being trained in the United States from 168 to 514. Finally, the administration asked Congress to authorize $100 million in military credits for Morocco in 1983.

The Moroccan government was not eager to offer military facilities to the United States, because the issue of foreign bases has long been a controversial one in Morocco. Hence Morocco's need to minimize the import of the agreement and link it to "territorial integrity." The United States on the other hand was not eager to become deeply embroiled in what it considers an unwinable war (see, for example, the statement of Robert Flaten, director of the North African desk at the State Department: "We have repeatedly stated that we do not believe this conflict is winnable in a military sense"(Flaten 1982). At the same time, the American government did not wish to see Hassan lose the war, because it did not want to lose a "friend." The Reagan administration was predisposed to giving Hassan a helping hand, but the king was obliged to reciprocate the friendship by acknowledging U.S. strategic interests.

Officially Morocco was not given any additional military or economic aid or any other commitment in return for its agreement to U.S. use of the airfields during emergencies. Just as Morocco insisted on the limited nature of the agreement—no permanent stationing of American personnel, no granting of extraterritorial rights—the United States desired to separate Rapid Deployment Force policy from Western Sahara policy. Yet obviously the joint military commission, under whose auspices an eighty-member American delegation, including eight generals, traveled to Fez in April, embodies a new U.S.-Moroccan military relationship.

The training arrangements already mentioned constitute significant assistance to the Moroccan forces. The United States has demonstrated its willingness to counter Polisario escalation by this aid and by dropping its former restraints on the use of American-supplied equipment in the annexed territory. Even though the transit facilities agreement may not contain an explicit quid pro quo, Morocco has gotten the military boost that it so desperately needed. The desire to implement the Rapid Deployment Force has raised the U.S. stake in its "friendship" with Morocco.

Although the American Congress cut back the administration aid request from $100 million to $50 million, Morocco got the essence of what it was looking for. Cognizant of his strategic value to the United States, Hassan is much less likely to compromise. However much congressional voices may be raised to say, as did the chairman of the House Subcommittee on Africa, "we do not want to see King Hassan's war become our war" (Wolpe 1982), the American government has assumed a share of the responsibility for the stalemate and bloodshed in Western Sahara.

THE SAHARAWIS IN A GLOBAL CONFLICT

In October 1982, Polisario held its fifth Popular Congress at Chahid El-Heddah, a site in "liberated territory" in Western Sahara. Six hundred delegates attended the four-day meeting, undisturbed by the Moroccan administration. They voted changes in the constitution of the SADR and established broad policy guidelines for the next three years. The motto of the occasion was "The entire nation or martyrdom." The meeting, as the motto, was designed to demonstrate that the Saharawi nationalists were not ready to give up their struggle to recover all their territory.

The meeting confirmed Mohamed Abdelaziz in his post as secretary-general of the Polisario Front. It elected a seven-man Executive Committee and a twenty-five member Political Bureau. A month later the Executive Committee made some changes in the composition of the government, naming Mahfoud Ali Beida prime minister and Mohamed Lamine (former prime minister) minister of education. Whatever the internal significance of these changes, their external significance was to reaffirm the juridical claim to a Saharawi state with governmental responsibilities. For Morocco this state was a fiction, and Polisario a band of mercenaries; for Algeria, the SADR was the expression of an authentic nationalist movement. The rest of the world has been called upon to choose sides.

The entanglement of the OAU in the web of conflict between traditional desert peoples, Moroccan nationalism, and Algerian geopolitical interests is one dimension of the internationalization of the Western Saharan question. The OAU could hardly ignore hostilities of this scale on the African continent, but its involvement was assured by the Algerian insistence that other states take a stand. Algeria successfully sold its interpretation of the matter to the majority of OAU member states. In this, to be sure, it was greatly aided by the Polisario leadership, which fervently presented its case to all who would listen. Yet it appears evident that governments were not necessarily moved by the merits of the case so much as by their general international alignments. In general, as has been seen, radical or progressive states rallied to the Polisario cause as championed by Algeria, a prominent leader of the progressive camp.

Those states that apparently found Moroccan arguments persuasive were as a general rule pro-Western in their overall international orientation. They backed Morocco because Morocco was one of them. Their concern for Moroccan interest was a function of their interest in having a group of like-minded states present in the larger international system. The split between moderates and radicals, however oversimplified these labels may be, is a structural attribute of the diplomatic framework in which the Saharawi nationalists have waged their politico-military struggle for independence. There is relatively little that Polisario can do to alter this structure, which reflects a larger global distribution of power.

Admission to the OAU was an attempt to force a structural pattern into a new shape. The structure resisted the pressure, because Morocco was able to call forth one-third of the members to its support. As Morocco proved capable of bringing the OAU to a halt, Polisario was obliged to revise its diplomatic tactics, as it did by the end of the year. Polisario was by then ready to "suspend" its participation for the sake of getting the OAU back into session, but the group formed by Morocco was now mobilized to inflict another defeat on Libya.

Morocco took the lead on the Chad question because it provided an unhoped-for opportunity to immobilize the OAU a little longer. Yet Morocco's willingness to take a stand on behalf of Hissen Habré stemmed from its new confidence in the American connection. The United States did not want Habré undermined, nor did it want Qaddafi to accede to the acting presidency of the OAU. The American partnership with Morocco facilitated the attainment of these objectives.

At the foundation of the reinforced U.S.-Moroccan relationship is the Rapid Deployment Force accord. Morocco stands militarily strengthened by virtue of its strategic value to American military planners. U.S. fears of Soviet aggression in the Persian Gulf have thus affected the course of a conflict in northwest Africa. The clansmen of Western Sahara are caught up in global political forces.

Nonetheless, neither Morocco nor Algeria nor the Saharawi people nor the United States can blithely envisage an unending war of attrition. The stakes remain high for all concerned: in Morocco, the stability of the throne and national honor; in Algeria, geopolitical objectives and respect for the principle of self-determination; among the Saharawi nationalists, recognition of their claim to a homeland. The stakes for the United States are of a different order: extrication of its strategic partner from a crisis whose long-term consequences remain highly risky, and reestablishing some degree of balance with Algeria, an influential third world state. All the parties have a stake in a settlement that would be humiliating to none. The rough shape of such a settlement is not beyond diplomatic imagination—however arduous the diplomatic process of getting there would certainly be. As the defender of the status quo, Morocco must begin that process, perhaps with a little help from its friend.

REFERENCES AND ADDITIONAL READINGS

Barbier, Maurice. 1982. *Le conflit du Sahara occidental.* Paris: L'Harmattan.

Boucetta, M'hamed. 1982. "Interview." *Africa Report* 27 (July/August): 12–14.

Flaten, Robert. 1982. "Interview." *Africa Report* 27 (July/August): 12–14.

Hodges, Tony. 1982a. *Historical Dictionary of Western Sahara.* Metuchen, N.J.: Scarecrow Press.

———. 1982b. "Le nouvel axe stratégique entre Washington et Rabat." *Le Monde Diplomatique* 27, no. 340 (July): 6–7.

———. 1982c. "Western Sahara: The Endless War." *Africa Report* 27 (July/August): 4–11.

Kodjo, Edem. 1982. Interview in *Jeune Afrique,* no. 1105 (10 March): 20–22.

Lewis, William H. 1981. "Western Sahara: Compromise or Conflict?" *Current History* 80 (December): 410–13, 431.

Mortimer, Robert. 1978. "Western Sahara: The Diplomatic Perspectives." *Africa Report* 23 (March/April): 10–14.

———. 1981. "Politics in Trans-Saharan Africa." *Africa Report* 26 (May/June): 47–52.

Novicki, Margaret. 1980. "Assessing the Freetown Summit." *Africa Report* 25 (September/October): 39–43.

"Sahara: en ignorance de cause." 1980. *Jeune Afrique,* no. 1012 (28 May): 17–32, 97–112.

Schulman, Jeffrey. "The Legal Issues of the War in Western Sahara." See U.S. Congress 1979.

Thompson, Virginia, and Richard Adloff. 1980. *The Western Saharans: Background to Conflict.* Totowa, N.J.: Barnes and Noble Books.

U.S. Congress. House. Committee on Foreign Affairs. Subcommittees on Africa and on International Organizations. 1979. *U.S. Policy and the Conflict in Western Sahara.* 96th Cong., 1st Sess.

———. ———. Committee on Foreign Affairs. Subcommittees on International Security and Scientific Affairs and on Africa. 1981. *Arms Sales in North Africa and the Conflict in the Western Sahara: An Assessment of U.S. Policy.* 97th Cong., 1st Sess.

Weexsteen, Raoul. 1978. "L'OUA et la question Saharienne." *Annuaire de l'Afrique du Nord* 17:213–37.

———. 1979. "La question du Sahara occidental, 1978–1979." *Annuaire de l'Afrique du Nord* 18:415–42.

Wolpe, Harold. 1982. "Interview." *Africa Report* 27 (July/August): 12–14.

Zartman, I. William. 1979. "Conflict in the Sahara." See U.S. Congress 1979.

Turkey:
The Reshaping of Domestic and External Politics

Ilter Turan

During the several decades that preceded its demise, the Ottoman Empire was referred to as the "sick man of Europe." Long since forgotten, the expression appeared to be regaining currency during the late 1970s for describing the Turkish republic. Three interrelated but distinct phenomena were implied in this designation: a faltering economy, a rising wave of terrorism and domestic strife, and, finally, a series of unstable governments incapable of dealing with these problems.

On 12 September 1980, the Turkish armed forces assumed political power. In this action, they were led by the National Security Council (NSC), comprising the top officers in the existing chain of command. The Turkish chief of staff, General Kenan Evren, headed the council. Other members were General Nurettin Ersin, the commander of the army; General Tahsin Şahinkaya, the commander of the air force; Admiral Nejat Tümer, the commander of the navy; and General Sedat Celasun, the commander of the gendarmerie. The purpose of this intervention, the military leadership explained, was to put an end to developments leading to fratricide and to lead the country back to a democratic system and a democratic way of life. Since the introduction of praetorian rule in Turkey, terrorism has been brought under control, and the performance of the Turkish economy has improved remarkably. With the ratification of a new constitution through a national referendum (7 November 1982), a process that will lead to the restoration of civilian politics has begun.

When compared with the turbulent domestic politics, Turkish foreign policy may appear to be uneventful. Yet the gradual but steadily increasing interest of Turkey in Middle Eastern affairs, a growing trade with the countries in the region, and the emergence of many problems between Turkey and its European partners have given way to speculation that a fundamental shift in Turkish foreign policy is in the making.

This article will examine the factors that have led to the reshaping of both Turkish domestic and external politics, and the nature of the changes that are occurring, their limits and the implications they may have for the future. In the domestic area, the context within which the military has intervened, the policies it has pursued, and its activities leading toward a restoration of civilian politics will be discussed. Special attention will be given to the new Turkish constitution, its features and the problems that might emerge in its application. In the area of foreign policy, an analysis of Turkey's close economic, political, and defense ties to the Western bloc will be presented. Then, forces promoting shifts in Turkey's external relations will be reviewed. Finally, an attempt will be made to identify the limits of change in Turkish foreign policy.

DOMESTIC POLITICS

Background to the Military Intervention

When the Turkish armed forces assumed direct political power on 12 September 1980, Turkey had reached a state of being nongoverned. The erosion of governance was the culmination of developments in various domains of political life that had gained momentum particularly after the elections of 1977.

The first election after the military revolution of 1961 had produced a multiparty system. In the elections of 1965, however, the Justice party (JP) managed to obtain a majority of parliamentary seats. For two consecutive terms (until 1973), the JP formed the government and the Republican People's party (RPP) served as the major opposition party.

The elections of 1973 reflected a realignment of political forces. The Justice party experienced significant electoral losses. The Republican People's party became the plurality party. Two parties of the radical right, the National Salvation party (NSP) and the Nationalist Action party (NAP), also considerably improved their standing. The elections of 1977 reflected a similar trend. The RPP, while continuing to increase its plurality, could not achieve a majority. The NAP and JP improved their positions slightly. Other small parties, including the NSP, lost votes and seats.

This realignment of political forces was accompanied by increasing ideological differentiation among political parties. Although each political party contained both supporters and members whose political orientations deviated significantly from the central tendency of their party, the place of each party in the ideological spectrum was not difficult to identify. The Justice party resembled in many ways the conservative parties of Western Europe, combining a preference for economic liberalism with social conservatism. The Republican People's party was similar to European Social Democratic parties, with which it identified. The center right was occupied, along with the JP, by two small parties, the Republican Reliance party and the Democratic party. The first, owing its existence mainly to the prominence of its leader, Professor Fevzioglu in Kayseri province, appeared to be more secularist in its orientation than the JP. The second had been established by a group of deputies who left the JP in 1969 in a factional fight with Prime Minister Demirel. How it differed from the JP was less clear.

Farther to the right of JP were the NSP and the NAP. The NSP appeared to favor a greater role for religion in public life and to oppose the strict secularist policies that had been followed since the founding of the republic. It also desired closer Turkish cooperation with Islamic countries. The NAP defended a nationalism that required unquestioned dedication to service to the nation and obedience to the party leader.

To the left of the RPP was a group of political parties and political organizations that lacked parliamentary representation. Marked by their tendency to be plagued by constant factionalism, they represented political orientations reflecting that of the Communist Party of the Soviet Union (CPSU), the various factions in Chinese politics, European left, and even those of tiny Albania. Some among them appeared to be favorably disposed toward ethnic separatism. Disparate as they were in their orientations, they were not favorably disposed toward the existing parliamentary system.

In earlier Turkish political experience, small political parties had not fared well. That they managed to survive and grow during the 1973 and 1977 elections, mainly at the expense of the JP, led that party to adopt a strategy of polarizing the electorate to reduce the likelihood of the defection of both its deputies and supporters to other parties. The RPP, under similar pressures from the left, did the same thing. After the 1973 elections, the center in Turkish political life gradually eroded and a right-left polarization emerged.

At about the same time that the political polarization of the public was proceeding, the employment of violence and terrorism on political grounds was also becoming more widespread. Clandestine groups, claiming this or that radical ideology, began to conduct abductions, tortures, armed attacks, and assassinations of political opponents with increasing frequency. Gradually law enforcement officers, civil servants, leaders of voluntary organizations such as labor and employer unions, journalists, university professors, businessmen, and even military officers became targets of these acts. Although the targets were usually accused of being sympathetic to the opposing side, in many instances such allegations appeared to be unfounded. Public buildings and private property also constituted targets for terrorist acts, sometimes to shock the public and other times to intimidate the owners. Spectacular robberies of banks, public agencies, corporate headquarters, shops, and homes were also staged in part to undermine public confidence in government and in part to finance future terrorist actions.

The increasing polarization of the policy fostered by the two major political parties made their cooperation and collaboration on the fundamental problems of the economy and on political terrorism impossible. Each party, afraid that close cooperation with the other would cost it the support it enjoyed from its extremist factions, tried to render these major problems a vehicle through which the other could be blamed and undermined.

After 1973, Turkey had to be ruled by coalition governments. The RPP-NSP coalition that was established following the 1973 elections collapsed not long after Turkey's intervention on Cyprus during the summer of 1974. After that, with the exception of a brief interlude during which an RPP-led coalition supported by independent deputies who had defected from the JP ruled the country, in 1978–79, the country was ruled by JP-led governments, often coalitions in which the NSP and NAP also participated.

Some basic factors threatened the stability and undermined the effectiveness of coalition governments. Small parties in coalitions, for example, experienced two conflicting pressures. On the one hand, to establish their identity and visibility vis-à-vis the electorate, they emphasized publicly, and in the day-to-day operation of the government, the differences between themselves and their coalition partners. On the other hand, they felt intensely the need to maintain their involvement in coalition governments, because being in office appeared to be the most efficient way of maintaining their organization and developing it, through the distribution of public resources that accrued to them as a result of their participation in government.

The smaller parties were difficult to work with in coalitions. Furthermore, polarized politics stood in the way of a coalition between the two major parties. One may ask why the two major parties did not at least agree on early elections as a possible formula for reducing the political role of the small parties. Some answers may be found in a study of the legislature, the legislators, and the costs of being in and out of power.

To counter the excessive power the national leadership of political parties had enjoyed in the determination of candidates for parliamentary office, the constitution of 1961 had introduced provincial primaries. The system of primaries did not serve its intended purpose, but rather produced a number of unintended consequences. The first of these was a rise in the turnover rate of deputies. At any legislative term after 1961, more than 50 percent of the deputies were usually freshmen and expected to leave Parliament without ever having a chance to earn seniority. Such high turnover rates stood in the way of the institutionalization of the legislature, that is, its development of a corporate identity, rules, norms, specialized structures, and traditions. Again, in contrast to what was intended by primaries, the rank and file, mostly newcomers, became highly dependent on the guidance of party leaders. The role of the legislature, as shall be explained later, in the political decision-making processes of the country, on the other hand, began a steady and rapid decline.

A second consequence of the primary system was an indirect one. The Turkish administrative unit il ("province") constituted at the same time the electoral district. Because the provinces varied in size of population, they had to be organized as multimember districts in which the number of deputies to be elected was calculated before each election according to the most recent census. A system of proportional representation was employed in the election to determine how many deputies each party would place in the National Assembly from each province.

Each political party competing in a province would put up as many candidates as the number of deputy positions allotted to that province. The primary elections were intended as a method through which delegates elected from among the members of provincial party organizations would determine the candidates of their party and rank them, so that when the seats won by each party became known, it would be possible to identify the winners. This meant that in addition to getting on the party ticket, a candidate had to attain a certain rank. Because provincial branches of political parties were narrowly based and intermittently active organizations, a limited number of activists, interested in getting personal rewards for their support of particular candidates, were able to dominate the nomination process. Those aspiring to candidacy had to engage in acts of personal generosity and entertain the party activists who would determine a candidate's chances of being elected. This was a costly operation and affected the behavior of those who were elected deputies.

The newly elected deputy would usually have a campaign debt, which he would try to meet out of his personal income. This situation rendered him overly concerned with questions of income. He would also usually be highly concerned with his reelection. Therefore, most of his time and effort would be devoted to securing services for his constituents, especially those who helped him attain a spot on the party ticket. For securing constituency services, he was heavily reliant on the government and the bureaucracy. This created pressures on him to curry the favor of the party leadership, especially when his party was in power.

The absorption of the time and energies of the deputy by constituency concerns left him little time to participate in the deliberative activities of the legislature, and the legislature was often paralyzed for lack of a quorum. Moreover, an inactive legislature was promoted by the leadership of member parties in coalition governments, who had discovered that it was very difficult to achieve intragovernmental consensus. Attempts to legislate only helped expose the prevailing dissension. The solution was to avoid legislation and let each ministry run its own affairs, creating what might be best described as a confederation of ministries. On occasion, legislative sessions were held, but only to attack, harass, and embarrass opponents and solidify individual ranks.

Not only was success in the elections costly, but the tenure of a deputy tended to be brief. Encountering what might be termed high-risk circumstances, many deputies tried to maximize their gains in office. Membership in the government party considerably enhanced the opportunity of deputies to maximize their political and sometimes material gains. This development occurred in a context in which the cost of being out of power was already perceived to be unacceptably high for a number of reasons.

The Turkish government, to begin with, is heavily centralized, and the distribution of public funds, goods, and services is tied into a network in which the locus of decision is the national capital. Second, the economic role of the state in Turkish society is greater than in most other nonsocialist societies for historical reasons. Private enterprise has developed under the protective arm of the state, and it has depended on governmental support for its successful operation. The central political and economic role of the state in Turkish society has meant that, relatively speaking, those in government have, directly and indirectly, access to an immense amount of resources to distribute. Because they are backed by constituents who stand to lose much if their party fails, political parties tend to use any means possible to get into government.

In a society whose tradition of self-supporting, autonomous associations is of recent origin, political parties have come to rely on being in power for acquiring resources such as funds, favors, and services that make it possible for them to survive and prosper as organizations. The JP and the small parties appeared initially to be more reliant on being in government for their continuation than the RPP. The latter, after the transition to competitive politics, had perceived its mission to be the defense of the modernist principles of the republic. This ideological orientation provided the cement that held the party together in many years of opposition. Interestingly, as the RPP evolved after the late 1960s into a more pragmatic political party, it was infected by the same ailment, namely, the need to achieve power in order to flourish as an organization. No Turkish political party during the 1970s felt that it could stay away from power for long periods and still hope to retain the support of its electorate and maintain itself as an active organization.

In summary, inexperienced deputies, seeing their tenure as limited and in a mood to maximize their gains, operating in an institutional context that discouraged deliberation and compromise, led by people who did not even pretend to form a coherent administration but felt the need to be in government to perpetuate their organizational bases, did not characterize a political system that would be capable of coping with major problems.

The Advent of the Military Regime

The preceding discussion was intended to analyze the process of the erosion of governance in Turkey. Let us now turn to the specific developments that led to the assumption of political power by the leadership in the armed forces.

Changing governments had failed to arrest the rising wave of terrorism. In 1979, communal riots and fighting in various parts of Turkey led to the reluctant imposition of martial law in the several provinces that seemed to be particularly problematic. The national political leaders did not appear to treat the deteriorating domestic peace, however, as an emergency. The polarized political conflict appeared to be so intense that each incident of social turmoil was viewed as another reason for the government and the opposition to attack each other vehemently. Even a series of warnings by the Turkish chief of staff, General Evren, went unheeded and became a part of a political football game in which parties argued that the warnings were intended for the others but not for them.

In the meantime, soldiers and officers became targets of acts of terrorism, a development that the military leadership perceived as a challenge to the integrity of the armed forces and their credibility as a deterrent to violence. Aspects of the domestic struggle also assumed dimensions that appeared to be threatening to the central values of the republic, such as secularism, nationalism, republicanism, and modernism. Intracommunal riots in which some political parties were suspected of complicity carried religious overtones, posing a fundamental challenge to the republican principle of secularism. The principle of nationality based on citizenship rather than ethnic or racial origin was challenged by persistent activities of ethnic separatists.

Of equal importance was the fear that the divisive tendencies in societal life would gradually appear among the members of the armed forces, threatening its unity as an institution. The conditions suggested that if the leadership did not intervene, attempts by lower-ranking officers to form secret committees and assume political power would not be unlikely.

The Turkish public, as it had done before, had come to expect that the armed forces would save Turkey from political crisis. These expectations were matched by the orientation of the officers corps, which felt that the Turkish military was ultimately responsible for the survival of the republic.

Therefore, the assumption of political power by the Turkish military did not come as a surprise, and it appeared to have been met, generally, with a sense of relief that a bloody domestic strife had been averted.

The Military in Power

In conformity with the general rule of behavior observed in other military regimes, as well as in the 1960–61 Turkish experience, the military leadership defined their intervention as a temporary state of affairs, and promised to return to civilian politics after eradicating terrorism and restoring political peace and stability.

The first year of military rule was devoted to coping with the problems inherited from the past requiring immediate attention. Of highest priority was ending terrorist activities, which had claimed, prior to the intervention, as many as twenty-five lives a day. By mobilizing military resources and improving the capabilities of the other law enforcement agencies, the military leadership initiated extensive efforts to combat terrorism. During 1980–81, many terrorists were caught; organizational networks were uncovered and destroyed. As terrorist activities became costlier and less productive their incidence subsided to negligible dimensions. The trials of those who had engaged in or supported acts of terrorism continue as of this writing.

As has already been noted, during the period preceding the military rule, almost no laws had been enacted because the legislature had, for all practical purposes, ceased to function. Assuming both legislative and executive powers, the National Security Council promulgated a series of new laws, in part, to provide a legal framework within which the military government would operate and, for the most part, to fill the legal vacuum created by the prolonged legislative inactivity that had characterized the period before 12 September 1980. Covering such diverse topics as taxation, labor-industry relations, retirement benefits, and authorization to bear arms, these laws responded to a long acknowledged need for legislation in many areas of public life.

The promulgation of laws was rapid. In many instances, legislative proposals prepared by the bureaucracy prior to the advent of the military government were taken as the basis for the legislation. This rapidity, while understandable after years of nonlegislation, proved on occasion to be problematic. Some proposals prepared by high-ranking bureaucrats without political inputs encountered significant practical difficulties and had to be amended within weeks. In other instances, laws were thought to be incomplete and inconsistent, failing to achieve the purposes for which they were intended. Many, however, appear to have worked without causing major problems.

Of longer-lasting interest are, of course, the attempts of the military leadership to restructure the Turkish political system. The NSC, upon taking over the government, had dissolved the legislature, taken leaders of political parties into custody, and banned political activity. Soon a government led by a retired commander of the navy, Admiral Bülent Ulusu, and comprising mainly persons of military, bureaucratic, or academic backgrounds was formed. While this government was charged with the day-to-day duties of governance, the NSC began to map out a strategy for the future.

In their deliberations, the members of the NSC were constrained by several considerations. The military leadership appeared to feel that all political organizations, public institutions, and interest groups had contributed to and exacerbated the political crisis that preceded the intervention. The leadership had also been impressed by the fact that after the 1960 revolution, the cooperation of the military leadership of that time with certain parties, organizations, and groups, such as the RPP, the Turkish Textile Workers Federation, and National Federation of Students of Turkey, while rejecting others, often affiliated with the Democratic party, had had a highly divisive impact on the Turkish polity. Therefore, the NSC was inclined not to include, for the most part, organized groups in Turkish society in planning the future.

An example of the above orientation is the manner of recruitment for the Consultative Assembly, which started to function in the fall of 1981 in order to prepare a draft constitution. The Constituent Assembly of 1960–61 had been staffed largely by representatives of political parties and institutional and associational interest groups. The members of the Consultative Assembly, on the other hand, were individually appointed by the NSC. Persons closely affiliated with political parties of the immediate past were not qualified to apply or to be considered for appointment.

Another constraint affecting the behavior of the military leadership has been their concern with the reemergence of "old politics." This concern appears to have been justified: each time political life was liberalized after the 1980 intervention, the political atmosphere repolarized. In addition, pre-1980 political groups and organizations now wanted to hasten the disengagement of the military from politics. The NSC appeared to feel, however, that too hasty a disengagement would undermine their own commitment to the restructuring of politics. Eventually, all political parties were abolished, and their organizations dismantled, to pave the way to a new environment in which competitive politics would eventually be reintroduced.

Politics in the era that preceded the military intervention was couched in ideological terms. The NSC leadership felt constrained to express and legitimize actions in ideological terms. The ideas of Atatürk, the founder of the republic, were strongly emphasized as state ideology. Some of Atatürk's major ideas include dedication to a sovereign nation-state and a republican form of government, a strong commitment to the separation of religion and state, and the recognition of religion as a private, personal matter; an intense desire to integrate Turkey into the Western community of nations; and a concern with the achievement and the retention of national unity accompanied by a tendency to view society as a homogeneous collectivity in which cleavages do not exist.

That the military leadership turned to the ideas of the founding father of the republic is understandable. Officers are socialized into thinking of themselves as the bearers of the legacy of Atatürk throughout their educational experience. The ideas themselves are seen to constitute a national ideology, an answer to internationalist ideologies such as Socialism, Communism, and Pan-Islamism, which were making rapid headway in Turkish society prior to the military intervention.

This emphasis on a national ideology after 12 September 1980 seems also to be the manifestation of a deep concern with maintaining national unity. The intensity of domestic tensions, the ever-hardening political polarization in the country, and the appearance of separatist ideas during the 1970s probably impressed upon the military leadership that some formula for reintegrating the polity was needed. Whether the specific formula adopted will provide the cement for an increasingly differentiated society with a multiplicity of functional and nonfunctional cleavages remains to be seen.

A final constraint has been the awareness of the military leadership that their tenure is not unlimited. While the public distrust of ordinary politics has provided the military leadership with high levels of political support, many forces operate in favor of their gradual disengagement from politics. One such force is the desire to retain the credibility of the armed forces in the public eye. The unusually high levels of public support the NSC has been accorded are a result of the conviction that the military had intervened to bring solutions to major national problems within a reasonable time. If this public confidence is undermined by prolonging military rule, the armed forces are likely to lose some of their credibility and be reduced to the level of an ordinary actor in Turkish politics with all the implications of that status.

A second factor in making the NSC want to move with reasonable speed is related to the consequences of a political intervention on the military itself. A long period of intervention, for example, tends to reduce upward mobility in the higher ranks of the military. Those who initiate the intervention assume political positions without relinquishing their military duties until a formula for transition to civilian politics is developed. The formulation and the implementation of a transition plan may require a longer period than the ordinary tenure commanders may traditionally enjoy in their military positions. If a conflict between political imperatives and military traditions develops, the former, inevitably, tend to determine the outcome. The slowing down of promotions and the appearance of unexpected retirements tend to undermine the morale of the officers.

The administration of civilian duties on a regular basis tends also to reduce the military preparedness of the armed forces. Nonmilitary activities take time away from training and practice. Daily contact with civilian life may lead to corruptive influences, particularly among the soldiers. In the Turkish armed forces with its highly professionalized cadre of officers, who feel they have a mission to protect the country from external aggression, there is high sensitivity to retain the esprit de corps, the morale and combat effectiveness. These concerns promote inclinations against permanent or long-term involvement in politics.

A final factor limiting the tenure of the armed forces in government is Turkey's external relations. Turkey is connected to Western Europe and the United States through membership in NATO, the Council of Europe, and the Organization for Economic Cooperation and Development (OECD). The country holds associate member status in the European Economic Community, with plans to become a full member in the future. These organizations assume a communality of interests among members, including the existence of a market economy and a competitive political system. While the determination of the nature of the Turkish political system and the speed with which it will be constructed is an internal Turkish concern, it is natural that Turkey's external relations are taken into consideration in this process.

The New Turkish Constitution

The constraints discussed above have constituted part of an environment within which the shaping of the future political structure of the country has taken place. During the first eight months of 1982, the Consultative Assembly prepared a draft constitution, which it submitted to the NSC. Following a monthlong review of the draft by the NSC, including some revisions, it was submitted to a national referendum on 7 November 1982. Rates of voter participation were extraordinarily high, 90 percent or higher in many instances, as were the rates of approval, which reached a national level of 91 percent. The text of the constitution was discussed in public extensively until a ban was introduced by the NSC within less than a month of the referendum. The voting process itself, administered by the judiciary, was free and honest, reflecting a tradition of open and fair elections.

The recently ratified constitution not only defines what the future political system in Turkey will look like, but also lays out a series of steps for the restoration of civilian-based politics. This section will be devoted to a discussion and analysis of the new constitution.

The new constitution is a lengthy and highly detailed document. This is in part a reflection of the Turkish tradition of preparing detailed constitutional texts. These texts lend themselves only to strict interpretation and serve as a source of what might be termed a traditional Turkish problem: many issues, which under more flexible systems would be the subject of legislation, are elevated to the level of constitutional matters. To cite an example, Article 51, dealing with labor unions, requires that a person who wants to be an elected officer of a labor union be an active worker for the ten preceding years. If for any reason a future government would want to reduce, increase, or eliminate this qualification, it could only do so by amending the constitution. Changing the constitution requires that a bill be introduced by one-third of the legislature and be approved by two-thirds of the entire membership. Laws, however, require only a simple majority of those attending a session, provided there is a quorum.

The length of, and the kind of detail in the new constitution are also due in part to the mood in which the constitution was drafted. Like the 1961 constitution, the 1982 draft was prepared in an atmosphere in which the paramount concern was to prevent the recurrence of the problems of the immediate past. Such an approach appears to have stood in the way of anticipating the future impact of many constitutional provisions. A case in point is Article 84, which deals with the conditions under which a deputy may lose his membership in the National Assembly. Among other things, it is apparent that the article is trying to deal with two problems of the immediate past: lack of attendance to legislative sessions and defections from parliamentary parties. A simple solution is proposed: if a deputy fails to attend without excuse five sessions a month, or if he leaves his party to join another during his term in office, he may be dismissed from his parliamentary seat by a decision of a simple majority of the entire membership.

The lack of attendance to legislative sessions has received attention because it had often proved difficult to raise a quorum in the legislature during the pre-1980 period, which immobilized the legislature. Yet one wonders whether the cure will be an effective one. A party that holds a majority of the parliamentary seats may tolerate or even encourage its members not to attend sessions, if it so chooses, assuring them no sanction will be forthcoming. The same party, however, may try to oust opposition members who are lax in their attendance. Another article (Article 96), in fact, appears to provide a sufficient solution. In contrast to the constitution of 1961, which defined the parliamentary quorum as a simple majority of the entire membership, the new constitution reduces the number to one-third of the whole house. Thus, a large and committed minority can initiate parliamentary sessions that would, almost certainly, force the majority party or parties to attend the session. The new measure would have been appropriate only if most deputies failed to come to legislative sessions because they were personally irresponsible and lax. It may be recalled from the discussion of pre-1980 developments, however, that coalition governments with very low levels of cohesion chose not to promote parliamentary activity.

The concern with defections from parliamentary parties can be traced to the strategies adopted by political parties after the elections of 1977. Coalition governments of this period enjoyed small majorities. Oppositions tried to persuade deputies to defect from government parties by promising them such rewards as ministerial positions, guaranteed reelection, and, allegedly, personal benefits. A study of defections from the parliamentary parties, by this author, shows that the highest numbers of defections took place from 1961 to 1965, the first legislative term following the 1960 revolution. This was a time when many parties had emerged to claim the votes of the defunct Democratic party. The opportunity for deputies to change parties had helped consolidate the party system in the legislature, since many deputies eventually joined the most promising heir of the Democratic party, the Justice party. It is not unlikely that the oncoming transition to competitive politics will resemble the 1961–65 period rather than the 1977–80 period. If this analysis is correct, then rendering a change in party affiliation difficult may contribute to the perpetuation of political fragmentation in the legislature. Deputies will be reluctant to leave their own to join other parties that appear to have a better future if such an action brings only risks and not sufficient rewards. The propensity of the constitution makers to design laws to prevent the recurrence of the problems of the past is manifest throughout the constitution. The above discussion provides only a few examples.

The length and the detailed nature of the new constitution appear also to derive from the inclination of the Consultative Assembly to formalize a set of duties for future governments that, in many other systems, are policy decisions left to governments. Article 41 directs government, for example, to offer education and help in the implementation of family planning. Article 45 is concerned with governmental support of the development of animal husbandry and the improvement of grazing grounds. While Article 59 instructs government to promote sports and recreation and to extend support to successful athletes, Article 64 extends governmental protection to artists and works of art.

In the fourth section, concerned with financial and economic matters, the inclination to formulate governmental policies is particularly manifest. Article 166, for example, mandates that economic, social, and cultural development be realized according to an economic development plan, then proceeds to say:

> The plan contains measures designed to promote savings and production, to stabilize prices, to achieve a balance in the balance of payments, to encourage expansion of investments and employment.

Article 171 directs government to promote the development of cooperatives as a desirable form of economic organization.

The inclusion in the constitution of directives to future governments is a particularly problematic approach, as has been demonstrated in the past. The constitution of 1961 contained a set of articles directing governments to provide social security, health services, and employment, and to conduct land reforms, as well as to do other things. Not only did governments not always share the policy goals laid out for them, but the resources of the economy would not allow any government to fully accomplish all the constitutionally defined policy goals. The result was to provide oppositions with a tool to undermine the legitimacy of those in power: many acts of government (sometimes the governments themselves) were branded unconstitutional because they did not pursue specific policies with which they sometimes disagreed and for which government often lacked the resources. The inclusion of policy directives in the new constitution may well raise problems similar to those observed when the 1961 constitution was in effect.

To summarize, the constitution is too detailed and specific, and, therefore, low in adaptability. It is designed with a short-term perspective of trying to ensure that the conditions that led to the near collapse of the Turkish polity should not recur. Finally, it contains policy directives that may or may not be shared by future governments. Given these qualities, it should not be surprising if the transition to competitive politics is followed by never-ending constitutional debates and efforts to effect constitutional amendments.

The general orientation of the constitution reflects a tendency to restrict, rather than accommodate, political conflict. This is realized in several different ways. Chapter 2, from Article 12 through Article 74, deals with fundamental rights and duties of citizens. Article 12 states that citizens not only have inalienable individual rights and liberties, but also have obligations to society, family, and other individuals. Before these rights and obligations are explained, Articles 13 to 15 introduce certain qualifications. Article 13 defines the contingencies under which liberties may be limited; Article 14 explains that they may not be used for purposes destructive of the republic; and Article 15 cites the situations under which the liberties may be partly or fully suspended. The articles describing the liberties themselves often allude to their limits. Reading these, one cannot escape the impression that centrist political ideologies and positions constitute the framework within which politics is expected to occur.

Second, there is a clear-cut preference for limiting political activity to political parties. Article 33, dealing with freedom to associate, specifies:

> Associations . . . cannot pursue political purposes, cannot
> engage in political activities, cannot receive support from
> political parties, nor extend support to them.

The same restrictions are imposed on labor unions (Article 52). Both voluntary associations and labor unions are also prohibited from collaborating for political purposes with other associations, quasi-public professional organizations (such as the Bar Association and Medical Association), and foundations (Articles 33 and 52).

Third, political parties are banned from forming specialized branches. Article 68 prohibits them from establishing youth, women's, and similar supportive organizations. The following article (Article 69) restates the restriction on associations and labor unions regarding collaboration for political purposes, extending these restrictions to political parties.

The orientation to confine political life to activities of political parties may have consequences unforeseen by the makers of the new constitution. The approach adopted in the constitution was motivated by the earlier excessive politicization of all aspects and institutions of public life. Yet, whether the particular solution offered will be successful or will create more problems than it may solve remains to be seen. It is to be remembered that political processes in Turkey have occurred within the context of a highly sophisticated network of political parties, voluntary associations, and professional organizations. These have created opportunities for political participation and the transmitting of demands or needs to the decision makers. Organization-based politics in Turkey existed long before the demise of the political system in 1980. An understanding of politics as organizational action is likely to assert itself after the transition to competitive politics. Attempts to contain it, in addition to creating political tensions, may encourage "covert" politics.

One may also wonder whether Turkish political parties by themselves will be capable of responding to the political needs of the country. Until 1980, Turkish political parties did not seem to possess organizational structures, particularly below the national headquarters level, that would be capable of serving a multiplicity of political functions in Turkish society. These parties have now been dissolved. Their leadership has been banned from forming or assuming the leadership of new parties and becoming candidates for public office for some time after the transition to competitive politics. Their financial wealth and other assets have been nationalized. It will take time for new political parties to form and then acquire the capabilities to articulate and aggregate interests. In the meantime, groups whose interests may not be tended may feel frustrated. The new constitutional order may be the most readily identifiable target of their frustrations.

It is also not difficult to anticipate extensive conflict revolving around the question of what is "political." In the previous system, associations were banned from engaging in "political activities" by law. Governments tended to interpret "political" to mean that which they found detrimental to their interests. There is no reason to think that the elevation of the ban to the level of the constitution will render the term clearer or reduce the problems that may stem from it.

Next to the tendency to restrain rather than to accommodate political conflict is the preference to solve certain problems by the application of decisional rule rather than by the building of political consensus. This approach becomes very evident in Articles 94 and 102, pertaining to the election of the president of the National Assembly and the president of the republic, respectively. In the election of the president of the National Assembly (Article 94), only four rounds of voting are allowed. A qualified majority of two-thirds of the whole house is required for the first two rounds. If no person is elected, a simple majority of the total membership becomes sufficient to conclude the election in the third round. If that does not produce a result, those two candidates who have obtained the highest number of votes are permitted to compete in a fourth round. The candidate who gets the higher number of votes is then elected. It should be added that the entire process is limited to twenty days, ten days to identify the candidates, another ten within which to elect the president.

The election of the president of the republic is designed along similar lines, except a simple majority of the whole house is still required in the fourth round. Failure to elect a president in that round leads to the dissolution of the legislature. The election of the president is to be concluded within thirty days.

The rigidity of the rules described above is a response to the failure of the legislators prior to the 1980 intervention to elect their officers and a new president of Turkey. One would find it difficult to argue, however, that the rules of election were responsible for the indecision that prevailed. From 1961 until 1978, it had proved possible for the legislature to elect its own officers and presidents of the republic under the same rules. For a series of reasons, some of which have been discussed earlier, the consensus on the nature of the Turkish political system and the rules of its operation had broken down in the late 1970s. Substituting decisional rules for consensus building may facilitate producing results in formal elections, but it may not ensure a political tranquility, peace, and stability. In fact, a political party holding a majority in the National Assembly would have no stake, under the current rules, in seeking to accommodate other parties, since it can win all by itself if it refuses to cooperate with them. Such a possibility would expose the Turkish political system to the tensions that marked the period preceding the 1960 military revolution. During that period, the Democratic party, holding a majority of seats in the National Assembly, had not felt that a broader consensus might be needed to govern the country. A growing polarization between government and opposition leading to civil strife was eventually ended by a military intervention.

Finally, another tendency manifest in the new constitution is a reliance on presidential checks on the legislature and the parliamentary government. This is achieved in a number of ways. First, the president is given the power to make appointments to positions that the current leadership feels should be separated from partisan politics: the presidents of universities and the members of the Constitutional Court would be examples. Second, he is empowered to exercise oversight on any governmental institution or agency through the State Auditing Council. This authority extends also to nongovernmental organizations of a public nature such as labor unions, management associations, professional organizations, and voluntary associations that have been granted public service status. The members of the council are appointed by the president and are accountable to him. Third, he is empowered to submit constitutional amendments accepted by the legislature to a national referendum if he deems it necessary. Fourth, he may decide under certain conditions to call new parliamentary elections. Finally, in the exercise of prerogatives given to him alone, the president's decisions are final.

What a strengthened presidency will mean in practice remains to be seen. That the essence of the system remains parliamentary suggests the possibility of power contentions between the president and parliamentary governments after the transition to competitive politics. Though not probable, the authority vested in the president could also be used arbitrarily.

The Transition to Competitive Politics

The transition to civilian-based competitive politics started with the appointment of a Consultative Assembly in October 1981 and continued with the drafting and the ratification by popular referendum of the new constitution in November 1982. Though not specifying a timetable, the constitution describes in fifteen provisional articles the additional steps to be taken to continue the transition.

The head of the NSC and the state, General Evren, has become the president of the republic for a period of seven years with the ratification of the constitution (Provisional Article 1). The NSC will continue to function as the supreme authority until a new National Assembly is elected and convenes. Elections to the new legislature will be held after laws on political parties and elections are enacted by the Consultative Assembly and approved by the NSC (Provisional Article 2).

With the convening of the new legislature, the members of the NSC will become, for a period of six years, members of the Presidential Council, with the same rights and privileges accorded to the members of the National Assembly. The council will advise the president on the laws that are submitted for his approval and on other duties he is constitutionally required to discharge (Provisional Article 2). It appears that the creation of a Presidential Council is intended to serve two purposes. First, it projects the collegial nature of the leadership of the NSC into the new system. Second, it creates essentially a team that will see that the laws referred to in the constitution and other laws are enacted in a fashion that complies with constitutional provisions. Differently expressed, along with the president, the members of the Presidential Council will act as the trustees of the system they helped to create during this prolonged period of transition.

To avoid the reemergence of pre-1980 political organizations under new names and the immediate reappearance of old personalities, both of which might help reintroduce the politics of confrontation characterizing the period, certain restrictions are depicted in Provisional Article 4. Accordingly, persons who were occupying leadership positions in political parties at the time of the NSC intervention are barred from establishing or joining new political parties or from becoming candidates for public office for a period of ten years. [The article actually posits a set of conditions to identify those who may not actively participate in politics. Some leaders of small parties, therefore, remain outside this ban.] Similarly, all those who were members of the most recent legislature, which was dissolved by the NSC, are prohibited from engaging in active politics for five years. While it is true that these restrictions will prevent some whose experience might have been beneficial initially from becoming involved in politics, there exists a pool of others who were not deputies in the most recently elected legislature.

President Evren has indicated that, barring unusual developments, elections for the single chamber, four-hundred-member new legislature will take place before the end of 1983, possibly in October 1983.

EXTERNAL RELATIONS

After the Second World War, Turkey shifted from a policy of neutrality to one of close relations with the emergent Western bloc. Because the overriding foreign policy concern initially was to resist Soviet expansionary moves toward Turkey, and because the Western alliance was seen as the only instrument that would provide Turkey with the needed protection, the commitment to the alliance was unqualified.

Concomitant with the growth of the defense relationship, Turkey also began to receive economic aid from its new Western partners, mainly the United States. This aid was used to improve or develop infrastructures such as roads and dams, and gradually to launch an industrialization effort based on an import substitution strategy. Within a decade some questionable consequences of unqualified commitment to Western defense systems and to an exclusive reliance on Western generosity to finance an industrialization effort focusing on the domestic market had become apparent.

The Defense Connection

The Turkish integration into the Western defense system coincided with the struggle of many countries, including some neighbors of Turkey, to liberate themselves from colonial or quasi-colonial domination by Western powers. In the process of trying to establish credibility as a reliable ally, Turkey behaved very much like other members of the Western bloc toward these countries. As a consequence, it became apparent in the long run that Turkey had almost totally isolated itself from its neighbors and most members of the developing world.

The alliance affiliation enabled Turkey to modernize the armed forces. To maximize military assistance, all Turkish units were placed under NATO command. So long as no non-NATO purpose could be envisioned for the Turkish armed forces, this heavy reliance on NATO, and the United States as the dominant element behind it, was not problematic. But the emergence of the Cyprus problem and, later, the Aegean dispute demonstrated that some military capability for coping with non-NATO conflicts was needed. The 1974 Turkish intervention on Cyprus to protect the Turkish community there and the subsequent U.S. arms embargo against Turkey finally prompted Ankara to develop a new army outside the NATO-committed military force.

The all-encompassing nature of the defense relationship and Turkey's exclusive reliance on it reduced the nation's leverage vis-à-vis its allies. When Jupiter and Thor missiles were withdrawn in 1962 from Turkey, the government was not consulted. Again, without consultation, the United

States utilized facilities, established to serve NATO purposes, to supply Israeli needs, a non-NATO concern. In 1964, Turkey was told that Soviet actions prompted by a Turkish intervention on Cyprus might not be covered by NATO.

Turkey's commitment to NATO and an exclusive reliance on that connection for security had not proven entirely satisfactory. It appeared necessary, from a Turkish perspective, to introduce changes in its foreign policy that, while preserving the central role of the Western defense system, would enable Turkey to pursue more independent policies in areas not of immediate concern to NATO and to act more autonomously in areas where alliance interests and Turkish national interests were not fully convergent.

The Political Economy of Development

Achieving economic development by establishing industries oriented to import substitution, with funds coming from external sources, appeared to be a painless formula to Turkish political leaders during both the 1950s and 1960s. Although it was clear that developing in this fashion would necessitate assuming long-term availability of external economic support, there did not appear to be convincing reasons as to why it would not be available. Economic assistance to Turkey had been extended by allied governments mainly because the country was considered strategically important; it was unlikely that this strategic importance would change rapidly in the short run.

The Turkish economic development efforts did not proceed as smoothly as the preceding analysis might lead us to predict, however. The growth of the Turkish economy was marked by ever-increasing needs for external funds. These increases were not always matched by a corresponding increase in the availability of funds. Thus, a cyclical pattern in Turkish economic performance developed: so long as external resources were readily available to support the hard currency needs of the Turkish economy, the country would enjoy a period of economic expansion. At some point (1957–58, 1969–70, 1979–80) the Turkish economic burden would reach levels deemed unacceptable by Western supporters. Then, an economic crisis would ensue, marked by economic stagnation, shortages of critical goods, expansion of black market operations, and high rates of inflation. To end the crisis, a set of policy recommendations would be produced by the creditors. These would usually include a major devaluation of the Turkish lira, a downward revision of the rate of economic growth, limiting the expansion of governmental expenditures, introduction of measures to reduce the deficits of state economic enterprises, and a moderation of the increases in the support prices of agricultural commodities. In return for Turkey's implementation of these policy recommendations, which would be expected to lead to structural changes in the economy so as to reduce the reliance on external support, the Western allies would make new funds available.

The achievement of economic stability would, at the same time, mark the beginnings of a development toward the next crisis. As the conditions of the Turkish economy improved, the vigilant mood of Turkey's allies to promote structural changes so as to reduce reliance on external support would begin to weaken. The determination of the Turkish political leaders to effect structural changes would not last either, since prolonged measures of economic austerity would not prove popular with the electorate. Slowly, the economy would deteriorate.

When the petroleum crisis of 1973 erupted, the Turkish economy was recovering from a crisis and appeared to be performing well. But the cost of energy increased so suddenly that foreign exchange reserves were quickly exhausted and the country eventually began to experience external deficits that the economy could not bear. Turkey's Western partners appeared reluctant to come to Turkey's support, however. They were also experiencing inflation, declining production, and rising unemployment.

The implications of the economic reality facing Turkey were clear. The Turkish economy had to be reorganized in order to be more competitive in the international markets and to become an earner of hard currency rather than being just a spender of it. Yet, because of the political immobility and fragmentation that had come to characterize the political system, Turkish governments could not produce action even when the crisis had become an emergency. To cite an example, the country went through days without fuel until enough hard currency could be collected to purchase oil on the spot market to be imported. During the period without fuel, there were power shortages, factories stopped their production, transportation was paralyzed, and homes and buildings were unheated.

The intensity of the economic crisis finally aroused international interest. If Turkey were to default on its payments, retrieving loans made to Turkey would be impossible, setting off financial repercussions in the international banking system. Turkey's economic collapse would also threaten the survival of the Turkish political system and destabilize the entire region. Therefore, despite the initial reluctance mentioned earlier, Turkey's traditional allies, working through the International Monetary Fund, produced an economic recovery program. Turkey undertook to implement the program late in 1979. According to the agreement reached with the International Monetary Fund (IMF), Turkey's economic policies and performance would come under periodic IMF review, and credits would be made available upon certification that the government had complied with the conditions outlined in the agreement.

The assumption of power by the NSC has not affected the implementation of the agreement reached with the IMF. In fact, to symbolize the continuity in Turkey's external commitments, the minister of state for economic affairs under the Demirel (JP) government, which preceded the NSC rule, Turgut Özal, was asked to continue in the same capacity in the new government. The economic policies Turkey has been pursuing during the past three years have been in harmony with the commitments made to the IMF. Although it is probably too early to judge the extent to which the Turkish economy has transformed itself to become more competitive internationally, the recent performance of the economy has been impressive despite the adverse conditions prevailing in the international economy. Both the volume and the dollar value of exports have registered significant increases. The share of industrial products in total exports has grown rapidly and has begun to exceed regularly the external earnings from raw materials and agricultural products, which Turkey has traditionally exported. The black market for hard currencies has all but disappeared; remittances from Turkish workers abroad have reached unprecedented levels; and Turkey's ability to finance its external needs has approached 90 percent. The economic growth rate in 1982 is expected to be more than 4 percent, making Turkey the fastest growing economy among the OECD countries.

The improved performance of the Turkish economy has been, to a major extent, a result of the expansion of economic relations with the countries of the Middle East. A report in the Istanbul daily *Cumhuriyet* (6 October 1982, 6) related that between June 1981 and June 1982 Turkish exports to Iran increased by 180 percent; those to Saudi Arabia, by 121 percent, and to Iraq, by 49 percent. During the same period, exports to Germany, with whom Turkey has close relations, had increased 16 percent. Similar increases were seen in exports to Great Britain, Italy, and Switzerland. To the United States, the increase was below 3 percent.

As of December 1982, Turkish construction companies held contracts with a total value exceeding $12 billion. Many of these companies use Turkish workers whose remittances home also provide an important source of invisible external income.

In a way that resembles the change in Turkey's alliance relations, greater variety and flexibility are coming to characterize Turkey's external economic relations. Will these changes eventually lead to a fundamental shift in Turkish foreign policy? What are the time limits of change?

Is the Turkish Foreign Policy Changing?

Turkey has shown in recent years a renewed interest in developing closer relations with its Middle Eastern neighbors. This has come at a time when Turkey's relations with its western partners, with the exception of the United States, have been plagued with problems. After the repeal of the arms embargo, initiated in response to the Turkish intervention on Cyprus, Turkish-American relations continued to improve. Relations with the countries of Western Europe, however, have been deteriorating. The poor performance of European economies that has led to the application of restrictive practices to Turkish labor and products, the desire of European governments to eventually repatriate the migrant Turkish workers, the introduction of visa requirements for Turkish citizens traveling in certain European countries, social and sometimes physical hostility directed against residents of Turkish origin, and the unfriendly attitude some European politicians have displayed against the current Turkish government despite the high support it has enjoyed at home have been some of the reasons behind this deterioration.

In contrast with the problem-ridden nature of Turkey's relations with its Western European friends and allies, Turkey's relations with the Arab Middle East and Iran appear to be exemplary. Economic relations have grown rapidly. Turkey has gradually reduced, in recent years, its relations with Israel to a diplomatic minimum, and has become more actively involved in regional activities that bear the title "Islamic." All these indicators have led to the speculation that a fundamental shift in Turkish foreign policy, establishing the Middle East as a focal point, is in the process of unfolding. That the importance of the Middle East in Turkish foreign relations is increasing is clear. But to identify the nature, the magnitude, and the limits of change requires a more careful analysis.

Let us begin by examining the growing economic relationship. The growth of Turkish trade to the Middle Eastern countries results from several factors. Some of the increase is due to economic policies pursued by the Turkish government to promote exports. With the daily adjustment of the exchange rate of the lira, for example, the prices of Turkish products have become more competitive. Earlier governments had tried to preserve a fixed exchange rate. The lira was usually overvalued, rendering Turkish products too expensive to export. Similarly, the extension of credit with low interest to exporters has made exporting economically more appealing now than in the past.

A second factor contributing to the increase in Turkish trade with the Middle East has been the continuing war between Iraq and Iran. Both countries have encountered difficulties in using their port facilities in the Persian Gulf. This has not only made them reliant on Turkey as an alternate route for their supplies, but has also made it possible for Turkish products to acquire a larger share of their markets. A barter arrangement of petroleum for Iranian and Iraqi economic needs usually proves possible and has further promoted the existing trade.

A final factor contributing to increasing Turkish economic activity in the Middle East has been the interest some countries have shown in having Turkey be an economically sound and politically stable country. The preferential treatment given Turkish construction companies in the awarding of certain Saudi and Libyan contracts may be attributed to this factor.

The order in which the three factors contributing to the expansion of Turkish trade to the Middle East have been examined also indicates their order of importance. The first factor, clearly economic in nature, will determine more than the others the level and volume of Turkish economic relations with other countries of the region in the future. Current indicators suggest that these relations will continue to grow.

The second factor, the Iran-Iraq war, is political. Although it might be tempting to predict that this factor will cease to play a role once the hostilities have ended, it appears likely to produce longer-lasting effects. Iran and Iraq have both appreciated Turkey's political and military neutrality toward their struggle, and have been impressed with the consistency and stability of the Turkish position. They have seen that Turkey possesses the potential to meet many of their economic needs. Iraq has also discovered that while it had difficulty shipping oil from the Gulf area, it could send part of the oil through the Turkish-Iraqi pipeline without interruption. Iraq has recently signed an agreement with Turkey to more than double the capacity of the pipeline. Iran and Turkey have also initiated talks for the construction of pipelines for oil and gas that would ensure safe transport of Iranian products to Turkish ports and then on to European markets. In brief, the war may have drawn attention to certain options that both countries would like to have and retain even in the long run.

The third factor, the interest of some countries in the prosperity and stability of Turkey, is likely to continue. Yet, the effect this factor will have in the determination of Turkey's economic relations is probably limited unless it converges with other economic interests.

The preceding discussion would suggest that, on the whole, Turkey's growing economic relationship with the countries of the Middle East is beneficial. But before judging the effect of economic relations on foreign policy, other constraints that affect the overall relationship of Turkey to countries in the region should be examined. Let us first look into other economic considerations.

Turkey's efforts toward economic development, impressive as some of the achievements may have been so far, continue to require capital, investment goods, and technology imports. It also appears necessary for Turkey to be a borrower of hard currency for some time to come, until the structural transformation of the economy to a more competitive and industrialized one is completed.

In the development process, Turkey is more likely to engage in close cooperation with the countries of the West for several reasons. To begin with, technology and know-how for industrialization, as well as capital goods, have to be imported for the most part from Western countries. Similarly, the Western industrialized nations have been the traditional suppliers of Turkey's capital needs, as our earlier discussion noted. Although some Middle Eastern countries have accumulated sizable capital holdings after the rapid rise of petroleum prices, these funds have usually been treated as economic resources to be invested in the international capital markets. The latter are located in Western commercial centers and run mainly according to economic criteria. In them, a country's credit worthiness is often established by the judgments of the International Monetary Fund, an organization dominated by Western countries. Recent developments indicate, in any case, that the surplus funds from oil are declining rapidly and that some of the oil producers themselves are becoming important borrowers, suggesting that long-term reliance on oil-exporting countries for capital imports may not be prudent. In summary, even within the limits of only economic considerations, some limits to change in Turkey's external orientation may be identified.

A set of ideological-political constraints also affects Turkish foreign policy dispositions toward the Middle East. First, it should be recognized that ever since the founding of the republic, the Turkish political elite have striven to construct a secular society and to develop a Turkish national identity distinct from the nonnational, Islamic identity. Nationalist-secularist attitudes are not only held by the key segments of the Turkish political elite, including the military and the bureaucracy, but are also strongly propagated through education. Every constitutional arrangement Turkey has had since the founding of the republic has been based on the existence of a secular national community. Therefore, Turkey has been slow and shy in getting fully involved in organizations and activities that are based exclusively on Islamic credentials. Yet the common force that has appeared behind many efforts of regional cooperation and joint action in the international stage has been Islam. Thus, a constant tension is to be found between fundamentals of the Turkish political system and the politico-cultural basis of developing closer relations with the countries of the region. Significant changes in Turkish foreign policy that would bring Turkey into the Middle Eastern-Islamic group of nations could prove to be divisive in Turkish society itself.

Most Middle Eastern societies do not subscribe to the ideology of a secular nation-state that accepts a competitive political system as the most desirable form of political organization. In fact, the political systems of the region are quite diverse. Some systems are revolutionary Islamic, others are Islamic Socialist, and still others are traditional Islamic. Many try to export their ideologies to their neighbors with a view to undermining the latters' regimes. Various levels of hostility mark the relationships between them. This means that closer relations with the countries in the region may not be possible without identifying with one group of countries at the expense of friendship with the others. It seems, on the other hand, that Turkey's ability to stay out of intraregional conflicts is a major source of respect that may prove influential in the region.

Turkey's perceptions of its security needs and concerns do not often coincide with those of other Middle Eastern countries. Historically and currently, the Soviet Union has been seen as the major threat to Turkish territorial integrity and independence. Turkey also fears that what could be interpreted as Greece's expansionary tendencies may gain the support of one or more of the great powers. At the symbolic level, Arab countries of the area are agreed that Israel is their major security threat, but beyond that, Arab unity tends to break down. Many neighbors such as Syria and Iraq, or Egypt and Libya, see each other as major security threats. While some, such as Saudi Arabia, see the United States as the major guarantor of their security, others such as Libya see that country as the major threat.

Given these circumstances, Turkey would not be inclined to loosen ties to its traditional allies and base its overall security on a group of countries that cannot agree on a common security need, do not have high defense capabilities, and are reliant on superpowers, some of which Turkey sees as the major threat to its security, for their military equipment and supplies.

All of this suggests that there are some important political, ideological, and security limitations to the reorientation of Turkey's foreign policy away from the traditional Western connection to a new Middle Eastern connection, even if there were a strong desire on the part of Turkey to initiate such a change. Although certain problems exist between Turkey and its Western partners, there are no indications that these are of a magnitude that warrants major shifts in foreign policy. The relations with Europe and the United States have been cultivated for decades. They reflect a convergence of not only economic but also political, cultural, and security interests of Turkey. Greater variety in a nation's external relations does not necessarily imply a reordering of priorities, but rather the introduction of more flexibility within the existing set of priorities.

What inferences can be made in light of the preceding discussion? What has changed in Turkish foreign policy and how can we characterize such change?

The major change is the very fact that Turkey finds it important to be cognizant of the desires and aspirations of the countries in the area and is interested in developing more ties with them. Until the mid-1960s, Turkish interest in the area was almost nonexistent. To the extent some interest was shown, it was generally defense or security related. Current Turkish governments are inclined to take into account the concerns and desires of Middle Eastern countries as well as their responses to Turkish actions.

The characteristics of the evolving relationship can be summarized briefly. First, Turkey tends to be more sensitive in responding to the countries of the region on issues on which they have wide agreement. Needless to say, such responsiveness is even greater if regional aspirations coincide with Turkish foreign policy interests. Second, in intraregional conflicts, Turkey is strongly inclined not to take sides. This covers not only the inter-Arab conflicts but also the Arab-Israeli conflict. The Turkish decision to reduce relations with Israel to the minimum diplomatic level is intended to keep Turkey out of that conflict rather than render the country a party to it. Third, Turkish interest in the region can best be understood if viewed from the perspective of a member of the Western bloc with a special relationship to the area, rather than being viewed as the beginning of the departure of Turkey from the Western group of nations. Furthermore, Turkey is viewed as an important country in the region by others only to the extent that Turkey's foreign policy orientation is not considered to be exclusively committed to the Middle East, but to the West.

The implications of these observations for Turkish foreign policy as it relates to the Middle East can be better understood if applied to a specific example. Let us examine the changing Turkish relations with Israel.

Turkey recognized Israel shortly after its founding and maintained regular diplomatic relations with that country despite the disapproval of Arab countries. The Turkish stand was due in part to the fact that Turkey perceived relations with Israel to be a normal extension of its relations with the West. That Turkey continues to retain diplomatic relations with Israel and does not support efforts that would challenge the legitimacy of the existence of the latter is further indication that Turkey is not inclined to pursue policies in the region that are totally contradictory to those of its Western allies. The lowering of the level of diplomatic relations is a special case, but not outside the boundaries of Western relations to the Middle East.

The recognition of Israel and the maintenance of diplomatic relations with that country reflected Turkish impartiality and a policy of noninvolvement in conflicts within the region, a clear characteristic of the regional Turkish foreign policy. This operational principle was based on the assumption that involvement in regional conflicts would sap Turkish resources without producing results that Turkey would desire, such as the de-escalation of conflicts, the reduction of the probability of great power intervention in the area, and the achievement of long-term stability.

Turkey has, in past experience, discovered that the United States has often expected Turkey to be supportive of measures and willing to extend facilities to help realize the American defense commitments to Israel. The Turkish-American relationship is based on NATO, which does not cover Israel. Because Turkish relations with the countries of the Arab Middle East were limited and did not appear to constitute a major concern in the formulation of Turkish foreign policy, the United States seemed to assume that Turkey would cooperate closely in the implementation of American plans for supporting Israel.

From a Turkish perspective, however, involvement in the major conflict in the region, even if indirect, did not serve any readily identifiable national interest. It brought with it the danger of Turkey's being pulled into a major struggle against its desires. Becoming somewhat more responsive to

Arab preferences provides a way to counter pressures to be deeply involved in the conflict.

Other considerations have probably affected Turkish policies as well. Arab-Israeli relations carry the constant possibility of a conflagration that could escalate to worldwide proportions. The possibility of Turkey's remaining outside such a conflict would be enhanced by establishing clearly the differences between Turkey and its major ally, the United States, on this matter.

Arab-Israeli relations have created a permanent destabilizing influence in the area. The gradual change in Turkish regional policy may enable Turkey to have a stronger moderating influence on the Arab countries. It is also meant to communicate to Israel that expansionary actions rationalized on the basis of security needs are strongly disapproved of by a generally non-hostile power.

The inference from the examination of Turkey's relations with Israel is simple: Turkish foreign policy toward the Middle East is carried out in accordance with a set of rules that have been observed over a long period. While these rules may not tell us the specific foreign policy actions Turkey will carry out, they enable us to predict the context and the limits within which these actions will occur.

The highest priority in Turkish external relations remains the continuation of the Western connection. Yet, similar to its partners in the Western community, Turkey now seems intent on pursuing special relations in areas that remain outside the concerns of the Western system of alliance, and in ways that are not destructive of Turkey's relations with the Western community of nations.

ADDITIONAL READINGS

Ahmad, Feroz. 1977. *The Turkish Experiment in Democracy: 1950–1975.* London: C. Hurst.

Berberoglu, B. 1979. "Post War Integration of Turkey Into the World Economy." *Journal of Asian and African Studies* 14 (July-October): 258–74.

Boll, M.M. 1979. "Turkey's New National Security Concept: What It Means for NATO." *Orbis* 23 (Fall): 609–31.

Burrows, B. 1978. "Community of Thirteen: The Question of Turkish Membership of E.E.C." *Journal of Common Market Studies* 17 (December): 143–50.

Ciller, T. 1976. "Economics of Exporting Labor to the E.E.C.: A Turkish Perspective." *Middle Eastern Studies* 12 (October): 173–85.

Hale, W.M. 1980. "Role of the Electoral System in Turkish Politics." *International Journal of Middle East Studies* 11 (May): 401–17.

————. 1981. *The Political and Economic Development of Modern Turkey.* London: Croom Helm.

Harris, G.S. 1972. *Troubled Alliance: Turkish-American Problems in Historical Perspective, 1947–1971.* Washington, D.C.: American Enterprise Institute.

_____. 1980. "Left in Turkey." *Problems of Communism* 29 (July): 26–41.

Heper, M. 1976. "Recalcitrance of the Turkish Public Bureaucracy to 'Bourgeois Politics': A Multi-Factor Political Stratification Analysis." *Middle East Journal* 30 (Autumn): 485–500.

_____. 1981. "Islam, Polity and Society in Turkey: A Middle Eastern Perspective." *Middle East Journal* 35 (Summer): 345–63.

Henze, P. 1981/82. "Long Effort to Destabilize Turkey." *Atlantic Community Quarterly* 19 (Winter): 468–73.

Karpat, K.H., ed. 1973. *Social Change and Politics in Turkey: A Structural-Historical Analysis.* Leiden: E.J. Brill.

_____. 1975. *Turkey's Foreign Policy in Transition. 1950–1974.* Leiden: E.J. Brill.

Karpat, K.H. 1981. "Turkish Democracy at Impasse: Ideology, Party Politics and the Third Military Intervention." *International Journal of Turkish Studies* 2: 1–43.

Keyder, C. 1979. "Political Economy of Turkish Democracy." *New Left Review* 115 (May): 3–36.

Klieman, A.S. 1980. "Confined to Barracks: Emergencies and the Military in Developing Societies." *Comparative Politics* 12 (January): 143–63.

Landau, J.M., E. Özbudun, and F. Tachau, eds. 1980. *Electoral Politics in the Middle East: Issues, Voters, Elites.* Stanford: Hoover Institution Press.

Leder, A. 1979. "Party Competition in Rural Turkey: Agent of Change or Defender of Traditional Rule?" *Middle Eastern Studies* 15 (January): 82–105.

Levy, V. 1981. "Oil Prices, Relative Prices, and Balance of Payments Adjustments: The Turkish Experience." *European Economic Review* 15 (March): 357–72.

Mardin, S. 1977. "Religion in Modern Turkey." *International Social Science Journal* 29, no. 2: 279–97.

_____. 1979. "Youth and Violence in Turkey." *European Journal of Sociology* 19, no. 2: 229–54.

Nye, R.P. 1977. "Civil-Military Confrontation in Turkey: The 1973 Presidential Election." *International Journal of Middle East Studies* 8 (April): 209–28.

Okyar, O. 1979. "Development Background of the Turkish Economy." *International Journal of Middle East Studies* 10 (August): 325–44.

Özbudun, E. 1966. *The Role of the Military in Recent Turkish Politics.* Cambridge, Mass. Center for International Affairs of Harvard University.

_____. 1976. *Social Change and Political Participation in Turkey*. Princeton: Princeton University Press.

_____. 1981. "Turkish Party System: Institutionalization, Polarization, and Fragmentation." *Middle Eastern Studies* 17 (April): 228–40.

Özbudun, E., and F. Tachau. 1975. "Social Change and Electoral Behavior in Turkey: Toward a Critical Realignment." *International Journal of Middle East Studies* 6 (October): 460–80.

Özbudun, E., and A. Ulusan, eds. 1979. *The Political Economy of Income Distribution in Turkey*. New York: Holmes and Meier.

Sayari, S. 1978. "Turkish Party System in Transition." *Government and Opposition* 13 (Winter): 39–57.

Sezer, D.B. 1981. *Turkey's Security Policies*. London: International Institute of Strategic Studies.

Turan, Ilter. 1979. "The Development of Violence as a Feature of Turkish Political Life." In *Proceedings of the VIIth International Conference on the Unity of the Sciences*. New York: International Cultural Foundation.

_____. 1980. "Political Perspectives." *Current Turkish Thought* 44–45 (Fall–Winter): 1–47.

_____. 1980b. "Whither Turkish Foreign Policy?" *Conflict* 2, no. 1: 17–29.

_____. Forthcoming. "The Evolution of Political Culture in Turkey." In *Modern Turkey: Continuity and Change*, edited by Ahmet Evin. Philadelphia: University of Pennsylvania Press.

Turan, Ilter, J.D. Barkan, M. Jewell, and C.L. Kim. Forthcoming. *The Legislative Connection: The Representatives and the Represented in Kenya, Korea, and Turkey*. Durham, N.C.: Duke University Press.

Völker, G.E. 1976. "Turkish Labor Migration to Germany: Impact on Both Economies." *Middle Eastern Studies* 12 (January): 45–72.

Weiker, W.F. 1981. *The Modernization of Turkey from Atatürk to the Present Day*. New York: Holmes and Meier.

Wilson, A. 1979. *The Aegean Dispute*. London: International Institute of Strategic Studies.

U.S. Economic Ties with the Gulf Cooperation Council and Egypt

Ragaei El Mallakh

For the United States, the Arab states of the Gulf and Egypt form the fastest growing market for American goods and services and, in absolute terms, one of the largest markets. While petroleum immediately comes to mind in assessing this relationship, there are other economic factors and political issues that make this group of countries a principal trading partner for the United States.

The Gulf states, basically the members of the Gulf Cooperation Council (GCC)—Bahrain, Kuwait, Oman, Qatar, Saudi Arabia, and the United Arab Emirates—rank among the countries with the world's highest per capita incomes. Bahrain and Oman are the GCC's "poorer" members, but when compared with other developing nations, they appear reasonably well off. The affluent members (Kuwait, Qatar, Saudi Arabia, and United Arab Emirates), who also belong to the Organization of the Petroleum Exporting Countries (OPEC), hold 62 percent of that organization's proven oil reserves. When the smaller reserve holdings of Bahrain and Oman are added, the GCC as a group accounts for almost 47 percent of the oil reserves in the free world and over 40 percent of the world's total oil reserves.

One reflection of this oil wealth, made possible in part by these countries' small populations, is the significant foreign exchange reserves and growing investments abroad that characterize most of the Gulf states. Kuwait and Saudi Arabia had total official foreign assets of almost $199 billion in 1982—an amount greater than the foreign assets held by the industrial countries (Abed 1982/83, 29). This estimate, moreover, is conservative for it does not include private holdings.

Egypt also plays an important economic role for both the Gulf nations and the United States. To its Arab neighbors to the east, it is no small fact that Egypt is the world's largest volume transmitter of petroleum. A respectable oil and natural gas producer in its own right, Egypt consumes about half of its output at present. The strategic transport activities of the Suez Canal and Sumed (Suez to Mediterranean) pipeline are likely to be expanded, in part due to Saudi Arabia's development of the Red Sea port of Yanbuʿ. By the end of 1982, three major petroleum projects were ready for inauguration there: the Petromin refinery, Aramco's liquefied gas plant, and Petroline (the east-west crude oil pipeline, linking the vast oil fields in the east to a western processing and export point, which will lessen dependence on tankers loaded in and moving through the often tension-filled Gulf). As seaborne carriers of refined products decrease in size, greater use will be made of the Suez Canal.

In addition, Egypt is linked with the Gulf states through its contribution of skilled labor and professional expertise. More than one million Egyptian nationals work in the GCC countries in such capacities as advisers, engineers, doctors, teachers, and professors. Even in the Gulf's limited agricultural sector Egyptian farmers are surprisingly widespread.

To the United States, Egypt offers a major market and appears as a vital element in the region's stability, both economic and political. Egypt is the second largest importer of U.S. commodities among the twenty-seven countries of North Africa and the Middle East (See table 1). The movement in Egypt toward an expanded private sector and an open-door policy for foreign investment has strengthened American involvement in Egyptian development. Moreover, Egypt's geographical location, its leading role in the area due to history, culture, and population size (it is the Arab world's most populous nation, with four times the number of inhabitants of the GCC countries, and its control of the Suez Canal combine to make Egypt of strategic and economic importance.

THE UNITED STATES AND THE GCC

Established just two years ago by six Gulf states, the GCC was spurred by the turbulence in the Arabian/Persian Gulf marked by the continuing Soviet presence in Afghanistan, internal security issues in some member countries, and the outbreak of the Iran-Iraq war.

Originally conceived as a security umbrella for these small but strategically significant Arab states in the Gulf, the alliance has moved ahead in the economic sphere. An economic agreement initialed in November 1981 specified the goal of *eventual* economic, financial, and industrial integration. As a first step, the GCC scheduled implementation of several measures in 1982, including the abolition of customs duties within the group and the establishment of a common external tariff. Another step in the near future involves the elimination of infant industry protection between members. In the financial sphere the GCC's agency for joint investment, capitalized at $3 billion, is mandated to invest both in the Gulf and abroad. A portion of this body's funding is expected to spearhead projects in the relatively poor (by Gulf standards) members such as Bahrain and Oman.

A principal economic concern behind the GCC's formation is the encouragement of mobility of both capital funds and labor (including expatriates, on whom most depend) and closer coordination to optimize industrial development and reduce project duplication. Greater coordination in industry could diminish or halt the negative consequences of excessive competition in certain areas (such as petrochemicals) and lead to a larger domestic or regional market for industrial output that would otherwise be more export oriented and thus more vulnerable.

The problems of petroleum-based industries worldwide in the early 1980s are directly relevant to the industrial diversification programs of the GCC. First, as more and more major oil-producing countries expand "downstream" operations (such as refining and petrochemicals), the traditional centers for these activities, until recently located primarily in the consuming industrialized nations (United States, Japan, and Western Europe), are undergoing fundamental structural change. That established pattern, now under pressure, developed during an era of easy access to—and even control over the production of—foreign crude oil; the infrastructure, technology, and markets of the industrialized countries gave them a comparative advantage over oil-producing countries. Now most major oil-exporting nations have not only assumed control over their output but have also undertaken industrial programs based on their petroleum resources; the advantage now lies with the oil-producing nations.

Yet the oil-exporting developing countries, including those in the GCC, are confronted with a shrinking demand for petroleum. Part of the drop in oil consumption between 1981 and 1983 was due to the recession, and is therefore temporary; demand for refined products and petrochemicals should rise with economic recovery. But part of the decline in consumption is of a permanent nature, involving fuel switching, increased plant and process efficiency, and conservation. Thus, the expected slow growth in the market for petroleum products in the 1980s, compared to growth in the 1960s and even the 1970s, places a greater burden on the newly industrializing oil producers to increase efficiency and competitiveness in "downstream" operations.

In general, the diversification of the GCC members' economies most likely will continue to be handicapped by specific constraints: (1) limited natural resources other than oil and natural gas; (2) inadequate indigenous technological bases; (3) shortages in entrepreneurial and managerial capabilities; (4) severe sectoral imbalances in that some members are essentially without agriculture because of fresh water limitations and climate; and (5) small domestic markets. Not all GCC states, of course, suffer to the same extent from each of these constraints; thus, coordination can help to overcome some of the consequences of small size and limited nonoil resources.

It may be helpful to review briefly the economic conditions and outlook in the GCC countries and delineate their links with the United States.

Saudi Arabia

Saudi Arabia's dominant role in the GCC is conditioned by both physical and population size, its proximity to and shared borders with all other member states, and its enormous wealth. A recent estimate puts Saudi Arabia's proven and probable oil reserves at 178.9 billion barrels, or almost one-quarter of the total world proven and probable reserves (734.7 billion barrels). By comparison, Kuwait and Iran rank next, with almost 80 billion barrels each; the USSR, Mexico, and the United States follow, in that order (El Mallakh 1982a, 294). If produced at the rate of 6.2 million barrels per day, Saudi reserves

TABLE 1
U.S. Exports to the Middle East, 1978–1982 ($ million)

	Jan–Sept 1982	Jan–Sept 1981	1981	1980	1979	1978
Algeria	602.8	519.9	717.3	541.8	404.1	374.0
Bahrain	200.0	176.2	296.5	196.7	159.5	157.1
Djibouti	6.4	6.3	7.2	11.6	8.0	4.0
Egypt	2,186.0	1,698.3	2,159.4	1,873.6	1,433.3	1,134.1
Iraq	698.0	750.9	913.6	724.3	441.6	316.6
Jordan	408.6	442.6	726.5	407.3	333.7	235.0
Kuwait	737.0	700.7	976.4	886.1	764.7	744.8
Lebanon	201.5	232.5	295.7	303.0	227.4	142.2
Libya	224.8	610.1	813.4	508.8	468.1	425.0
Mauritania	25.4	24.0	26.9	20.1	7.0	8.0
Morocco	326.8	359.3	429.0	344.4	271.3	406.4
Oman	127.1	140.4	180.4	94.9	87.9	65.1
Qatar	118.2	106.5	157.2	128.8	138.3	76.7
Saudi Arabia	6,679.0	5,447.7	7,327.4	5,768.5	4,875.0	4,370.1
Somalia	41.0	55.5	58.8	55.8	32.0	21.0
Sudan	187.1	160.0	208.4	142.5	103.0	157.0
Syria	101.8	106.1	142.7	239.2	229.3	142.5
Tunisia	152.2	178.6	222.2	173.5	175.1	83.0
United Arab Emirates	850.7	814.4	1,007.0	997.9	666.8	493.2
Yemen (Aden)	6.7	4.5	5.6	6.5	214.1	30.6
Yemen (Sana'a)	28.7	33.5	43.9	77.4	13.7	25.1
Israel	1,734.7	1,783.5	2,520.7	2,045.0	1,856.6	1,925.1

Afghanistan	9.1	5.0	6.4	11.3	66.0	17.0
Cyprus	72.4	64.1	85.5	69.5	42.0	25.0
Ethiopia	27.7	28.9	62.2	71.9	104.0	24.0
Iran	79.0	218.1	300.3	23.1	1,019.4	3,684.4
Turkey	696.9	554.7	789.1	539.8	354.0	358.0
Middle East total	16,529.6	15,222.3	20,479.7	16,263.3	14,495.9	15,445.0
World total	158,661.7	172,217.3	223,739.1	220,782.5	181,637.0	143,577.0
Middle East % of world	10.4	8.8	7.1	7.3	8.0	10.8
Arab % of world	8.7	7.3	7.2	6.1	6.09	6.56
GCC+Egypt % of world	6.9	5.3	5.4	5.1	4.6	4.9

Source: U.S. Department of Commerce, Bureau of the Census, *Highlights of U.S. Export and Import Trade*, various issues.

U.S. Economic Ties with the Arab States of the Gulf and Egypt

would last for nearly eighty years. This is in stark contrast to the life span of petroleum reserves of such North African countries as Algeria and Libya.

Oil far surpasses all other means of generating foreign exchange earnings, accounting for about 90 percent. Moreover, much of the oil-generated income has been invested abroad and no longer brings in insignificant returns; returns on investments have risen from 14.7 billion Saudi riyals in fiscal year 1979/80 to 35 billion SR in 1982/83, according to the International Monetary Fund. And these are only official returns; they do not include those from private sector investment. It has been projected that for 1983 income on foreign investments by the Saudi Arabian Monetary Agency (SAMA) could rise to $80 billion (*Financial Times* [London], 15 March 1983, 4).

International trade, based on the export of oil, is the foundation of the Saudi economy and the engine of growth. As noted above, the petroleum sector accounts for over 90 percent of the country's foreign exchange earnings, more than 85 percent of government revenues, and about 60 percent of the gross national product. (El Mallakh 1982b, 338). The level of Saudi imports was valued at $30 billion in 1980, rising to $36 billion in 1981, and $42 billion in 1982. The United States retains its main supplier role, accounting for one-fifth of Saudi Arabia's imports, followed closely by imports from Japan, then the United Kingdom, West Germany, and Italy. Nevertheless, the U.S. balance of trade with Saudi Arabia has not been positive for well over half a decade (See table 2), although the United States came close to balance in 1982 due to a drop in oil imports.

Saudi Arabia is not expected to drastically reduce its import levels through 1985, because projects are already underway in the Third Five-Year Development Plan (1980–85) and government revenues, even with lower oil prices and production rates, are expected to be sufficient to underwrite the development program (*Business America*, 8 February 1982, 30). The two industrial complexes of Jubail (on the eastern coast) and Yanbuʿ (on the Red Sea) are the heart of the Saudi industrialization drive, with an estimated cost of $70 billion (in 1980 constant dollars). American firms have been the overall planners for both Jubail and Yanbuʿ.

The long-term strategy for industrialization is woven around hydrocarbon-based enterprises; the main projects include a system to utilize gas now flared, increased refining capacity for domestic and export needs, the creation of energy-intensive industries (such as steel and iron), and the establishment of petrochemical industries and control of 4 percent of the world petrochemicals market by 1990. The industrialization process is expected to take three decades.

The leadership of the United States in oil and petrochemical technology and industrial management is likely to reinforce the economic and trade relationship between Saudi Arabia and the United States.

Another area of rapid growth has been agriculture; Saudi Arabia has been importing U.S. manufactured agricultural machinery in order to develop its arid lands and water resources. In fact, Saudi Arabia has become the sixth largest trading partner of the United States, surpassing Italy, the Netherlands, and France. The U.S. interest in strengthening this relationship has been reflected in the creation of the U.S.-Saudi Joint Economic Commission, seen by the former nation as a means of making an official American contribution to the latter's economic development.

Saudi investment in the United States has been conservative not so much in amount as in placement, mostly in government securities and in banks. The general policy has been to emphasize high liquidity and low risk; a good example is U.S. treasury bills. Moreover, the Saudi goal of investment diversification coincides with U.S. concern with maintaining the free world's financial stability. Billions of dollars have been advanced to Japan and to West Germany, France, and other European countries for the purchase of government securities. Although this was a means to diversify Saudi monetary investments, it also bolstered these industrialized countries' economies and, since 1980, has been a positive element in a negative period of recession.

The same could be said of Saudi Arabia's expanded contributions to the International Monetary Fund (IMF) and World Bank. In 1981 the IMF concluded a $10 billion loan from Saudi Arabia that raised that country's voting position to sixth place among the 141 IMF members and led to a permanent seat on the twenty-two-member board of directors. Yet another factor in maintaining international financial stability has been Saudi foreign aid, which amounted to about $5 billion in 1980 alone.

Kuwait

Kuwait is the first oil-exporting nation to attain "capital-surplus" status. Lying at the head of the Gulf and bordered by Iraq and Saudi Arabia, this small country is estimated to have proven and probable oil reserves more than double those of the United States (El Mallakh 1982a, 294). Kuwait is the second oldest oil producer among GCC states (the discovery of oil was made in 1938 and production begun in 1946). Because of the early availability of petroleum-generated revenues and the country's small population (in 1982 about 1.4 million people, of whom nearly half are indigenous), Kuwait's economic development was begun well before that of most other GCC states. By the mid–1950s, rapid increases in oil production and revenues had led to a high per capita income (now over $20,000) and the initiation of sorely needed infrastructure projects such as roads, port facilities, and electricity.

Rapid economic growth made Kuwait an early market for goods and services from the United States and other industrialized nations. For example, the average annual growth rate of the gross domestic product (GDP) for 1970–75 was 30 percent. For the following five years, until 1980, the rate slowed to an average of 16.6 percent per annum. Only in 1981 was the upward spiral in growth checked, with an estimated 20 percent decline in oil GDP due to lower production and petroleum prices, even though the nonoil sectors' contribution to the GDP increased in that year (Central Bank of Kuwait 1981, 31).

Thus, despite its active and relatively longstanding development and economic diversification efforts, Kuwait remains dependent on a single product: 70 percent of the GDP results from petroleum, as does 97 percent of government revenues. Yet this dependence has been changing qualitatively: Kuwait has moved to reduce the proportion of revenues derived from sales of crude oil by moving into "downstream" operations—a policy of diversifica-

TABLE 2
U.S. Imports from the Middle East, 1978–
1982 ($ million)

	Jan–Sept 1982	Jan–Sept 1981	1981	1980	1979	1978
Algeria	1,850.6	4,074.0	5,038.1	6,576.8	4,940.2	3,481.6
Bahrain	30.2	24.4	34.8	15.5	10.6	28.8
Djibouti	a	a	a	a	b	b
Egypt	425.8	318.2	397.3	538.5	318.0	105.0
Iraq	37.6	163.4	164.2	459.6	618.4	243.4
Jordan	4.8	1.2	1.5	2.5	4.1	0.6
Kuwait	37.5	66.1	86.2	493.9	86.6	49.6
Lebanon	15.1	11.9	18.5	32.6	14.6	14.8
Libya	493.5	4,916.9	5,300.9	8,594.7	5,256.0	3,779.3
Mauritania	0.4	0.2	0.2	0.4	b	1.0
Morocco	37.2	25.3	36.2	35.3	39.3	43.5
Oman	278.7	296.1	347.8	344.3	316.7	354.0
Qatar	105.5	111.0	114.6	236.6	279.1	318.0
Saudi Arabia	6,221.4	10,390.7	14,391.3	12,648.2	7,983.4	5,306.5
Somalia	0.9	a	0.2	0.4	b	b
Sudan	12.5	53.6	58.0	17.3	16.0	14.0
Syria	9.9	82.2	83.0	25.9	165.2	36.8
Tunisia	36.8	5.7	10.4	59.9	95.4	21.1
United Arab Emirates	1,823.4	1,428.5	1,992.7	2,985.2	1,971.0	1,857.9
Yemen (Aden)	0.5	0.7	1.3	18.5	1.5	0.4
Yemen (Sana'a)	0.3	0.3	0.4	0.8	4.0	4.7

Israel	904.5	934.0	1,243.0	949.9	749.1	719.4
Afghanistan	8.5	7.1	12.5	5.9	13.0	12.0
Cyprus	2.7	3.2	4.0	5.6	5.0	6.0
Ethiopia	84.6	69.3	83.0	86.8	109.0	96.0
Iran	305.9	49.7	63.8	457.7	2,783.7	2,877.4
Turkey	217.7	183.5	261.0	174.6	201.0	175.0
Middle East total	12,947.5	23,217.2	29,744.9	34,767.4	25,980.9+	19,546.8+
World total	185,010.4	195,531.4	261,304.9	244,870.6	206,326.0	171,978.0
Middle East % of world	7.0	11.8	11.4	14.2	12.6	11.4
Arab % of world	6.1	11.2	10.7	13.5	10.72	9.11
GCC+Egypt % of world	4.8	6.5	6.6	7.0	5.3	4.7

Source: U.S. Department of Commerce, Bureau of the Census, *Highlights of U.S. Export and Import Trade*, various issues.
a/Less than $100,000   b/Less than $50,000

U.S. Economic Ties with the Arab States of the Gulf and Egypt

tion within the petroleum sector. For the 1980s Kuwait's plans include a $2 billion expansion of the existing refinery at Mina Ahmadi, modernization of the Mina Abdullah refinery, and construction of a $1 billion olefins/aromatics complex and expansion of the gas-gathering system into the Neutral Zone (established and jointly administered by Kuwait and Saudi Arabia). Kuwait now has the most effective gathering system for "associated" gas (gas produced in conjunction with the lifting of crude oil) in the Middle East, thereby utilizing a hydrocarbon resource that earlier (and in many producing countries, still is) was flared or burned at the wellhead.

As tables 1 and 2 indicate, the United States maintains favorable balance of trade with Kuwait; it is second only to Japan as a supplier to Kuwait. Unlike the United States, Japan is a major purchaser of Kuwaiti oil. The type of development underway, that is, in areas such as housing, telecommunications, petrochemicals, and educational and health facilities, as well as massive power and desalination plants, seems to depend heavily on American technology and equipment. Despite the growing strength of the U.S. dollar in 1982, which reduces the competitiveness of American commodities overseas, Kuwait continues to provide an excellent market, albeit a very competitive and price sensitive one. After all, the Kuwaitis retain their historical and traditional expertise in trade and commerce, making them the most accomplished mercantilists of the Gulf.

Accumulated financial reserves by the end of 1981 were over $65 billion, with estimates of up to $80 billion for the end of 1982 (including privately held assets) (Stoga, 1982/83, 65). Kuwaiti investors in overseas opportunities are more aggressive than their Saudi counterparts, and more interested in acquiring participation in foreign manufacturing and service corporations. The most recent notable transaction in the United States by Kuwait was the acquisition of Santa Fe International Corporation for $2.5 billion. This investment reflected the Kuwaiti objective of being a part of oil exploration, production, and distribution operations in both the United States and elsewhere.

Kuwaiti investment is not linked solely to energy, as is demonstrated by Kuwait's participation at varying levels in most of the five hundred largest U.S. industrial firms. Kuwaiti investment also includes real estate, the best-known transaction being the purchase of Kiawah Island in South Carolina.

U.S. companies are not the only recipients of Kuwaiti investment; reportedly, 25 percent of Hoeschst is owned by Kuwait, as are portions of other German industrial firms, including Daimler Benz, Metallgesellschaft, BASF, and Korf Stahl. In addition, there is Kuwaiti investment in such Japanese companies as Hitachi, Mitsubishi Electric, and Toshiba. This trend of worldwide investment is expected to continue: negotiations were under way in 1982 for the purchase by Kuwait Petroleum Corporation (KPC) of two of Gulf Oil Corporation's European refineries and their network of 1,575 gasoline stations in Western Europe. Thus, KPC would join the ranks of the international integrated oil companies.

Finally, Kuwaiti foreign aid, although less in absolute terms, is generally similar in kind and destination to that of Saudi Arabia. Kuwait was the first of the GCC members to institutionalize such assistance through its Kuwait Fund for Arab Economic Development. The World Bank and IMF are major beneficiaries of Kuwaiti subscriptions, which indicate Kuwait's interest in maintaining monetary and economic stability worldwide.

United Arab Emirates

During the nineteenth century, the small emirates along the Gulf were the site of strife and maritime raiding until Great Britain enforced a truce, giving this area the colorful title of Trucial States, a designation that remained until December 1971, when the seven coastal emirates of Abu Dhabi, Dubai, Sharjah, Ajman, Ras Al-Khaimah, Umm Al-Quwain, and Fujairah (the latter on the Batinah coast of the Gulf of Oman) combined to become the United Arab Emirates (U.A.E.). Abu Dhabi, the largest (82 percent of the federation's total area) and westernmost emirate, granted its first oil concession in 1939; commercial oil production did not begin until 1960. Due to its oil wealth (around 80 percent of the U.A.E.'s oil production) and size, Abu Dhabi is the most important single member of the federation. The second emirate to begin oil production was Dubai, which accounts for about 18 to 20 percent of the total U.A.E. production and has about one-third of the federation's population. Dubai's long tradition as the major entrepôt and port of entry to the emirates makes it second in importance. Although there have been concessions granted and some exploration activities in the remaining five emirates, only Sharjah has joined the producer club. With a population of eighty-eight thousand people and oil production of about twenty-five thousand barrels per day, Sharjah needs little economic aid from Abu Dhabi aside from the large-scale, intraemirate infrastructure projects. The other emirates receive support from Abu Dhabi and, to a lesser extent, from Dubai through the federation. Recent reports indicate a good potential for petroleum exists in Ras Al-Khaimah (El Mallakh 1981).

With a total population smaller than Kuwait's (the vast majority of whom are expatriates) and with proven and probable oil reserves of 29.5 billion barrels—almost equal to that of the United States—the U.A.E. 1980 per capita income of $23,000 is no surprise. The U.A.E. is now the third largest market in the Arab world (after Saudi Arabia and Egypt) for U.S. exports (see tables 1 and 2), and represents about 12 percent of that regional market. The U.A.E. is still completing its expensive and infrastructure projects, including airport construction, road improvements, and power, water, and sewage facilities; the industrial city of Ruwais in Abu Dhabi is being developed along lines similar to Shuaiba in Kuwait and Jubail and Yanbu' in Saudi Arabia. A gas-gathering project now underway and being supervised by an American company is expected to provide the energy for Ruwais and serve as the basis for petrochemical production and a gas liquefaction plant. Total investment in Ruwais for the industrial facilities, the support industries and infrastructure, and the housing, water, and other services for the work force is expected to reach $20 billion upon completion in the early 1990s. In addition to oil, Abu Dhabi has substantial "nonassociated" gas potential in the onshore Thamama C field.

The U.A.E. (specifically Abu Dhabi) is a "capital-surplus" nation. Current account surpluses for the U.A.E. for the past nine years have been estimated at $30 billion. Abu Dhabi itself directs its investment through the Abu Dhabi Investment Authority, which does not publicize its activities. The

U.A.E. is involved in U.S. financial institutions through such agencies as the Abu Dhabi International Bank (Washington, D.C.) and the Dubai Bank Ltd. (New York).

Like Kuwait and Saudi Arabia, although on a smaller scale, the U.A.E. extends economic aid; in 1979 foreign assistance from the U.A.E. was estimated at $1.5 billion. The Abu Dhabi Fund for Arab Economic Development, patterned after the Kuwait Fund, is expanding its number of loan recipients and continues to be the primary agency for project lending.

Qatar

U.S. exports to Qatar, a member of both the GCC and OPEC, have been rising in recent years (see table 1). American trade with that country could be greatly expanded, since new discoveries of natural gas have made Qatar one of the major holders of gas reserves in the world. To date, U.S. goods sold to Qatar have been primarily related to oil production, but have also included autos, parts and accessories, and medical equipment. Domestic consumption needs are largely met at present by other suppliers (Japan, the United Kingdom, and West Germany). In short, about 12 percent of Qatari imports in 1980–1981 came from the United States.

The Qatari government encourages foreign investment, specifically in industrial ventures. All domestic companies must have a 51 percent Qatari ownership, although exemptions can be arranged. Equipment and other imports directly related to new industries are exempted from duties, and there is a renewable five-year tax holiday for industrial projects, as well as government aid through capital participation, loans, and provision of land.

The Qatari market is not insignificant. The nation's population is about a quarter of a million people, of whom about half are not indigenous. Development expenditures on major projects in 1981 amounted to $1.6 billion. As noted earlier, future development is expected to be centered around "nonassociated" natural gas reserves in the northern fields and to cost $6 billion. If schedules are maintained, the first liquefied natural gas (LNG) conversion unit (one thousand cubic feet per day) may be ready in late 1986 or early 1987.

Qatari investment abroad is modest compared to Saudi Arabia's and Kuwait's, but is expanding. Qatar can boast, however, of a foreign aid program that, as a share of its gross national product, is the world's highest; between 1973 and 1976 Qatar disbursed on average 12 percent of the country's GNP. During the period of the IMF's Oil Facility, in 1975 and 1977, Qatari contributions to that agency totaled $237 million.

Along with fellow OPEC members Saudi Arabia, Kuwait, and United Arab Emirates, Qatar has been adversely affected by the oil price instability and declines of 1982. Nonetheless, there are several positive factors pointing to continued strong and even expanded trade and investment with these nations. As capital-surplus countries, they can still afford to continue their key development projects. Also, economic recovery definitely appears to be taking hold in the United States and other industrialized countries. Accordingly, higher levels of economic activity will be reflected in greater demand for petroleum. The "soft" oil market should see significant firming of demand and stability of prices.

Bahrain

The oldest producer of oil among GCC states is the island nation of Bahrain. Its petroleum reserves were never vast, and in 1982 revenues from oil amounted to only 34 percent of total revenues (*Financial Times* [London], 15 March 1983, 4). Nevertheless, Bahrain has been able to initiate modest development efforts earlier than other GCC members, leading to a slower but progressive diversification of its economy. United States-Bahraini ties are longstanding. The first Western school and medical dispensary was begun by American missionaries in the 1890s; the American Missionary Hospital still operates today. The Bahrain Petroleum Company, a subsidiary of Standard Oil Company of California, brought in the first well, in 1932.

Bahrain is the financial, industrial, and service core of the Gulf. Some sixty-two licensed offshore banking units give Bahrain a notable role in recycling petrodollars. In industry, Bahrain's aluminum smelter, ship repair yard, and gas refinery have been in operation since the 1970s and service much of the Gulf. Almost eighty U.S. companies have offices and industrial or service operations in addition to businesses represented by local agents. Major projects include a Pan-Gulf petrochemicals venture to produce one thousand tons of ammonia and methanol per day by the mid–1980s as well as construction of the Gulf University campus, which will eventually serve ten thousand students.

Bahrain's refinery (Bapco), which is the largest single industrial employer in the country, at full capacity receives 80 percent of its feedstock by pipeline from Saudi Arabia. Moreover, the major Bahraini oil field (Abu Safa), operated by Aramco, is shared with Saudi Arabia, with the latter nation controlling production levels. Bahrain's share in that field is taken in cash, not in oil. Thus, Bahrain's ties with other GCC states are substantial in both the petroleum and nonpetroleum sectors. Although Bahrain does not have the vast financial surpluses of other Gulf producers, its net official reserves at the beginning of 1982 were considered sufficient to cover a year of nonoil imports at the 1981 level of $1.6 billion. This would indicate that projects will go ahead on schedule and that imports will not be drastically restricted.

Oman

The remaining GCC country, Oman, may be the most important member in strategic terms because of its control of the narrow Strait of Hormuz and its outlets along the Gulf of Oman and Arabian Sea. One of the earliest treaties of the fledgling United States, negotiated by Edmund Roberts in 1833 and confirmed by the Senate, was with Muscat and was designed to free American trade from annoying restrictions. Today, the United States is Oman's third largest supplier of goods, holding 8 percent of the market, after Japan and the United Kingdom. Omani imports more than doubled between 1978 and 1981 (from 327.2 million Omani riyals to 790.3 million). The U.S. trade balance with Oman is negative (see tables 1 and 2), with the United States primarily importing oil from Oman.

Despite lower oil production and hence lower revenues (the petroleum sector generates 85 percent of total revenues), Oman imported through the first half of 1982 30 percent more than in the first half of the preceding year (*Financial Times* [London], 13 January 1983, supplement, VI). Not only was the market for manufactured goods, machinery, and transport equipment an expanding one, but the ranking of the suppliers showed an abrupt reversal between Japan and the United Kingdom; Japan's share of Omani imports rose from 13.6 percent to 22.6 percent between 1977 and 1981, while the United Kingdom's share fell from 23.1 percent to 14.5 percent in the same period. More than half of Oman's oil is exported to Japan.

Because of the Iran-Iraq war and the risk of transport through the Strait of Hormuz, Oman could become an entrepôt for reexports to the Gulf states, particularly the U.A.E. and Saudi Arabia, capturing part of the trade traditionally directed through Dubai. For this reason, development of ports, roads, and airports continues to hold a high priority in Omani expenditures. Thus, about half of both U.K. and U.S. exports to Oman fall into the area of construction equipment.

Aside from the import requirements needed to implement the development plan for 1981–85, military cooperation between the United States and Oman has increased, leading to a number of military projects, with costs in excess of $200 million for facilities at Masirah Island and Khassub, Thumrait, and Seeb.

THE UNITED STATES AND EGYPT

U.S. economic ties with Egypt are more diversified than those with the GCC states due to the relatively large size of the Egyptian economy and market, its economic diversification, and its large population of over forty-five million. While Egypt is at present a modest petroleum exporter, its role in oil transmission is enormous. Moreover, there are promising new finds of oil and gas in the Gulf of Suez, the western desert, and the Nile delta, and offshore in the Mediterranean.

Egypt's economy has a solid manufacturing and assembly capability, a sizable agricultural sector, which could benefit from mechanization and expanded agribusiness, and a developed service sector as exemplified by Egypt's international tourism industry. Egyptian infrastructure, which was the most advanced within the region at the turn of the century and even at the end of World War II, now requires massive improvements. Because of overpopulation, housing and urban services (water, electricity, transport, sewage) are strained. The Egyptian economy, therefore, can now easily absorb capital and advanced technology.

The economy moved toward a greater role for private enterprise and increased mobility of capital under President Sadat, an open-door policy continued by President Mubarak. As a result, by the spring of 1982 approximately three hundred U.S. firms had established offices in Egypt in the fields of tourism, construction, trade, accounting, and oil exploration and production. The United States remains Egypt's major single trading partner (supplying one-fifth of Egypt's total imports); almost 50 percent of U.S. exports to that country in 1981 were agricultural commodities and products. (The European Economic Community as a bloc holds about half of the Egyptian market.)

Egypt has always been an outlet for regional investment and trade by neighboring Arab states. Even when the Camp David accords brought severed diplomatic relations with most Arab countries, private capital continued to flow into Egypt. The Iran-Iraq war, Iranian agitation in the Gulf, and the devastation of Lebanon all serve to enhance Egypt's position as a haven for investment. Egypt also possesses other economic advantages, including a relatively skilled labor force and an experienced professional and managerial class. In 1982 Egypt sponsored several investment meetings with U.S., European, and regional companies, including a seventy-six-member group from the Arab states of the Gulf.

The great stumbling block in Egypt is an ineffective and sluggish bureaucracy. Under the guidance of the minister of investment, who directs the Egyptian Investment Authority, a number of steps have been designed to speed up the bureaucratic process: a commitment that the Investment Authority will either accept or reject a proposal within a four-month period; clear delineation on customs exemptions; and no retroactive application of new laws or regulations on foreign investors that runs counter to initial agreements by the Investment Authority. Equally important is the recent announcement that capital imports will receive a higher priority than consumption imports; the objectives of this policy are to maximize the available foreign exchange and to bring about a more equitable distribution of the nation's financial resources.

The construction sector remains the fastest growing sector in the Egyptian economy, indicating potential markets for U.S. equipment and building materials. Food processing is also a growth sector, with about one-third of agricultural equipment imports in 1981 coming from the United States. Companies dealing in data processing and computers are just beginning to find viable markets. Finally, the hotel and tourist industry is robust, with plans for expanded or upgraded facilities along the Red Sea, in Sinai, and in upper Egypt.

The U.S. aid program to Egypt is currently substantial, reaching about $1 billion annually. This, of course, underwrites a portion of U.S. exports to Egypt and encourages U.S. private investment. In 1982 a bilateral investment treaty was concluded between the United States and Egypt, asserting each government's commitment to protect foreign investment and encourage private sector activities domestically.

The United States-Egyptian relationship goes beyond economic and commercial ties, and involves cultural exchange and influence. The American University in Cairo, for example, is one of the oldest U.S. institutions of higher learning outside the United States. It serves as a regional as well as an Egyptian training and educational center. Such economic and cultural relationships with Egypt are of a stabilizing nature, and stability in the Eastern Mediterranean and in the Gulf is a vital concern to the United States.

The Gulf Cooperation Council states and Egypt are the most important Middle Eastern economic partners of the United States. Oil is indisputably a major catalyst in the relationship. However, American export trade, the two-way investment between them and the U.S., and economic aid continued to be vigorous and, in some cases, even to expand despite the impact of the 1982 global recession. In addition, the GCC-Egyptian relationship itself has been improving through 1982, advancing political moderation and stability in the region—issues of critical significance to the United States.

REFERENCES

Abed, George. 1982/83. "The Arab Oil-Exporting Countries in the World Economy." *American-Arab Affairs*, no. 3 (Winter): 26–40.

Central Bank of Kuwait. 1981. *Annual Report*. Kuwait.

El Mallakh, Ragaei. 1981. *The Economic Development of the United Arab Emirates.* London: Croom Helm Ltd.; New York: St. Martin's Press.

_____. 1982a. "Hydrocarbons in a Changing World: Some Future Strategies."*OPEC Review* 6, no. 3 (Autumn): 287–94.

_____. 1982b. *Saudi Arabia: Rush to Development/Profile of an Energy Economy and Investment.* Baltimore: Johns Hopkins University Press.

International Monetary Fund. 1982. *IMF Survey*. 15 November.

Stoga, Alan. 1982/83. "The Foreign Investments of OPEC and Arab Oil Producers." *American-Arab Affairs*, no. 3 (Winter): 60–67.

Bibliography: The Year's Publications in Middle Eastern Studies, 1982

Eric Ormsby, with David H. Partington

The bibliography lists monographs and serials in English, French, and German on the modern Middle East that appeared in 1982. Certain 1981 imprints, which could not be included in volume 1 of the *Middle East Annual* are also listed and identified by year of publication. Annotations in brackets are based on information derived from such secondary sources as publishers' catalogs, national bibliographies, and reviews; all other annotations are based on examination of the books themselves. The alphabetical arrangement disregards the Arabic article "al" in its various permutations (al, Al, el, El, etc.); thus, El Mallakh will be found under M, Algosaibi under G, and so on.

MONOGRAPHS

Abadan-Unat, Nermin, ed. *Women in Turkish Society*. Social, Economic, and Political Studies of the Middle East, 30. Leiden: E.J. Brill. 350 pp. Tables.
[A collection of fourteen papers, originally presented at the Conference on Women in Turkish Society, in Istanbul, May 1978. The book is divided into four broad subjects: population and health; labor and education; continuity and change in sex roles; and religion and political behavior.]

Abdullah, Muhammad Salim. *Islamische Menschenrechtserklärung*. Aktuelle Fragen, 6. Altenberge: Verlag für Christl.-Islam. Schrifttum. 32 pp.

Abou Rizk, Joseph. *La politique culturelle au Liban*. Politiques culturelles: études et documents. Paris: Presses de l'Unesco. 90 pp.

Abrahamian, Ervand. *Iran between Two Revolutions*. Princeton Studies on the Near East. Princeton: Princeton University Press. 574 pp. Maps; tables; bibl.; index.

An exhaustive study of modern Iran, based on archival sources, Iranian parliamentary debates, and the Iranian press from 1905 to 1980, that focuses on three broad areas: historical background, especially the Constitutional Revolution and the period of Reza Shah; the "politics of social conflict" from 1941 to 1953, with emphasis on the Tudeh party; and contemporary Iran, with attention to the subjects of development, political and clerical opposition to the shah, and the 1978 revolution.

Abu Eishe, Anwar. *Mémoires palestiniennes: La terre dans la tête*. Mémoire pour demain. Paris: Clancier-Guénand, distributed by Distique. 210 pp.

Abu-Ihya, Sami. *Religionsunterricht an den öffentlichen Knabenschulen des Königreichs Saudi-Arabien*. Schriften zur Islamkunde, 1. Frankfurt: R.G. Fischer. 218 pp. Map; bibl.
A study of religious education in Saudi Arabian secondary schools for boys, the work includes a discussion of the role of religion in Saudi history and life; a historical survey of education in Saudi Arabia; and an analysis and description of current teaching and curriculum. Excerpts from textbooks on traditional religious subjects, at various levels, are included, as well as the Arabic text and German translation of an interview with the director of Islamic education. The work is the author's dissertation.

Abu Izzeddin, Nejla M. *Nasser of the Arabs: An Arab Assessment*. London: Third World Centre for Research and Publishing, 1981. 475 pp. Bibl.; index.

Abu-Lughod, Ibrahim, ed. *Palestinian Rights: Affirmation and Denial*. Wilmette, Ill.: Medina Press. 233 pp.
Sixteen essays on various aspects of the Palestinian problem, such as the PLO; the UN and the Palestinians; international law in the occupied territories; the legal structure of West Bank settlements; human rights; African opinion on the issue; and the formation of American public opinion. Henry Cattan, Michael Adams, Ibrahim Abu-Lughod, Janet Abu-Lughod, John Quigley, and Edward Said are among the contributors.

Abu Zahra, Nadia. *Sidi Ameur: A Tunisian Village*. St. Antony's Middle East Monographs, 15. London: Ithaca Press. 254 pp. Illus.; tables; map; bibl.; index.

Afanasyan, Serge. *L'Arménie, l'Azerbaïdjan et le Georgie: De l'indépendence à l'instauration du pouvoir soviétique 1917–1923*. Paris: L'Harmattan.

Akiner, Shirin. *Islamic Peoples of the Soviet Union, with an Appendix on the Non-Muslim Turkic Peoples of the Soviet Union*. London and Boston: Kegan Paul. Bibl.; index.

Alazar, Daniel J., ed. *Israeli Views on Judea, Samaria, and Gaza: The Present and the Future*. AEI Studies, 334. Washington, D.C.: American Enterprise Institute, 1981.

Alem, Jean-Pierre. *La Déclaration Balfour, 1917: Aux sources de l'État d'Israël*. Mémoire du siècle, 20. Paris: Complexe. 160 pp.
[The emergence of the Balfour Declaration in its diplomatic and political context.]

Alexander, Yonah, and Ebinger, Charles K., eds. *Political Terrorism and Energy: The Threat and Response.* New York: Praeger. 272 pp.

Algérie 20 ans. Paris: Le Seuil.

Āl-i Ahmad, Jalāl. *Gharbzadegi [Weststruckness].* Translated by John Green and Ahmad Alizadeh. Lexington, Ky.: Mazda Publishers. 204 pp. Tables; illus.
[A critique of social conditions in Iran, written in 1962 by the influential author (1923–69).]

————. *Iranian Society: An Anthology of Writings by Jalal Al-e Ahmad.* Edited by Michael C. Hillmann. Lexington, Ky.: Mazda Publishers. 158 pp.
[A collection of sixteen short stories and essays.]

Ali-Toudert, Abdallah. *Le coût de la vie en Algérie depuis 1962.* Paris: Economica. 124 pp.

Allan, J.A. *Libya since Independence: Economic and Social Development.* New York: St. Martin's Press.

Alleg, Henri, ed. *La Guerre d'Algérie.* T. 3, *Des complots du 13 mai à l'Indépendance.* Paris: Temps actuels. 600 pp.

Allen, Peter. *The Yom Kippur War.* New York: Scribner. 288 pp. Illus.; maps; bibl.; index.
A popular account of the 1973 Arab-Israeli war.

Allen, Roger. *The Arabic Novel: An Historical and Critical Introduction.* Journal of Semitic Studies Monographs, 4. Manchester: University of Manchester. 181 pp. Bibl.; index.
Traces the rise of the modern Arabic novel and discusses eight important recent novels by such authors as Najīb Mahfūz, Ghassān Kanafānī, Halīm Barakāt, and Jabrā Ibrāhīm Jabrā; includes a bibliography of Arabic works, as well as of translations and critical studies.

Almana, Mohammed. *Arabia Unified: A Portrait of Ibn Saud.* London: Hutchinson Benham. 321 pp. Ilus.; maps; index.
[A revised edition of the biography first published in 1980.]

American Friends Service Committee. *A Compassionate Peace: A Future for the Middle East.* New York: Hill and Wang. 240 pp. Illus.; maps; bibl.
A report on the major areas of conflict in the Middle East, with special emphasis on Israel and the West Bank; Lebanon; Iran and Afghanistan. The work seeks to offer proposals that will be conducive to peace in the region, and strives to be both "visionary" and "realistic" at once.

Amin, Samir. *Irak et Syrie, 1960–1980: Du projet national à la transnationalisation.* Documents/Editions de Minuit. Paris: Editions de Minuit. 160 pp. Tables; illus.; bibl.

Amin, S.H. *The Iran-Iraq War: Legal Implications.* Glasgow: S.H. Amin.

_____. *Trading with Iran*. Glasgow: S.H. Amin.

Andersen, Roy; Seibert, Robert F.; and Wagner, Jon G. *Politics and Change in the Middle East: Sources of Conflict and Accommodation*. Englewood Cliffs, N.J.: Prentice-Hall. 317 pp. Bibl.; index.

Anderson, Norman, et al. *The Kingdom of Saudi Arabia*. 6th rev. ed. London: Stacey International. 256 pp. Illus.; bibl.; index.

Antes, Peter. *Ethik und Politik im Islam*. Stuttgart: Kohlhammer. 112 pp. Notes; index.
    A succinct survey and analysis of traditional Islamic ethics and political thought in confrontation with contemporary, westernizing trends; based on two previously published studies by the author.

Les Arabes dans les territoires occupés par Israël. Paris: Editions ouvrières. 308 pp.

Arab Resources: The Transformation of a Society. London: Croom Helm. 320 pp.

Argov, Shlomo. *Europe and Arab-Israeli Peacemaking: A Critique*. The 22d Selig Brodetsky Memorial Lecture. Leeds: University of Leeds. 12 pp.
    [The text of a lecture given at Leeds on 18 May 1981.]

Assersohn, Roy. *The Biggest Deal*. London: Methuen. 320 pp.
    [On the release of the American hostages in Iran in 1981.]

Atallah Daad Bou Malhab. *Le Liban: Guerre civile ou conflit international (à partir du milieu du XIXᵉ siècle)*. [Paris]: Lib. gen. de droit et de jurisprudence. 284 pp.

Atiya, Nayra. *Khul-Khaal: Five Egyptian Women Tell Their Stories*. Syracuse: Syracuse University Press.

Ayoun, Richard. *Les juifs d'Algérie: 2000 ans d'histoire*. Judaïques. Paris: J.C. Lattès.

Aziz, Tareq. *The Iraq/Iran Conflict: Questions and Discussions*. London: Third World Centre for Research and Publishing, 1981. 92 pp.
    [The author is deputy premier of Iraq and a member of the Revolutionary Command Council, and was formerly editor of *al-Thawrah*, the official Baʿth party newspaper.]

Azoy, G. Whitney. *Buzkashi: Game and Power in Afghanistan*. Symbol and Culture. Philadelphia: University of Pennsylvania Press. 158 pp. Illus.; bibl.; index.

Azzam, Hamdy. *Über Anwar el Sadat*. Biographische Skizzen. Stuttgart: Poller. 70 pp. Illus.
    Written in October 1981 by the press secretary of the Egyptian embassy to West Germany and Austria, this brief biography relates the principal events of Sadat's career, with particular attention to his relations with Germany; contains numerous photographs.

Bahrain: A MEED Practical Guide. Boston and London: Kegan Paul.

Baer, Gabriel. *Fellah and Townsman in the Middle East: Studies in Social History.* London: Frank Cass. 330 pp.
[A collection of studies, by the late professor of Middle Eastern history at the Hebrew University, that center on the history of the common people of the Middle East. Topics covered include Turkish guilds, the village *shaykh* in Palestine, and popular movements and rebellions.]

Balta, Paul, and Rulleau, Claudine. *La vision nassérienne.* La Bibliothèque Arabe. Paris: Sindbad.

Balta, Paul; Rulleau, Claudine; and Duteil, Mireille. *L'Algérie des algériens vingt ans après* . . . . Enjeux internationaux. Paris: Les Editions ouvrières, 1981. 288 pp. Maps; bibl.
A strongly sympathetic account, written from a Socialist viewpoint, of the political and economic development of Algeria since independence; includes a "succinct chronology" of Algerian history to 1 December 1981.

Banks, Lynne Reid. *Torn Country: An Oral History of the Israeli War of Independence.* New York: Franklin Watts. 416 pp. Map; index.
An account of the founding of Israel drawn from interviews with participants and observers. The statements of more than sixty individuals interviewed are interspersed in a narrative beginning in November 1947 and continuing into the early years of statehood. Those interviewed range from private citizens to well-known figures.

Barbier, Maurice. *Le conflit du Sahara occidental.* Paris: L'Harmattan. 418 pp. Bibl.

Bassiouni, M. Cherif, ed. *The Islamic Criminal Justice System.* London, Rome, and New York: Oceana Publications. 255 pp. Bibl.; glossary.
Eleven essays by Muslim professors, attorneys, and judges on Islamic criminal law; topics treated include the sources of Islamic law, rights of the accused, principles of evidence, and punishments. There is a useful, brief glossary and a short bibliography of classical Arabic works of *fiqh*, arranged by *madhhab*.

Bayat, Mangol. *Mysticism and Dissent: Socioreligious Thought in Qajar Iran.* Syracuse: Syracuse University Press. 245 pp. Bibl.; index.
Examines the tradition of dissent in Shiite thought in the Qajar period (1785–1925), with chapters on Shaykhī thought, Babism, and secularization; an epilogue discusses such dissent in the light of the 1978 revolution.

Bazak, Yaacob. *Réflexions sur Israël.* Haifa: Tamar Editions. 299 pp.

Bazin, Marcel. *Le Tâlech, une région ethnique au nord de l'Iran.* Collection Recherche sur les grandes civilisations, serie Synthèse, 1. Paris: Editions ADPF, distributed by Boccard. 534 pp. Illus.; tables.
[The author's revised dissertation on a unique and isolated ethnic group in Iran.]

Behn, Wolfgang H., and Floor, Willem M., comps. *Twenty Years of Iranian Power Struggle: A Bibliography of 951 Political Periodicals from 1341/1962 to 1360/1981, with Selective Locations.* Berlin: Adıyok. 159 pp.
Covers underground and ephemeral radical publications in Persian, including anti-shah and anti-Khomeini materials, with dates of publication, pagination, and size supplied for many titles; includes a subject index and locations of titles at eighteen European and North American libraries. Titles are given in Persian and in transliteration; facsimiles of selected title pages are also included. (This work was listed under a slightly different title in the *Middle East Annual,* vol. 1, but did not appear until 1982.)

Behrens, Henning. *Die Afghanistan-Intervention der UdSSR.* Munich: Tuduv-Verlagsgesellschaft.

Ben-Ami, Yitshaq. *Years of Wrath, Days of Glory: Memoirs from the Irgun.* New York: R. Speller. 601 pp. Illus.; maps; bibl.; index.
A personal, firsthand account of the Irgun by an early participant.

Bendt, Ingela, and Downing, James. *We Shall Return: Women of Palestine.* Translated by Ann Henning. London: Zed Press. 132 pp. Illus.

Ben Jelloun, Tahar. *Haut Atlas, l'exil de pierres.* Les Grands Albums. Paris: Le Chêne/Hachette. 108 pp. Contains eighty color photographs by Philippe Lafond.

Bennigsen, Alexandre. *The Islamic Threat to the Soviet State.* Croom Helm Series on the Arab World. London: Croom Helm. 192 pp.

———. *Les musulmans oubliés: L'Islam en U.R.S.S. aujourd'hui.* Paris: Maspero, 1981.

———. *The Soviet Union and Muslim Guerrilla Wars, 1920–1981: Lessons for Afghanistan.* A Rand Note, N–1707/1. Santa Monica, Calif.: The Rand Corporation, 1981.

Berberoglu, Berch. *Turkey in Crisis: From State Capitalism to Neo-Colonialism.* Middle East Series.
London: Zed Press. 153 pp. Illus.; map; bibl.; index. [A Socialist view of Turkish economic conditions.]

Beshir, Mohamed Omer. *Terramedia: Themes in Afro-Arab Relations.* London: Ithaca Press. 205 pp. Bibl.
[On the foreign relations of Arab countries with Africa.]

Bhargava, G.S. *South Asian Security after Afghanistan.* Lexington, Mass.: Lexington Books.

Bidwell, Robin Leonard. *The Two Yemens.* Harlow, Essex: Longman; Boulder, Colo.: Westview Press. 250 pp. Bibl.; index.
[A history of North and South Yemen by a Cambridge University scholar with long familiarity with the area.]

Bielenstein, Dieter, ed. *Europe's Future in the Arab View: Dimensions of a New Political Cooperation in the Mediterranean Region*. Schriften des Instituts für Internationale Begegnungen, 7. Saarbrücken and Fort Lauderdale, Fla.: Breitenbach. 166 pp. Bibl.
[Nine essays by Egyptian authors, and four essays by German authors, on the prospects for a new European-Arab political and economic cooperation. Contributors include Udo Steinbach, Rushdi Said, Mourad Wahba, and Friedemann Büttner.]

Blumberg, Stanley A., and Owens, Gwinn. *The Survival Factor: Israeli Intelligence from World War I to the Present*. New York: Putnam. Index.

Blumenkranz, B., and Klatzmann, J., eds. *Histoire de l'état d'Israël*. Paris: Privat. 416 pp.

Boisard, Marcel A. *Der Humanismus des Islam*. Kaltbrunn: Verlag zum Hecht. 432 pp. Bibl.
A broad introduction to Islamic culture and civilization by a Swiss professor and former Red Cross official; the original French edition appeared in 1979 under the title *L'humanisme de l'Islam* (Paris: Albin Michel).

Bonnenfant, P., ed. *La péninsule arabique d'aujourd'hui*. Paris: CNRS. 400 pp. Illus.; maps; tables; bibl.; index.
[Eleven articles on the development and current role of the Arabian peninsula, with discussions of Islam, oil, economics, and demography; the first volume in a series.]

Bouteiller, Georges de. *L'Arabie Saoudite: Cité de Dieu, cité des affaires, puissance internationale*. Préface de Henri Laoust. Paris: Presses universitaires de France, 1981.

Breznitz, Shlomo, ed. *Stress in Israel*. New York: Van Nostrand Reinhold.

Büren, Rainer. *Ein palästinensischer Teilstaat? Zur internen, regionalen und internationalen Dimension der Palästina-Frage*. Internationale Politik und Sicherheit, 8. Baden-Baden: Nomos. 347 pp. Tables; map; bibl.
A detailed analysis of the Palestinian question with special regard to West German foreign policy; the author draws on Arabic sources and includes a study of Palestinian society and political development. The position of the Soviet Union on the question is also treated; there is as well a critical analysis of the Camp David accords. The book contains an extensive bibliography (pp. 305–39), as well as useful appendixes and tables; abstracts in Arabic and English are provided.

Caplan, Neil. *Futile Diplomacy*. Vol. 1, *Early Arab-Zionist Negotiation Attempts, 1913–1931*. London: Cass. 296 pp.

Carré, Olivier, ed. *L'Islam et l'état dans le monde d'aujourd'hui*. Paris: Presses universitaires de France. 272 pp.

Carrère d'Encausse, Hélène. *Réforme et révolution chez les musulmans de l'empire Russe Bukhara, 1867–1924*. Paris: Presses de la fondation nationale des sciences politiques.

Chaliand, Gérard. *Report from Afghanistan*. Translated by Tamar Jacoby. New York: Viking. 100 pp. Maps; bibl.; index.
[An account of the Soviet invasion of Afghanistan in the context of Afghan internal politics.]

Chalvron, Alain de. *Le piège de Beyrouth*. Paris: Le Sycomore. 200 pp.
[A journalist's eyewitness account of the Israeli siege of Beirut.]

Chevallier, Dominique. *Villes et travail en Syrie du XIXe au XXe siècle*. Paris: Maisonneuve et Larose. 168 pp. Illus.

Cigar, Norman L., comp. *Agriculture and Rural Development in the Arabian Peninsula*. Monticello, Ill.: Vance Bibliographies, 1981. 4 pp.

Clarke, Peter B. *West Africa and Islam*. London: Edward Arnold.

Clarke, Thurston. *By Blood and Fire*. London: Hutchinson, 1981. 346 pp. Illus.; maps; bibl.; index.
[On the bombing of the King David Hotel in 1946 by Jewish terrorists.]

Cohen, Michael Joseph. *Palestine and the Great Powers, 1945–1948*. Princeton: Princeton University Press. 417 pp. Maps; bibl.; index.
A detailed study, based on archival documents, of the attempts by the protagonists in the Palestine conflict—the Arabs, Jews, Britain, and the United States—to impose their own solutions on the area.

Cohen, Yona. *Jerusalem under Siege: Pages from a 1948 Diary*. Foreword by Yitzhak Rabin. Los Angeles: Ridgefield Publishing Co., 1981.

Cooley, John K. *Libyan Sandstorm*. A New Republic Book. New York: Holt, Rinehart and Winston. Bibl.; index.

Cooper, Mark Neal. *The Transformation of Egypt: State and State Capitalism in Crisis, 1967–1977*. Baltimore: Johns Hopkins University Press. 288 pp. Bibl.; index.
[A study of a crucial decade in Egyptian history that seeks to analyze that country's political economy on the basis of a new methodological framework combining Marxist and Weberian principles.]

Cragg, Kenneth. *This Year in Jerusalem: Israel in Experience*. London: Darton, Longman and Todd. 178 pp. Index.

Dadiani, Lionel, ed. *Zionism: Enemy of Peace and Social Progress*. Moscow: Progress, 1981.

Daly, Martin. *Sudan*. World Bibliographical Series, 40. Oxford: Clio Press. 180 pp.

Davies, William David. *The Territorial Dimension of Judaism*. Berkeley: University of California Press.

Dawisha, Adeed, and Dawisha, Karen, eds. *The Soviet Union in the Middle East: Policies and Perspectives*. London: Heinemann. 172 pp. Index.

Deeb, Marius, and Deeb, Mary Jane. *Libya since the Revolution: Aspects of Social and Political Development*. New York: Praeger. Bibl.; index.

De Gaury, Gerald, ed. *The Road to Kabul*. London: Quartet.

Deshen, Shlomo, and Zenner, Walter P., eds. *Jewish Societies in the Middle East: Community, Culture, and Authority*. Washington, D.C.: University Press of America.

Dessouki, Ali E. Hillal, ed. *Islamic Resurgence in the Arab World*. Praeger Special Studies. New York: Praeger. 286 pp. Bibl.; index.
A collection of eleven original essays that seek to define and describe "Islamic resurgence" in its contemporary social and historical context; the contributors include A.E. Hillal Dessouki, Daniel Pipes, Ismail Serageldin, R. Stephen Humphreys, Tawfic Farah, Ann Mayer, and Jean-Claude Vatin. The collection was prepared under the auspices of the Center of International Studies, Princeton University.

Devlin, John F. *Syria: Modern State in an Ancient Land*. Boulder, Colo.: Westview Press. 135 pp. Illus.; bibl.; index.
[A profile of the Arab Republic of Syria that surveys the country's history, peoples, culture, economy, and politics; the author was formerly an analyst for the CIA's Office of Political Research.]

Djalili, Mohammad-Reza. *Religion et révolution: L'Islam shi'ite et l'Etat*. Perspectives économiques et juridiques. Paris: Economica. 68 pp.

Documents and Statements on Middle East Peace, 1979–82. Report prepared for the Subcommittee on Europe and the Middle East of the House Committee on Foreign Affairs. Washington, D.C.: U.S.G.P.O. 350 pp. Bibl. [Supt. of Docs. no. Y 4.F 76–1:M 58/22/979–82]

Domb, Risa. *The Arab in Hebrew Prose, 1911–1948*. London: Vallentine Mitchell. 192 pp. Bibl.; index.

Droz, Bernard, and Lever, Evelyne. *Histoire de la guerre d'Algérie (1954–1962)*. Paris: Seuil. 384 pp.
[A history of the Algerian war of independence and the founding of the new state.]

Duncan, David Douglas. *Exploring the World of Allah*. Boston: Houghton Mifflin.

Dutey, Guy. *Le temps du mépris: Les maghrébins de la deuxième génération*. Paris: Les Editions ouvrières. 192 pp.

Enayat, Hamid. *Modern Islamic Political Thought: The Response of the Shi'i and Sunni Muslims to the Twentieth Century*. London: Macmillan; Austin: University of Texas Press. 237 pp. Bibl.; index.
A comparative study of Shiite and Sunnite doctrines of the state in their respective historical developments and contexts from the earliest period, but with emphasis on the last two centuries. Iran and Egypt receive special attention, but Pakistan, India, Lebanon, and Iraq are also considered.

Esposito, John L. *Women in Muslim Family Law*. Contemporary Issues in the
Middle East. Syracuse: Syracuse University Press. 170 pp. Bibl.;
index.
[A historical account of the role of women and the family in Islamic society
from the earliest period, with an analysis of contemporary efforts at reform
in Egypt and Pakistan.]

Evans, Stephen F. *The Slow Rapprochement*. Beverley: Eothen Press. 123 pp.
[On Great Britain's foreign relations with Turkey.]

Fage, J.D. *An Atlas of African History*. 2d rev. ed. London: Edward Arnold.

Farès, Abderrahmane. *La cruelle vérité. De l'Algérie de 1945 à l'Indépendance*.
Paris: Plon. 256 pp.
[Memoirs of the president of the provisional Algerian government.]

al-Farsy, Fouad. *Saudi Arabia: A Case Study in Development*. London and
Boston: Kegan Paul. 224 pp. Illus.; bibl.; index.
[The author's revised 1978 thesis.]

Feldman, Shai. *Israeli Nuclear Deterrence: A Strategy for the 1980s*. New
York: Columbia University Press.

Fernandez-Armesto, Felipe. *Sadat and His Statecraft*. London: Kensal Press.
196 pp. Illus.; bibl.; index.

Ferrier, R. W. *The History of the British Petroleum Company*. Vol. 1, *The Developing Years, 1901–1932*. Cambridge: Cambridge University Press.
831 pp. Illus.; maps; tables; index.
A massive and detailed study, profusely illustrated and extensively
documented, of the British Petroleum Company; the first volume, which
deals with the early years of the D'Arcy Concession, the formation of the
company, and the discovery of oil in 1908 and concludes with the
cancellation of the concession in 1932, will be followed by two further
volumes tracing the company's history up to the 1970s.

Findlay, Allan M.; Findlay, Anne M.; and Lawless, Richard I., comps. *Tunisia*. World Bibliographical Series, 33. Oxford: Clio Press. 279 pp.
Index.

Frangi, Abdallah. *PLO und Palästina: Vergangenheit und Gegenwart*. Frankfurt: R.G. Fischer. 312 pp. Maps; bibl.
A history of Palestine from ancient times, with emphasis on contemporary
events up to the Israeli invasion of Lebanon and the withdrawal of the PLO
from Beirut; the author takes a moderate, pro-Palestinian stand.

Freedman, Robert Owen, ed. *Israel in the Begin Era*. New York: Praeger. 288
pp. Bibl.; index.
Papers originally presented at a conference at the Baltimore Hebrew College
on 8 April 1979, and now updated; the volume includes eight essays on
such topics as the Likud party 1977–81 (by E. Torgovnik), the opposition
Labor party (by M. Aronoff), the religious parties (by D. Elazar), Israel's Arab
minority (by I. Lustick), U.S.-Soviet-Israeli relations during the Begin era (by
R.O. Freedman), and the question of Palestinian autonomy (by R.A.

Friedlander). There are also four useful documentary appendixes: the Soviet-U.S. joint statement of 1 October 1977; the Camp David agreements; the Israeli-Egyptian peace treaty; and preelection polls and Knesset results for the 1981 Israeli elections.

Freund, Wolfgang S. *Welche Zukunft für den Iran? Die entwicklungspolitischen Grundideen des Abolhassan Banisadr.* Aktuelle Zukunft, 1. Vienna: Wilhelm Braumüller, 1981. 53 pp. Bibl.
An introduction to the life and political thought of Abū al-Hasan Banī Sadr, former president of Iran, with special regard to his theories of economic development within the Islamic milieu; the author is a sociologist from the University of Strasbourg.

Freustié, Jean. *L'entracte algérien.* L'Instant romanesque. Paris: Balland. 112 pp.
[An account of the two years (1940–42) that the author, a physician, novelist, and critic, spent in Algeria.]

Friedman, Saul S. *Land of Dust: Palestine at the Turn of the Century.* Washington, D.C.: University Press of America. Bibl.

Georgeon, François. *Aux origines du nationalisme turc: Yusuf Akçura (1876–1935).* Paris: Ed. ADPF, distributed by Boccard. 154 pp.
[An intellectual biography of Yusuf Akçura, and a study of the development of Turkish nationalism; among the texts translated in the appendixes is the first manifesto of Pan-Turkism.]

Ghanem, Hanna. *Iran, Démocratie et technologie, une interaction explosive: Lutte pour une justice.* Sherbrooke, Québec: Didon. 224 pp. Maps; tables.

Ghantus, Elias T. *Arab Industrial Integration: A Strategy for Development.* London: Croom Helm. 240 pp. Bibl.; index.

Gilmour, David. *The Dispossessed: The Ordeal of the Palestinians, 1917–1980.* London: Sidgwick and Jackson.

Gilsenan, Michael. *Recognizing Islam: An Anthropologist's Introduction.* Croom Helm Series on the Arab World. London: Croom Helm. 295 pp. Bibl.; index.
Based on extensive fieldwork in Egypt, Lebanon, and Yemen, the study seeks to correct stereotyped views of Islam by considering Islamic beliefs and practices in the context of daily life, with particular regard to class tensions.

Gitelman, Svi. *Becoming Israelis: Political Resocialization of Soviet and American Immigrants.* New York: Praeger. 352 pp.

Glick, Edward Bernard. *The Triangular Connection: America, Israel, and American Jews.* London and Boston: George Allen and Unwin. 174 pp. Bibl.; index.
[A history of American Zionism, combined with an analysis of various problems in Israeli society and a proposal for resolving the Arab-Israeli conflict.]

Golan, Matti. *Shimon Peres: A Biography.* Translated from the Hebrew by Ina Friedman. New York: St. Martin's Press.

Algosaibi, Ghazi A. *Essays.* London and Boston: Kegan Paul.

Grandin, Nicole. *Le Soudan nilotique et l'administration britannique (1898–1956). Éléments d'interprétation socio-historique d'une expérience coloniale.* Social, Economic, and Political Studies of the Middle East, 29. Leiden: E.J. Brill. 362 pp.

Granotier, Bernard. *Israël: Cause de la Troisième Guerre mondiale?* Paris: L'Harmattan.

Granqvist, Hilma. *Portrait of a Palestinian Village: The Photographs of Hilma Granqvist.* Edited by Karen Segar, with a foreword by Shelagh Weir. London: Third World Centre, 1981. 176 pp. Illus.; bibl.

Grayson, Benson Lee. *Saudi-American Relations.* Washington, D.C.: University Press of America. Bibl.; index.

——. *United States-Iranian Relations.* Washington, D.C.: University Press of America.

Graz, Liesl. *Les Omanis: Nouveaux gardiens du Golfe.* Présence du Monde Arabe. Paris: A. Michel, 1981. 246 pp. Bibl.; index.

——. *The Omanis: Sentinels of the Gulf.* London and New York: Longman. 217 pp. Illus.; bibl.
[An English version of the preceding title.]

Green, Jerrold D. *Revolution in Iran: The Politics of Countermobilization.* New York: Praeger.

Gruen, George E., et al. *The Palestinians in Perspective: Implications for Mideast Peace and U.S. Policy.* New York: Institute of Human Relations Press, American Jewish Committee. 116 pp.
[Six essays on the Palestinian problem within the context of international politics, regional rivalries, and current Israeli attitudes; contributors include Yehoshafat Harkabi, Daniel L. Elazar, Galia Golan, and Rita E. Hauser.]

Grummon, Stephen R. *The Iran-Iraq War: Islam Embattled.* Washington Papers, 92. New York: Praeger. 111 pp. Maps; bibl.

Gubser, Peter. *Jordan.* London: Croom Helm; Boulder, Colo.: Westview Press. 128 pp. Map; illus.; bibl.; index.
[A profile of modern Jordan, with chapters on environment, people, economy, history, contemporary politics, and international relations; the author is the president of American Near East Refugee Aid.]

Guerin, Daniel. *Ben Barka, ses assassins: 16 ans d'enquête. . . .* Paris: Plon. 272 pp.

Habiby, Emile. *The Secret Life of Saeed, the Ill-fated Pessoptimist: A Palestinian Who Became a Citizen of Israel.* New York: Vantage Books.

Hakim, M.S. Abdel. *Some Aspects of Urbanisation in Egypt*. Occasional Papers Series, 15. Durham, England: Centre for Middle Eastern and Islamic Studies.

Halabi, Rafik. *The West Bank Story*. New York: Harcourt Brace Jovanovich.

Hanifi, Mohammed Jamil, comp. *Annotated Bibliography of Afghanistan*. 4th rev. ed. New Haven: HRAF Press. 560 pp. Index.
[A revised edition of Donald N. Wilber, *Annotated Bibliography of Afghanistan* (3d ed., 1968).]

Harkabi, Yehoshafat. *The Bar Kokhba Syndrome: Risk and Realism in International Politics*. Chappaqua, N.Y.: Rossel Books.

Harmon, Robert B., comp. *Administration and Government in Libya: A Selected Bibliography*. Monticello, Ill.: Vance Bibliographies. 10 pp.
Lists books and articles in English, with brief, occasional annotations; there is a short introduction and a succinct bibliographic essay as well.

Harrison, Selig S. *In Afghanistan's Shadow: Baluch Nationalism and Soviet Temptations*. New York: Carnegie Endowment, 1981. 228 pp. Maps; illus.; index.
[A study of the Baluch nationalist movement in Pakistan and Iran, with special reference to the effects of the Soviet-Afghan conflict; the author is a former *Washington Post* bureau chief in South Asia.]

Heard-Bey, Frauke. *From Trucial States to United Arab Emirates: A Society in Transition*. London: Longman. 548 pp. Bibl.; index; glossary.
A detailed and comprehensive account of the geography, tribal structure, Islamic traditions, economic bases, history, and recent development of the United Arab Emirates; includes a glossary of Arabic terms.

Heggoy, Alf Andrew, ed. *Through Foreign Eyes: Western Attitudes toward North Africa*. Washington, D.C.: University Press of America.

Heikal, Mohamed. *Iran, the Untold Story: An Insider's Account of America's Iranian Adventure and Its Consequences for the Future*. New York: Pantheon. 217 pp. Index.
An account by a well-known Egyptian journalist and former editor of *al-Ahrām* that seeks to trace the roots of American-Iranian relations; the author draws on his familiarity with Iranian internal politics, and especially his acquaintance with such figures as the shah, Ayatollah Khomeini, and Mehdi Bazargan, among others.

Heper, Metin. *State and Bureaucracy in Turkey*. N. Humberside [England]: Eothen Press, distributed by Humanities Press, Atlantic Highlands, N.J.

Herzog, Chaim. *The Arab-Israeli Wars: War and Peace in the Middle East*. London: Arms and Armour Press; New York: Random House. 368 pp. Bibl.; index.

al-Hibri, A., ed. *Women and Islam*. Oxford: Pergamon. 119 pp. Index.
[Published as a special issue of *Women's Studies International Forum*, vol. 5, no. 2.]

Hiro, Dilip. *Inside the Middle East*. London: Routledge and Kegan Paul. 490 pp. Maps; bibl.; index.
[A well-documented study of the Arab countries of the contemporary Middle East by a British journalist.]

Hooglund, Eric J. *Land and Revolution in Iran, 1960–1980*. Modern Middle East Series, 7. Austin: University of Texas Press. 208 pp. Illus.; bibl.; index.
A study of the Iranian government's land reform efforts between 1962 and 1971, based on fieldwork in Iranian villages. The author argues that the main purpose of land reform was to supplant the power of local landlords by a governmental presence. The author spent fourteen months in Iran during the revolution and provides valuable information on the effects of the revolution on the village level.

Hopwood, Derek. *Egypt, Politics and Society, 1945–1981*. London and Boston: Allen and Unwin. 224 pp. Bibl.; index.
[A survey of Egyptian politics and society from the end of the Second World War to the present, with special attention to the political thought of Presidents Nasser and Sadat and the role of Islam in Egyptian society.]

Hureau, Jean. *Jérusalem aujourd'hui*. Paris: Editions Jeune Afrique.

Hussain, Asaf, comp. *Islamic Movements: An Annotated Bibliography of Political Islam in Egypt, Pakistan and Iran*. London: Mansell. 192 pp.
[A bibliography of books and articles in English on the Ikhwān al-Muslimīn in Egypt, the Jamaat-i-Islami in Pakistan, and the Iranian revolution; with a general introduction on fundamentalist movements.]

Hütteroth, Wolf-Dieter. *Türkei*. Wissenschaftliche Länderkunden, 21. Darmstadt: Wissenschaftliche Buchgesellschaft. 569 pp. Illus.; maps; tables.

Ibrahim, Saad Eddin. *The New Arab Social Order: A Study of the Social Impact of Oil Wealth*. Westview Special Studies on the Middle East. Boulder, Colo.: Westview Press; London: Croom Helm. 222 pp. Bibl.; index.
[A study of the effects on Arab societies of the rising oil revenues of the 1970s; the author argues that these effects are creating a "silent social revolution."]

Imart, Guy. *Être Kirghiz au XXe siècle: le chardon déchiqueté (Le nomade et le commissaire)*. Aix-en Provence: Publications Université de Provence; Paris: Diffusion Champion, 1981.

Islam, contemporain dans l'océan indien: Les problèmes religieux et les minorités en océan indien à l'époque contemporaine. Paris: CNRS.

Der Islam in der Weltpolitik. Weltpolitik und Sicherheit, 1. Frankfurt: R.G. Fischer.

Islamic Council of Europe. *Islam and Contemporary Society*. Harlow: Longman. 289 pp. Index.

Ismael, Jacqueline S. *Kuwait: Social Change in Historical Perspective*. Syracuse: Syracuse University Press. 224 pp. Tables; figures; index.
[A history of Kuwait over the last three centuries, with emphasis on the social and economic impact of oil.]

Israeli, Raphael, ed. *The Crescent in the East: Islam in Asia Major*. London: Curzon; Atlantic Highlands, N.J.: Humanities Press. 245 pp. Bibl.

————. *"I, Egypt": Aspects of President Anwar al-Sadat's Political Thought*. Jerusalem: Magnes Press, 1981. 173 pp. Bibl.; index.

Issawi, Charles P. *An Economic History of the Middle East and North Africa*. The Columbia Economic History of the Modern World. New York: Columbia University Press. 317 pp. Bibl.; index.

al-Izzi, Khalid. *The Shatt al-Arab Dispute: A Legal Study*. London: Third World Centre for Research and Publishing, 1981. 310 pp.
[A historical and legal study of the dispute between Iraq and Iran, by an Iraqi scholar and government official.]

Jacob, Xavier. *L'enseignement religieux dans la Turquie moderne*. Islamkundliche Untersuchungen, 67. Berlin: Klaus Schwartz.

Jansen, Michael. *The Battle of Beirut*. London: Zed Press. 160 pp.

Jargy, Simon, ed. *Les Arabes et l'Occident: Contacts et échanges*. Collection Arabiyya, 4. Geneva: Labor et Fides. 131 pp.
Ten papers by Swiss and Italian scholars from a 1980–81 conference at the University of Geneva on various aspects of Islamic history and culture (Arabic poetry, philosophy, Islamic-Christian relations, medicine, etc.).

Joffe, E.G.H., and McLachlan, K.S., eds. *Social and Economic Development of Libya*. Cambridgeshire: Middle East and North African Studies Press.
[Papers presented at a conference at the School of Oriental and African Studies in July 1981.]

Johansen, Baber. *Islam und Staat: Abhängige Entwicklung, Verwaltung des Elends und religiöser Antiimperialismus*. Argument-Studienhefte, 54. Berlin: Argument Verlag. 55 pp. Bibl.
German translation of the revised version of a talk given in Berlin in 1981, the pamphlet provides a rapid survey of Islamic history and political thought, with special reference to contemporary developments; there is an excellent bibliography (pp. 46–55).

Johnson, Nels. *Islam and the Politics of Meaning in Palestinian Nationalism*. London: Kegan Paul. 118 pp. Bibl.; index.

Jordan: A MEED Practical Guide. Boston and London: Kegan Paul.

Joseph, John. *Muslim-Christian Relations and Inter-Christian Rivalries in the Middle East: The Case of the Jacobites in an Age of Transition*. Albany: State University of New York Press.

Joumblatt, Kamal [Junblāt, Kamāl]. *I Speak for Lebanon*. As recorded by Philippe Lapousterle, translated by Michael Pallis. London: Zed Press. 128 pp. Index.
[Translation of *Pour le Liban* (Paris: Stock, 1982?).]

Kahhaleh, Subhi. *The Water Problem in Israel and Its Repercussions on the Arab-Israel Conflict*. Beirut: Institute for Palestine Studies, 1981. 51 pp.

Kamil, Jill. *Upper Egypt*. London and New York: Longman.

Karpat, Kemal H., ed. *Political and Social Thought in the Contemporary Middle East*. Rev. and enl. ed. New York: Praeger. 601 pp. Bibl.; index.

Kaufman, Menahem. *America's Jerusalem Policy, 1947–1948*. Jerusalem: Alexander Silberman International Scholarship Foundation in Contemporary Jewry, Institute of Contemporary Jewry, Hebrew University of Jerusalem. 189 pp. Illus.; bibl.

Keddie, Nikki, and Hooglund, Eric, eds. *The Iranian Revolution and the Islamic Republic: New Assessments*. Washington, D.C.: The Middle East Institute.

Kedourie, Elie, and Haim, Sylvia G., eds. *Palestine and Israel in the 19th and 20th Centuries*. London and Totowa, N.J.: F. Cass. 286 pp. Bibl.
[Collection of articles reprinted from the journal *Middle Eastern Studies*.]

————, eds. *Zionism and Arabism in Palestine and Israel*. London and Totowa, N.J.: F. Cass. 265 pp. Maps; bibl.
A collection of ten studies, previously unpublished (though written for the journal *Middle Eastern Studies*), on the Palestinian problem from about 1920 to 1973. Contributors include Neil Caplan, Shai Lachman, Thomas Mayer, Aaron S. Klieman, Joseph Heller, Allen H. Podet, Amitzur Ilan, Yaacov Ro'i, Ibrahim A. Gambari, and Yael Yishai.

Kelley, Allen C.; Khalifa, Atef M.; and El-Khorazaty, M. Nabil. *Population and Development in Rural Egypt*. Studies in Social and Economic Demography. Durham, N.C.: Duke University Press. 294 pp. Illus.; bibl.; index.

Kennedy, William, ed. *Secret History of the Oil Companies in the Middle East*. 2 vols. Salisbury, N.C.: Documentary Publications.

Kerr, Malcolm H., and Yassin, El Sayed, eds. *Rich and Poor States in the Middle East: Egypt and the New Arab Order*. Westview Special Studies on the Middle East. Boulder, Colo.: Westview Press; Cairo, Egypt: American University in Cairo Press. 492 pp. Illus.; bibl.; index.

Khatib-Semnani, M.A. *Peripherer Kapitalismus—Der Fall Iran: Die strukturelle Unterentwicklung in einer peripheren Gesellschaft*. Frankfurt: Haag & Herchen. 370 pp.

Kieval, Gerson R. *Party Politics in Israel and the Occupied Territories*. Contributions in Political Science, 93. Westport, Conn.: Greenwood Press.

Kilmarx, Robert A., and Alexander, Yonah, eds. *Business and the Middle East: Threats and Prospects.* Pergamon Policy Studies on Business and Economics. New York: Pergamon Press. Bibl.; index.

Kitromilides, Paschalis, and Evriviades, Marios L., comps. *Cyprus.* World Bibliographical Series, 28. Oxford and Santa Barbara, Calif.: Clio Press. 213 pp. Illus.; maps; index.

Klein, Judith. *Der deutsche Zionismus und die Araber Palästinas: Eine Untersuchung der deutsch-zionistischen Publikationen, 1917–1938.* Campus-Forschung, 295. Frankfurt: Campus Verlag. 230 pp.

Koury, Enver M., and MacDonald, Charles G., eds. *Revolution in Iran: A Reappraisal.* Hyattsville, Md.: Institute of Middle Eastern and North African Affairs. 109 pp. Illus.; bibl.

Krämer, Gudrun. *Minderheit, Millet, Nation?: Die Juden in Ägypten, 1914–1952.* Bonner orientalische Studien, n.s., 27. Wiesbaden: Otto Harrassowitz.

Kravetz, Marc. *Irano nox.* Paris: B. Grasset. 272 pp.
[An account of the Iranian revolution and its leading personalities by a seasoned reporter.]

Lapidoth-Eschelbacher, Ruth. *The Red Sea and the Gulf of Aden.* International Straits of the World, 5. London and The Hague: Nijhoff. 279 pp. Maps; index.

Laskier, Michael M. *The Alliance Israélite Universelle and the Jewish Communities of Morocco, 1862–1962.* Albany: State University of New York Press.

Lauff, Rudolf J. *Die Aussenpolitik Algeriens, 1962–1978: Phasen und Bezugsfelder.* Afrika-Studien, 107. Munich and London: Weltforum Verlag, 1981. 231 pp. Bibl.

Layish, Aharon. *Marriage, Divorce and Succession in the Druze Family: A Study Based on Decisions of Druz Arbitrators and Religious Courts in Israel and the Golan Heights.* Social, Economic, and Political Studies of the Middle East, 31. Leiden: E.J. Brill. 499 pp.

Legum, Colin, ed. *Crisis and Conflicts in the Middle East: The Changing Strategy.* Mideast Affairs Series, 2. New York: Holmes and Meier, 1981. 159 pp. Maps; index.
[Articles reprinted from the current volume of the *Middle East Contemporary Survey.*]

LeLong, Michel. *Guerre ou paix à Jérusalem?* Préface de Habib Chatty; postface de Léon-Étienne Duval. Paris: Albin Michel. 192 pp.

———. *L'Islam et l'Occident.* Présence du monde arabe. Paris: Albin Michel. 260 pp.

Le Mire, Henri. *Histoire militarie de la guerre d'Algérie.* Paris: Albin Michel. 402 pp. Illus.; maps; bibl.

Lewis, Bernard. *The Muslim Discovery of Europe*. New York: Norton. 350 pp. Illus.; index.

A masterful examination of Muslim perceptions of, and reactions to, Western society and culture from the earliest period to recent times; the author, the leading English historian of the Near East, bases his study on original sources in Arabic, Persian, and Turkish, and discusses cross-cultural perceptions in such diverse areas as religion, government, science, technology, and scholarship itself.

Lieblich, Amia. *Kibbutz Makom: Report from an Israeli Kubbutz*. New York: Pantheon; London: Deutsch. 344 pp.

Lippman, Thomas W. *Understanding Islam: An Introduction to the Moslem World*. A Mentor Book. New York: NAL. 208 pp. Bibl.; index; glossary.

A popular survey of Islamic history and belief, by the former Cairo bureau chief of the *Washington Post*; includes a glossary of Arabic terms.

Long, David E., and Shaw, John A. *Saudi Arabian Modernization: The Impact of Change on Stability*. New York: Praeger.

[A study, based on fieldwork in Saudi Arabia, of the effects of development on the country's stability.]

Looney, Robert E. *Saudi Arabia's Development Potential: Application of an Islamic Growth Model*. Lexington, Mass., and Toronto: Lexington Books. 375 pp. Tables; bibl.; index.

A study of economic development in Saudi Arabia, with attention to the Islamic economic system and the issues attendant upon industrialization, agricultural development, and growth; the author provides a forecast of Saudi Arabian economic growth to the end of the century.

Maachou, Abdelkader. *L'O.P.A.E.P. et le pétrole arabe*. Paris: Berger-Levrault. 200 pp.

[An analysis of OPEC, by one of its consultants, with emphasis on its legal and economic aspects.]

Macfie, Alexander. *A Struggle for the Turkish Straits: A Study in International Relations, 1908–1936*. London: Prior. 240 pp.

Magnes, Judah Leon. *Dissenter in Zion: From the Writings of Judah L. Magnes*. Edited by Arthur A. Goren. Cambridge, Mass.: Harvard University Press. 554 pp. Illus.; bibl.; index.

[A collection of letters, speeches, papers, and sermons, accompanied by introductions and a biographical essay.]

Mahler, Gregory S., ed. *Readings in the Israeli Political System: Structures and Processes*. Washington, D.C.: University Press of America. 449 pp. Bibl.; index.

Mahrad, Ahmad. *Die Wirtschafts- und Handelsbeziehungen zwischen Iran und dem nationalsozialistischen Deutschen Reich*. Europäische Hochschulschriften, Reihe 31, Politikwissenschaft, Bd. 39. Frankfurt and Bern: Lang. 330 pp.

[On economic and commercial relations between Iran and the Third Reich.]

Makki, M.S. *Medina, Saudi Arabia: A Geographical Analysis of the City and Region.* Amersham: Avebury. 245 pp. Bibl.

Male, Beverley. *Revolutionary Afghanistan: A Reappraisal.* New York: St. Martin's Press; London: Croom Helm. 229 pp. Bibl.; index.
[An attempt to revise the current image of Hefizullah Amin and his role in the 1978 revolution; by a lecturer in Middle East politics at the Royal Military College in Australia.]

Malka, Victor, and Demigneux, Jean-Loup. *Histoire d'Israël, 1948–1982.* Paris: Janninck. 120 pp. Illus.

El Mallakh, Ragaei. *Saudi Arabia: Rush to Development.* Baltimore: Johns Hopkins University Press. 464 pp.
[An analysis of the problems and accomplishments of Saudi development, with a critique of the Third Development Plan.]

El Mallakh, Ragaei, and El Mallakh, Dorothea H., eds. *Saudi Arabia: Energy, Developmental Planning and Industrialization.* Lexington, Mass.: Lexington Books; Aldershot: Gower. 217 pp. Illus.; index.

Mansfield, Peter. *The New Arabians.* Chicago: J.G. Ferguson, distributed by Doubleday, 1981. 274 pp. Illus.; index.
A study of the nations of the Arabian Gulf, within the context of their historical development and future prospects, and with special emphasis on social change in Saudi Arabia, Kuwait, Bahrain, Qatar, and the United Arab Emirates. The study was suggested and supported by the Bechtel Power Corporation.

Maprayil, Cyriac. *The Soviets and Afghanistan.* London: Cosmic. 172 pp. Index.

Marcus, Harold G. *Ethiopia, Great Britain and the United States, 1941–1974: The Politics of Empire.* Berkeley: University of California Press.

Marmur, Dov. *Beyond Survival.* London: Darton Longman and Todd.

Martin, Richard C. *Islam: A Cultural Perspective.* Prentice-Hall Series in World Religions, 3. Englewood Cliffs, N.J.: Prentice-Hall. 191 pp. Illus.; maps; bibl.; index; glossary.
A compact, introductory presentation of Islamic belief and practice, with numerous illustrations and a useful glossary of key Arabic terms.

Martin, Richard C., ed. *Islam in Local Contexts.* Contributions to Asian Studies, 17. Leiden: E.J. Brill. 129 pp.
[A collection of ten essays on Islam in such areas as China, West Africa, and India; contributors include Dale Eickelman, Annemarie Schimmel, Raphael Israeli, and Marilyn R. Waldman.]

Matar, Fuad. *Saddam Hussein: The Man, the Cause and the Future.* London: Third World Centre for Research and Publishing, 1981. 200 pp.
[A biography, based on interviews with the Iraqi leader, by a well-known journalist and author.]

Mattes, Hanspeter. *Die Geschichte Libyens: Von den Anfängen bis zur Proklamation der Volksherrschaft 1977.* Nordafrika-Reihe, 1. Brazzaville and Heidelberg: Kivouvou, Editions Bantoues. 320 pp.

———. *Die Volksrevolution in der Sozialistischen Libyschen Arabischen Volksgamāhīriyya: die Entwicklung des politischen Systems nach al-fātiḥ und die Bedeutung Muʿammar al-Qaddāfīʾs für den gesellschaftlichen Transformationsprozess.* Nordafrika-Reihe, 2. Brazzaville and Heidelberg: Kivouvou, Editions Bantoues. 990 pp. Illus.
[The author's 1982 Heidelberg University dissertation.]

McCarthy, Justin. *The Arab World, Turkey and the Balkans, 1878–1914: A Handbook of Historical Statistics.* Boston: G.K. Hall. 309 pp. Bibl.; index.
[Statistical data on numerous aspects of modern Middle Eastern countries, drawn from Ottoman Turkish sources.]

McClintock, Marsha Hamilton. *The Middle East and North Africa on Film: An Annotated Filmography.* Garland Reference Library of the Humanities, 159. New York: Garland.

Meibar, Basheer. *Political Culture, Foreign Policy and Conflict: The Palestine Area Conflict System.* Contributions in Political Science, 63. Westport, Conn.: Greenwood Press. 326 pp. Tables; bibl.; index.
A detailed analysis, drawing on Arabic and Hebrew sources, of the Arab-Israeli conflict, based on a theoretical model of Palestine as a "conflict system."

Meiring, Desmond. *Since Sadat.* London: Wildwood House. 196 pp.

Mercier, Jacques. *Eli Cohen: Le combattant de Damas.* Paris: Laffont. 320 pp.
[The story of the confidant of Hafiz al-Asad, who was exposed as an Israeli agent and hanged in Damascus in 1965; by his lawyer.]

Messali Hadj, Ahmed. *Les mémoires de Messali Hadj, 1898–1938.* Paris: J.-C. Lattès.
[The autobiography of the father of Algerian independence, with a preface by Ben Bella.]

Metropolitan Museum of Art. *Islamische Kunst: Meisterwerke aus dem Metropolitan Museum of Art, New York/The Arts of Islam: Masterpieces from the Metropolitan Museum of Art, New York.* New York: Metropolitan Museum of Art, distributed by Abrams. 339 pp. Illus.
[Originally published as a catalog for the Berlin 1981 exhibition "The Arts of Islam," the volume was conceived by the late Richard Ettinghausen, who wrote several of the essays.]

Metzger, Annette. *Zur sexualspezifischen Rolle der Frau in der türkischen Familie.* Berlin: Express-Edition.

Meyer, Lutz. *Ziele, Konfliktbereitschaft und Bedingungen der iranischen Erdölpolitik, 1970–1980: Vom Schahregime zur Islamischen Republik.* Sozialwissenschaftliche Studien zu internationalen Problemen, 67. Saarbrücken and Fort Lauderdale, Fla.: Breitenbach. 407 pp.

Meynier, Gilbert. *L'Algérie révélée: La guerre de 1914–1918*. Travaux de droit, d'économie, de sociologie, et de sciences politiques, 130. Geneva: Droz. 824 pp.
[An analysis of Algerian society in the first quarter of the twentieth century.]

Miller, E. Willard, and Miller, Ruby M., comps. *The Middle East (Southwest Asia): A Bibliography on the Third World*. Public Administration Series—Bibliography. Monticello, Ill.: Vance Bibliographies. 110 pp.

————, comps. *Northern and Western Africa: A Bibliography on the Third World*. Public Administration Series—Bibliography. Monticello, Ill.: Vance Bibliographies, 1981. 96 pp.

Minces, Juliette. *The House of Obedience: Women in Arab Society*. Translated by Michael Pallis. London: Zed Press. 114 pp.

Mirel, Pierre. *L'Egypte des ruptures*. Paris: Sindbad.

Mizrahi, Rachel. *L'un meurt, l'autre aussi*. Paris: Hachette. 380 pp.
[A study of Israel, based on the author's experiences.]

Monteil, Vincent. *Les musulmans soviétiques*. Paris: Seuil. 264 pp.
[A completely revised edition, based on new research and on travels, of the work of the same title that first appeared in 1957.]

Al-Morayati, Abid A., ed. *International Relations in the Middle East and North Africa*. Cambridge, Mass.: Schenkman. Bibl.; index.

Mortimer, Edward. *Faith and Power: The Politics of Islam*. New York: Random House. 432 pp. Glossary; maps; index.
The author, Middle East specialist for the London *Times*, analyzes the concept and practice of political power within Islam. The treatment is historical and focuses on six contemporary Muslim countries and movements: Turkey, Saudi Arabia, Pakistan, Iran, Soviet Muslims, and the Muslim Brotherhood.

Moskin, J. Robert, *Among Lions: The Battle for Jerusalem, June 5–7, 1967*. New York: Arbor House. 401 pp. Maps; illus.; bibl.; index.
Dramatic, narrative account, by an historian and journalist, of the capture of Jerusalem by Israeli forces; includes detailed maps and vivid photos.

Mostyn, Trevor, ed. *UAE: A MEED Practical Guide*. London: Middle East Economic Digest, distributed by Kegan Paul. 332 pp. Illus.; bibl.; index.

Müller, Konrad. *Anwar Sadat: The Last Hundred Days*. Photographs by Konrad Müller, text by Mark Blaisse. London: Thames and Hudson, 1981. 75 pp. Illus.

Naïm Khader, le sens d'une vie. Paris: Editions ouvrières. 240 pp.
[On the life of a murdered Palestinian Christian.]

Nakhleh, Emile A. *The Persian Gulf and American Policy*. New York: Praeger.

Nash, G. *Iran's Secret Pogrom: The Conspiracy to Wipe out the Baha'is*. Sudbury: Spearman.

Nashat, Guity. *The Origins of Modern Reform in Iran, 1870–80*. Urbana: University of Illinois Press, 1981.

Neuberger, Gunter, and Opperskalski, Michael, eds. *CIA in Iran: Die Geheimdokumente aus der Teheraner US-Botschaft*. Bornheim: Lamuv-Verlag. 160 pp.
A collection, reproduced in facsimile, of secret American documents,
purportedly captured during the takeover of the U.S. embassy in Tehran;
each set of documents is preceded by a brief introduction and analysis.

Newman, David. *Jewish Settlement in the West Bank: The Role of Gush Emunim*. Occasional Papers Series, Centre for Middle Eastern and Islamic Studies, 16. Durham, England: Centre for Middle Eastern and Islamic Studies.

Niblock, Tim, ed. *Iraq: The Contemporary State*. London: Croom Helm. 283 pp. Map; index.
[Conference papers, published for the Centre for Arab Gulf Studies,
University of Exeter.]

————, ed. *State, Society and Economy in Saudi Arabia*. New York: St. Martin's Press. 314 pp. Maps; index.

Nienhaus, Volker. *Islam und moderne Wirtschaft: Einführung in Positionen, Probleme und Perspektiven*. Islam und westliche Welt, 6. Graz, Vienna, and Cologne: Verlag Styria. 260 pp.

Noyes, James H. *The Clouded Lens: Persian Gulf Security and U.S. Policy*. Hoover International Studies. 2d ed. Stanford, Calif.: Hoover Institution Press. 183 pp. Map; bibl.; index.

Oehring, Otmar. *Bibliographie zum türkischen Recht und den internationalen Beziehungen der Türkischen Republik: Titel in Fremdsprachen*. Islamkundliche Materialen, 8. Berlin: Klaus Schwartz.

Olson, William J. *Britain's Elusive Empire in the Middle East, 1900–1921: An Annotated Bibliography*. Garland Reference Library of Social Science, 109. New York: Garland.
[This is volume 2 in the series entitled Themes in European Expansion:
Exploration, Colonization and the Impact of Empire, and was compiled with
the assistance of Addeane S. Caelleigh.]

Orywal, Erwin. *Die Baluç in Afghanistan—Sistan*. Kölner ethnologische Studien, 4. Berlin: Reimer.

Al-Otaiba, Mana Saeed. *Essays on Petroleum*. London: Croom Helm. 176 pp.

Otto, Ingeborg. *Frauenfragen im Modernen Orient: Eine Auswahlbibliographie/Women in the Middle East and North Africa, a Selected Bibliography*. Dokumentationsdienst Moderner Orient, Reihe A, 12. Hamburg: Deutsches Orient-Institut. 262 pp. Index.

Owen, Roger, ed. *Studies in the Economic and Social History of Palestine in the Nineteenth and Twentieth Centuries*. London: Macmillan. 271 pp. Index.

Palmer, Monte; Nedelcovych, Mima S.; Khashan, Hilal; and Munro, Debra L., eds. *Survey Research in the Arab World: An Analytical Survey*. Cambridgeshire: Middle East and North African Studies Press. 379 pp. Index.
[Contains 360 abstracts of surveys carried out in Arab countries.]

Pantelidis, Veronica S., comp. *Arab Education, 1956–1978: A Bibliography*. London: Mansell. 570 pp.
Lists 5,653 English-language monographs, articles, dissertations, and microforms on education in all the Arab countries. Entries are annotated; arrangement is by country. There are separate author-title and subject indexes.

Peace and Security in the Middle East after Lebanon. Washington, D.C.: Middle East Institute.
[1982 annual conference résumé.]

Pean, Pierre. *Les deux bombes*. Paris: Fayard. 203 pp. Bibl.
[On French-Iraqi relations, with regard to atomic power.]

Peres, Shimon. *La force de vaincre: Entretiens avec Joëlle Jonathan*. Paris: Le Centurion, 1981.

Perlmutter, Amos; Handel, Michael; and Bar-Joseph, Uri. *Two Minutes over Baghdad*. London: Vallentine, Mitchell. 192 pp. Map.
The story of the bombing by Israel of the Iraqi nuclear reactor on 7 June 1981.

Peters, F.E. *Children of Abraham: Judaism/Christianity/Islam*. Princeton: Princeton University Press. 236 pp. Glossary; index.
A comparative study of the three monotheistic faiths in the light of their common origins; there is a useful glossary of Arabic, Greek, and Hebrew terms, as well as extensive documentation.

Peterson, John E. *Yemen: The Search for a Modern State*. London: Croom Helm; Baltimore: Johns Hopkins University Press. 221 pp. Map; bibl.; index.
A study, based on European and Arabic documents and other sources, of the struggle in Yemen to develop a modern state; the author concentrates on the rule of Imam Yahya in the 1930s and 1940s and on the progress of the Yemen Arab Republic in the 1970s. Contains a glossary of Arabic terms and a chronology of events from 1918 to 1981.

Plascov, Avi. *Modernization, Political Development and Stability*. Security in the Persian Gulf, 3. London: International Institute for Strategic Studies. 191 pp. Index.

Politiques scientifiques et technologiques au Maghreb et au Proche-Orient. Les Cahiers du C.R.E.S.M., 14. Paris: CNRS. 380 pp.
[Contains nineteen papers from a conference of the Centre de recherches et

d'études sur les societes mediterraneennes held in Aix in May 1980, with particular emphasis on development, science, and technology in North Africa and the Near East; contributors include M. Benchikh, Jean-Robert Henry, Jean-Claude Vatin, and Noureddine Sraieb, among others.]

Pollock, David. *The Politics of Pressure: American Arms and Israeli Policy since the Six Day War.* Contributions in Political Science, 79. Westport, Conn.: Greenwood Press. Bibl.; index.

Porch, Douglas. *The Conquest of Morocco.* New York: Knopf. 320 pp. Bibl.; index.

Powell, William. *Saudi Arabia and Its Royal Family.* Secaucus, N.J.: L. Stuart.

Quandt, William B. *Saudi Arabia in the 1980s: Foreign Policy, Security and Oil.* Washington, D.C.: The Brookings Institution. 190 pp. Map; bibl.; index.
[A study of recent developments in Saudi Arabia and of U.S.-Saudi relations.]

Rabinowicz, Harry M. *Hasidism and the State of Israel.* Littman Library of Jewish Civilization. Rutherford, N.J.: Fairleigh Dickinson University Press.

Rahman, Fazlur. *Islam and Modernity: Transformation of an Intellectual Tradition.* Chicago and London: University of Chicago Press. 172 pp. Index.
A leading historian of Islamic thought surveys the major traditions and trends in Islamic education and intellectual history and offers a critique of both traditionalist and modernist tendencies; he argues for a distinction between "historical" and "normative" Islam and recommends a creative and a critical return to a fresh study of both the Qur'ān itself and the classical tradition.

Ramazani, Rouhollah K. *The United States and Iran: The Patterns of Influence.* Studies of Influence in International Relations. New York: Praeger. 176 pp.

Rash, Yehoshua. *Déminer un champ fertile: Les catholiques français et l'État d'Israël.* Rencontres, 25. Paris: Cerf. 212 pp. Bibl.

Razzak, Sufyan Abdul. *Die Interessen- und Konfliktkonstellationen in der arabischen Golf-Region: Eine Studie zu den Abhängigkeitsstrukturen der Peripherien.* Hamburg: Borg. 364 pp.

Revesz, Laszlo. *UdSSR über Afghanistan: Afghanistan im Spiegel der Sowjetpresse.* SOI-Sonderdruck, 19. Bern: Schw.-Ost-Institut, 1981. 109 pp.

Rezun, Miron. *The Iranian Crisis of 1941: The Actors—Britain, Germany and the Soviet Union.* Bohlau Politica, 6. Cologne and Vienna: Bohlau. 116 pp.

Riyad, Mahmud. *The Struggle for Peace in the Middle East.* London and New York: Quartet Books. Index.

Robbe, Martin. *Die Palästinenser: Ihr Kampf um nationale Identität und um Eigenstaatlichkeit.* Berlin: Dietz Verlag. 80 pp. Illus.
A brief history and analysis, from a pro-Palestinian viewpoint, of the Arab-Israeli conflict, by an East German academician.

Robinson, Francis. *Atlas of the Islamic World since 1500.* Oxford: Phaidon. 238 pp. Illus.; bibl.; index.

Rodinson, Maxime. *Marxism and the Muslim World.* Translated by Jean Matthews. New York: Monthly Review Press. Bibl.; index.

Roeh, Itzhak. *The Rhetoric of News in the Israel Radio: Some Implications of Language and Style for Newstelling.* Studies in International Communication, 3. Bochum: Brockmeyer. 209 pp.
[The author's Columbia University dissertation (1978).]

Roest Crollins, Ary A., ed. *Islam und Abendland.* Düsseldorf: Patmos-Verlag.

Roiter, Fulvio. *Le Liban.* Paris: Menges. 260 pp. Illus. (240 photographs).

Rondot, Philippe. *Le Proche-Orient à la recherche de la paix: 1973–1982.* Paris: Presses universitaires de France. 212 pp. Illus.; bibl.
[A study of the stages in the peace process from 1973 to 1982, with a preface by Jacques Vernant.]

Rubenstein, Alvin Z. *Soviet Policy toward Turkey, Iran, and Afghanistan: The Dynamics of Influence.* Studies of Influence in International Relations. New York: Praeger. 192 pp.

Ruud, Inger Marie. *Women's Status in the Muslim World: A Bibliographical Survey.* Arbeitsmaterialien zur Religionsgeschichte, 6. Cologne: E.J. Brill. 143 pp.

Rywkin, Michael. *Moscow's Muslim Challenge: Soviet Central Asia.* Armonk, N.Y., and London: M.E. Sharpe. 195 pp. Maps; tables; bibl.; index.
An analysis of Soviet policy in Central Asia, with emphasis on historical, economic, demographic, and ideological factors; the author, a professor of Russian at City College, New York, lived in Central Asia for several years.

Sabanegh, E.S. *Muhammad "le prophète." Portraits contemporains. Égypte 1930–1950. Jalons pour une histoire de la pensée islamique moderne.* Paris: Vrin.

Said Amer, Tayeb. *Le développement industriel de l'Algérie: Bilan de l'industrialisation.* Paris: Anthropos. 394 pp.

Salem, Elie Adib. *Prospects for a New Lebanon.* AEI Special Analyses, 81–84. Washington, D.C.: American Enterprise Institute.

Sanasarian, Eliz. *The Women's Rights Movement in Iran: Mutiny, Appeasement and Repression from 1900 to Khomeini.* New York: Praeger. Bibl.; index.

Sareen, Anuradha. *India and Afghanistan: British Imperialism vs Afghan Nationalism, 1907–1921.* Delhi: Seema Publications, 1981. 244 pp. Bibl.; index.

Saunders, Harold H. *Conversations with Harold H. Saunders: U.S. Policy for the Middle East in the 1980s.* AEI Studies, 346. Washington, D.C.: American Enterprise Institute. 101 pp.

_____. *The Middle East Problem in the 1980s.* AEI Special Analyses, 81–8. Washington, D.C.: American Enterprise Institute, 1981.

Sayigh, Yusif A. *The Arab Economy: Past Performance and Future Prospects.* Oxford: Oxford University Press.

Schall, Anton, ed. *Fremde Welt Islam: Einblicke in eine Weltreligion.* Mainz: Grünewald Verlag.

Schiller, David T. *Palästinenser zwischen Terrorismus und Diplomatie: Die paramilitarische palästinensische Nationalbewegung von 1918 bis 1981.* Munich: Bernard und Graefe. 480 pp. Illus.

Sears, William. *A Cry from the Heart: The Baha'is in Iran.* Oxford: G. Ronald.

The Security of Gulf Oil: An Introductory Bibliography. Occasional Papers Series, 13. Durham, England: Centre for Middle Eastern and Islamic Studies.

Seligmann, Rafael. *Israels Sicherheitspolitik—Zwischen Selbstbehauptung und Präventivschlag: Eine Fallstudie über Grundlagen und Motive.* Reihe Bernard und Graefe Aktuell, 30. Munich: Bernard und Graefe. 240 pp. Maps; tables.

Sen Gupta, Bhabani. *The Afghan Syndrome: How to Live with Soviet Power.* London: Croom Helm. 306 pp. Index.

Servan-Schreiber, Jean-Jacques. *La Guerre d'Algérie.* Paris: Paris-Match. 224 pp. Illus. (160 photographs).
Partial reedition of *Lieutenant en Algérie* (1957), with many previously unpublished photographs from the archives of *Paris-Match*.

Shayegan, Daryush. *Qu'est-ce qu'une révolution religieuse?* [Paris]: Presses d'aujourd'hui. 260 pp.
[The author, a student of the late Henry Corbin and former director of the Centre iranien pour l'étude des civilisations, studies current trends in traditional societies.]

Shehada, Raja. *The Third Way.* London: Quartet.
[On the Palestinian Arabs.]

Shokeid, Moshe, and Deshen, Schlomo. *Distant Relations: Ethnicity and Politics among Arabs and North African Jews in Israel*. New York: Praeger. 256 pp.

Shrar, S.A. *Afghanistan: Bericht eines Augenzeugen*. Hamburg: Verlag Hanseatische, 1981.

Siddiqi, Muhammad Nejatullah. *Issues in Islamic Banking*. Islamic Economics Series, 4. Leicester: Islamic Foundation. 152 pp.

Siddiqui, Kalim, ed. *Issues in the Islamic Movement, 1980–81 (1400–1401)*. London, Toronto, and Pretoria: Open Press. 409 pp. Index.
Selection of articles, from a pro-Khomeini viewpoint, drawn from the Toronto-based news magazine the *Crescent International*, from August 1980 to August 1981; also includes an index to other articles in the magazine.

Silberman, Neil Asher. *Digging for God and Country: Exploration, Archeology and the Secret Struggle for the Holy Land, 1799–1917*. New York: Knopf. Bibl.; index.

Silverburg, Sanford R., comp. *The Palestinian Arab-Israeli Conflict: An International Legal Bibliography*. Monticello, Ill.: Vance Bibliographies. 27 pp.

Simon, Merrill. *Oil, Money, Weapons . . . Middle East: At the Brink*. Introduction by Rev. Dr. Jerry Falwell, with a foreword by Dr. Yuval Ne'eman. Washington, D.C.: Center for International Security, distributed by Dean Books. 426 pp. Illus.
A collection of articles from the periodical *Israel Today*, covering the period from June 1976 to July 1981 and dealing mainly with Israeli foreign relations; the author, an electronics expert and self-professed authority on Israeli affairs, consistently presents a defensive and jingoistic viewpoint throughout.

Slaby, H. *Bindenschild und Sonnenlöwe: Die Geschichte der österreichisch-iranischen Beziehungen bis zur Gegenwart*. Graz: Akademische Druck-und Verlagsanstalt, 1981. 422 pp.
[On relations between Austria and Iran to the present.]

Sluglett, Peter, ed. *Theses on Islam, the Middle East and North-West Africa, 1880–1978*. London: Mansell. 154 pp.
[A list of theses accepted by British and Irish universities.]

Social, Economic and Political Institutions in the West Bank and the Gaza Strip. Prepared for, and under the guidance of, the Committee on the Exercise of the Inalienable Rights of the Palestinian People. New York: United Nations. 24 pp.

Souriau, C., ed. *Le Maghreb musulman en 1979: L'évolution des rapports entre les forces arabo-musulmanes et l'ordre islamique*. Paris: CNRS. 420 pp. Tables.

Spiegel, Steven L., ed. *The Middle East and the Western Alliance*. London and Boston: George Allen & Unwin. 256 pp.

Springborg, Robert. *Family, Power and Politics in Egypt: Sayed Bey Marei—his Clan, Clients and Cohorts*. Philadelphia: University of Pennsylvania Press.

Stark, Freya. *Rivers of Time: The Photographs of Dame Freya Stark*. Edinburgh: Blackwood.

Steinbach, Udo. *Der Islam und die Krise des Nahen Ostens*. Informationen zur politischen Bildung, 194. Munich: Franzis-Verlag. 32 pp. Illus.

Sterling, Martie, with Robin Sterling. *Last Flight from Iran*. Introduction by Leon Uris. New York: Bantam Books, 1981. 287 pp.

Steul, Willi. *Hilfe für Afghanistan*. Stuttgart: Verlag Bonn Aktuell, 1981.

Stewart, Desmond. *The Palestinians: Victims of Expediency*. London: Quartet. 160 pp. Map; index.

Stivers, William. *Supremacy and Oil: Iraq, Turkey and the Anglo-American World Order, 1918–1930*. Ithaca: Cornell University Press. Bibl.; index.

Stone, Russell A. *Social Change in Israel: Attitudes and Events, 1967–79*. New York: Praeger.

Stookey, Robert W. *South Yemen: A Marxist Republic in Arabia*. Westview Profiles: Nations of the Contemporary Middle East. Boulder, Colo.: Westview Press. 124 pp. Maps; bibl.; index.
[A concise introduction to the history, people, culture, economy, and international relations of South Yemen.]

Stora, Benjamin. *Messali Hadj, 1898–1974*. Paris: Le Sycomore. 296 pp.
[A biography of the founder of Algerian nationalism.]

Tahir-Kheli, Shirin. *The United States and Pakistan: The Evolution of an Influence Relationship*. Studies of Influence in International Relations. New York: Praeger. 192 pp. Bibl.; index.

Taleghani, Sayyid Mahmud. *Society and Economics in Islam: Writings and Declarations of Ayatullah Sayyid Mahmud Taleghani*. Translated from the Persian by R. Campbell, with annotations and an introduction by Hamid Algar. Contemporary Islamic Thought, Persian Series, 4. Berkeley: Mizan Press. 230 pp. Bibl.; index.
A careful, annotated translation of substantial portions of two influential works of the late *āyatallāh* Maḥmūd Ṭalaqānī (1911–79): "Islam and Ownership" (*Islām va Mālikīyat*) and "A Ray from the Qurʾān" (*Partavī az Qurʾān*). The volume includes a biographical essay on Ṭalaqānī and a bibliography of his works.

Tarbush, Mohammad A. *The Role of the Military in Politics: A Case Study of Iraq to 1941*. With a foreword by A.H. Hourani. London and Boston: Kegan Paul. 302 pp. Bibl.; index.

Tavin, Eli, and Alexander, Yonah, eds. *Psychological Warfare and Propaganda: Irgun Documentation*. Wilmington, Del.: Scholarly Resources. 309 pp. Bibl.

Taylor, Alan R. *The Arab Balance of Power*. Contemporary Issues in the Middle East. Syracuse: Syracuse University Press. 177 pp. Map; index.
A history and analysis of the relations and conflicts among Arab states from 1945 to the present; with extensive appendixes containing twenty-one key documents and charts of inter-Arab alignments from 1945 to 1982.

Teslik, Kennan Lee. *Congress, the Executive Branch and Special Interests: The American Response to the Arab Boycott of Israel*. Contributions in Political Science, 80. Westport, Conn.: Greenwood Press. 290 pp. Bibl.; index.
A study of the effects of the Arab boycott, from 1921 on, upon American policy, with special reference to internal American debates and responses.

Tessler, Mark A. *Secularism and Nationalism in the Israeli-Palestinian Conflict*. UFSI Reports, no. 9, Asia. Hanover, N.H.: Universities Field Staff International. 12 pp.

Tillman, Seth P. *The United States in the Middle East: Interests and Obstacles*. Foreword by J.W. Fulbright. Bloomington: Indiana University Press. 384 pp. Bibl.; index.

Timerman, Jacobo. *The Longest War: Israel in Lebanon*. Translated from the Spanish by Miguel Acoca. New York: Knopf. 167 pp.
An account of the Israeli campaign in Lebanon up to September 1982, based on the author's diary and visits to the front; the book is also a scathing denunciation of the policies of the Begin government.

Die Türkei und die Türken in Deutschland. Stuttgart: Kohlhammer.

Tworuschka, Monika. *Islam*. Religionen, 1. Göttingen: Vandenhoeck und Ruprecht. 115 pp.
A concise, but highly useful introduction to Islamic belief, duties, and practice that is based on analyses of original texts, presented in German translation, and on commentaries, especially by modern Muslim theologians.

Der unbekannte Islam. Cologne: Benziger.

Unwin, P.T.H., comp. *Qatar*. World Bibliographical Series, 36. Oxford: Clio Press. 187 pp.

Vaczek, Louis Charles, and Buckland, Gail. *Travelers in Ancient Lands: A Portrait of the Middle East, 1839–1919*. Boston: New York Graphic Society, distributed by Little, Brown and Co. 223 pp. Illus.; bibl.; index.

Voll, John Obert. *Islam: Continuity and Change in the Modern World*. Boulder, Colo.: Westview Press; Essex: Longman. 409 pp. Map; glossary; bibl.; index.
A broad, ambitious study of contemporary Islamic "resurgence" that seeks to understand the phenomenon by considering Islam itself in its historical

development; various Islamic groups and movements from the nineteenth century on in such areas as Africa, Iran, Egypt, and Palestine; and Western responses to Islamic countries and movements. The author argues that Islam is now entering a "new phase" in its development.

Wai, Dunstan, ed. *Interdependence in a World of Unequals: African-Arab-OECD Economic Cooperation for Development.* Westview Special Studies in Social, Economic, and Political Development. Boulder, Colo.: Westview Press. 252 pp. Tables; index.
[A collection of nine articles that explore the possibility of development in sub-Saharan Africa supported by surplus petrodollars from the Arab countries.]

Walther, Wiebke. *Woman in Islam.* Translated from the German by C.S.V. Salt. Montclair, N.J.: Abner Schram; London: G. Prior, 1981. 204 pp. Bibl.

Weinbaum, Marvin G. *Food, Development and Politics in the Middle East.* Westview Special Studies on the Middle East. Boulder, Colo.: Westview Press; London: C. Helm. 217 pp. Bibl.; index.

Welch, Anthony, and Welch, Stuart Cary. *Arts of the Islamic Book: The Collection of Prince Sadruddin Aga Khan.* Ithaca and London: Cornell University Press, for the Asia Society. 240 pp. Illus.
A sumptuous volume, containing eighty plates in color and black and white, that was prepared as a catalog for an exhibition at the Asia Society by two of the leading experts in Islamic art; the book contains an informative introduction as well as a detailed commentary on the plates.

Wheatcroft, Andrew. *Arabia and the Gulf in Original Photographs, 1880–1950.* London: Kegan Paul. 184 pp. Illus.

Wiethold, Beatrix. *Kadınlarımız—Frauen in der Türkei.* Hamburg: Rissen, 1981. 246 pp. Illus.

Wikan, Unni. *Behind the Veil in Arabia: Women in Oman.* Baltimore: Johns Hopkins University Press. 327 pp. Map; illus.; bibl.; index.
An anthropological study of Sohari society in Oman that is based on the author's fieldwork in 1974–76; the book is intended for the nonspecialist reader and pays particular attention to the lives and roles of women in a traditional Arabian culture.

Wilson, Sir Harold. *The Chariot of Israel: Britain, America and the State of Israel.* London: Weidenfeld and Nicolson, 1981. 406 pp. Illus.; bibl.; index.
Examines the British and American policies that contributed to the founding of the state of Israel; the former prime minister offers a broad, readable account, beginning in ancient times and the Diaspora and concluding in June 1980.

Winstone, Harry Viktor Frederick. *The Illicit Adventure: The Story of Political and Military Intelligence in the Middle East from 1898 to 1926.* London: Cape. 543 pp. Illus.; bibl.

Wolffsohn, Michael. *Politik in Israel: Entwicklung und Struktur des politischen Systems des Staates Israel.* Schriften des Deutschen Orient-Instituts. Opladen: Leske und Budrich. 780 pp.

Wright, John. *Libya: A Modern History.* Baltimore: Johns Hopkins University Press. 306 pp. Map; bibl.; index.
A history of Libya from 1900 to the present, with emphasis on the Libyan revolution of 1969, the leadership of Muammar Qaddafi, and the role of oil in Libyan development.

Yaacobi, Gad. *The Government of Israel.* New York: Praeger. 341 pp. Bibl.; index.

Yefsah, Abdelkader. *Le processus de légitimation du pouvoir militaire et la construction de l'Etat en Algérie.* Paris: Anthropos. 206 pp.

Yudkin, Leon I. *Jewish Writing and Identity in the Twentieth Century.* London: Croom Helm. 166 pp. Bibl.

Zabarah, Mohammed Ahmad. *Yemen: Traditionalism vs Modernity.* New York: Praeger. Bibl.; index.

Zabih, Sepehr. *Iran since the Revolution.* Baltimore: Johns Hopkins University Press; London: Croom Helm. 240 pp. Bibl.; index.

_____. *The Mossadegh Era: Roots of the Iranian Revolution.* Chicago: Lake View Press. 182 pp. Bibl.; index.
[An objective, historical account and analysis of the events of the years 1951–53 in Iran, by a former journalist who was an active participant in the events.]

Zartman, I. William, et al. *Political Elites in Arab North Africa: Morocco, Algeria, Tunisia, Libya, and Egypt.* New York and London: Longman. 273 pp. Bibl.; index.
Six essays on the ruling classes in contemporary North Africa by I. William Zartman (North Africa in general), Mark A. Tessler (Morocco), John P. Entelis (Algeria), Russell A. Stone (Tunisia), Raymond A. Hinnebusch (Libya), and Shahrough Akhavi (Egypt).

Zaza, Nourreddine. *Ma vie de Kurde ou le cri du peuple Kurde.* [Paris?]: P.M. Favre. 224 pp. Map; illus.
[A study of Kurdish society and history in Turkey, Syria, Iraq, and Lebanon.]

Zulfakar Sabry, Hussein. *Sovereignty for Sudan.* London: Ithaca Press. 136 pp.

SERIALS

Abu-Lughod, Janet. "Israeli Settlements in Occupied Arab Lands: Conquest to Colony." *Journal of Palestine Studies* 11, no. 2 (Winter 1982): 16–54.
This is a detailed exposition, with six plans and bibliography, of Israel's

settlement policy, which according to the author aims to *seize land* rather than to increase Jewish population in the West Bank.

Ajami, Fouad. "The Arab Road." *Foreign Policy*, no. 47 (Summer 1982): 3–25.
This is a rambling, poorly focused and often vague essay; yet the author, who is the director of Middle East studies at the School for Advanced International Studies, offers insights that are worthy of study by those concerned with America's role in the Middle East and our relations with the Arab states.

————. "The Shadows of Hell." *Foreign Policy*, no. 48 (Fall 1982): 94–110.
This essay, composed in response to the Israeli invasion of Lebanon, presents both a criticism of U.S. policy and a recognition of the centrality of U.S. policy. Much attention is paid to the motives and policies of Begin and Sharon and the total weakness of the Arabs. Many of the issues of the 1982 Middle East situation are succinctly presented.

Aly, Abd al-Monein Said, and Wenner, Manfred W. "Modern Islamic Reform Movements: The Muslim Brotherhood in Contemporary Egypt." *Middle East Journal* 36, no. 3 (Summer 1982): 336–61.
After a survey of the Brotherhood and an elucidation of political and economic factors of Egypt since 1952, this article concentrates on events of Sadat's Egypt. Sadat is found to have created the situation that inevitably led to his assassination.

Anderson, Lisa. "Libya and American Foreign Policy." *Middle East Journal* 36, no. 4 (Autumn 1982):516–34.
This is an information-filled review of Libya's recent past by a leading U.S. expert; not much is presented in the area of U.S. policy.

Aulas, Marie-Christine. "Soudan: le prix du 'consensus stratégique' dans le Golfe." *Le Monde Diplomatique*, no. 334 (January 1982): 14.
A summary analysis of the economic, military, and political situation in Sudan, indicating that the danger from Libya is utilized to prop up a government whose sole support is the army.

Avineri, Shlomo. "Beyond Camp David." *Foreign Policy*, no. 46 (Spring 1982):19–36.
Starting with the premise that the central Middle Eastern problem is the Arab world's recognition of Israel, the author, who once was director general of Israel's Ministry of Foreign Affairs, examines both the step-by-step and the comprehensive approaches to Middle Eastern problems and explores options to broaden participation in the peace process. Camp David, he argues, can be implemented if the United States resolves to support it.

Ayubi, Nazih N.M. "The Politics of Militant Islamic Movements in the Middle East." *Journal of International Affairs* 36, no. 2 (Fall/Winter 1982/83): 271–83.
A fairly detailed survey of recent involvement of militant Islamic groups in the Middle East that are seeking legitimacy and a share in political life. The author predicts increasing conflicts as the "religious trend" advances.

Barry, Michael. "Afghanistan—Another Cambodia?" *Commentary* 74, no. 2 (August 1982): 29–37.
The author is a member of the International Federation for Human Rights and has traveled in Afghanistan. He here details Russian oppression and torture in Afghanistan and draws upon interviews that he personally conducted.

Be'eri, Eliezer. "The Waning of the Military Coup in Arab Politics." *Middle Eastern Studies* 18, no. 1 (January 1982): 69–81.
A competent and interesting study. The decline of the officers' prestige is attributed to their failure to solve basic problems, create political stability, and achieve military victories. Their decline is countered by a rise in the prestige accorded to technocrats in the Arab world.

Bill, James A. "Power and Religion in Revolutionary Iran." *Middle East Journal* 36, no. 1 (Winter 1982): 22–47.
This article is valuable for its analysis of "neo-shi'ism" and of the mullahs who functioned in the First Iranian Islamic National Assembly (convened on 28 May 1980). Bill provides useful information on, and distinctions between, Khamenei (the president), Hujjati-Kirmani (a moderate), and Bahonar (former prime minister). The highlight of the article may be its deeply informed, clearsighted discussion of Ayatollah Khomeini's political strategy.

Borsten, Joan. "Kamil, an Israeli Arab." *Present Tense* 10, no. 1 (Autumn 1982): 31–33.
A sympathetic depiction of the personal and social disabilities of being a native Israeli Arab.

Brewer, William D. "The Libyan-Sudanese 'Crisis' of 1981: Danger for Darfur and Dilemma for the United States." *Middle East Journal* 36, no. 2 (Spring 1982): 205–16.
This short article, rich in detail, has two focuses: a political history and present position of Darfur province of Sudan, and relations between Chad and Libya, with attention to Libyan intervention. The author, a former ambassador to Sudan, urges caution in U.S. support of Sudan.

Brown, William R. "The Oil Weapon." *Middle East Journal* 36, no. 3 (Summer 1982): 301–18.
The author examines the present oil glut's effect on efforts to create an oil strategy (the use of oil as a weapon), and cautions that America's and Saudi Arabia's interests are interdependent.

Calder, Norman. "Accommodation and Revolution in Imami Shi'i Jurisprudence: Khumayni and the Classical Tradition." *Middle Eastern Studies* 18, no. 1 (January 1982): 3–20.
This is a scholarly and competent analysis of Ayatollah Khomeini's thought, particularly as expressed in his *Vilayet al-Faqih*, in relation to Imami Shi'i juristic tradition. The author suggests that the future of Iran will depend on an accommodation of juristic theories to practical exigencies.

Chaliand, Gerard. "L'Afghanistan deux ans apres." *L'Afrique et L'Asie modernes*, no. 132 (1ᵉʳ trim. 1982): 3–7.
A brief summation of the internal, military situation of the occupying Soviet forces and the various insurgent groups.

Chevallier, Dominique. "Liban: Un état non-militarisé sous surveillance militaire." *Le Monde Diplomatique*, no. 344 (November 1982): 6.
An analysis of the present situation in Lebanon under occupation by various military forces and of the Lebanese army. Special comment is made about the role of general Fu'ād Shihāb over the past three decades. A strong army (following the departure of foreign troops) is seen as a stabilizing factor in the Near East.

Corm, George. "Arab Social Scientists—Quo Vadis?" *Jerusalem Quarterly*, no. 23 (Spring 1982): 129–33.
This is a translation from an Arabic article published in 1980. It is a general criticism of the failure of social science research pursued by Arab scholars to understand the underdevelopment of the Arab world.

Ettinger, Shmuel. "Anti-Semitism in Our Time." *Jerusalem Quarterly*, no. 23 (Spring 1982): 95–113.
The author maintains that anti-Zionism is the same as anti-Semitism, and advocates that Israel preserve and nurture those values that distinguish it from other nations.

Faroughy, Ahmad. "Le guerre entre l'Irak et l'Iran." *Le Monde Diplomatique*, no. 344 (November 1982): 8.
Updates the military situation and assesses the war's impact on the Ba'th regime of Iraq.

Freedman, Robert O. "The Middle East—Another View." *Present Tense* 9, no. 4 (Summer 1982): 24–27.
Written by a leading academic expert on the international relations of the contemporary Middle East, this article is also a model of popular scholarly prose exposition. Freedman here outlines a plan for the United States to pursue: a Saudi-Egyptian rapprochement, pressure for continuation of the autonomy talks under Camp David, development of the Rapid Deployment Force, and provision in the United States for a strategic oil reserve.

Friedman, Murray. "AWACS and the Jewish Community." *Commentary* 73, no. 4 (April 1982): 29–33.

Gil, Ata. "Pouvoir militaire et 'dictature de la bourgeoise.' " *Le Monde Diplomatique*, no. 344 (November 1982): 9–10.
Surveys the political and financial situation in Turkey, with historical background. Stresses the repression of extremists of the left and right.

Goldberg, Jacob. "The PLO's Position in the Arab Israeli Conflict in the 1970s." *Orient* 23, no. 1 (March 1982): 81–92.
Offers a clear presentation of the official PLO policy and goals (up to early 1981) in contrast to public statements by various PLO officers.

Gruen, George E. "Israel and the War in Lebanon." *Present Tense* 9, no. 4 (Summer 1982): 27–29.
An account of a visit to southern Lebanon (Tyre and Sidon, on 16 June). The author assesses damage and casualties and is convinced the Israelis were very selective in inflicting damage.

Halliday, Fred. "The Iranian Revolution: Uneven Development and Religious Populism." *Journal of International Affairs* 36, no. 2 (Fall/Winter 1982/83): 186–207.
A highly competent and detailed analysis of the Iranian revolution and of the Ayatollah Khomeini.

Halperin, Morton H. "American Policy and the Security of Israel: The Hard Line is Not the Way." *Present Tense* 9, no. 3 (Spring 1982): 23–27.
Argues against the perception that a hard U.S. line with the Soviets is good for Israel. The author believes that U.S. support should be based on shared values.

Hanafi, Hasan. "Arab National Thought in the Balance." *Jerusalem Quarterly*, no. 25 (Fall 1982): 54–67.
This is an English translation of an article by a professor of philosophy at the University of Cairo. It is a thoroughgoing indictment of the state of intellectual life in the Arab world.

Heutsch, Thierry. "La cinquième guerre israélo-arabe." *Le Monde Diplomatique*, no. 338 (May 1982): 12.
After demonstrating that Egypt will not be a restraining factor on Israel, the author predicts that Israel, having a secure southern border, will strike against the PLO and Syria. The 21 April bombardment of Lebanon is seen as an announcement of this policy.

Hodges, Tony. "Le nouvel axe stratégique entre Washington et Rabat." *Le Monde Diplomatique*, no. 340 (July 1982): 6–7.
A detailed article on the causes and events leading to a closer U.S.-Morocco relationship.

Jarry, Emmanuel. "Prudence syrienne, craintes jordaniennes." *Le Monde Diplomatique*, no. 341 (August 1982): 3.
On the future of the PLO, now deprived of its base in Lebanon.

_____. "Sud Liban: le face à face." *Le Monde Diplomatique*, no. 338 (May 1982): 14–15.
Describes the Israeli military capacity to attack southern Lebanon and discusses the situation there, especially the growth of Shiite influence.

Kapeliouk, Amnon. "Le gouvernement israélien à l'heure des comptes." *Le Monde Diplomatique*, no. 343 (October 1982): 1, 3.
This is a well-informed discussion of the problem facing Israel as a result of its invasion of Lebanon. Emphasis is placed on the total rejection of President Reagan's peace plan, the future of U.S. aid to Israel, and the Labor party in Israel.

_____. "Israel: une stratégie radicale." *Le Monde Diplomatique*, no. 338 (May 1982): 12–13.
A detailed examination of Israeli actions and policies vis-à-vis the occupied territories as a prelude to incorporating them into Israel. The author also illustrates how the Old Testament is being used by some to justify eradication of Arabs from Samaria and Judea.

——. "La liquidation de l'obstacle palestinien: vers un nouvel ordre regional." *Le Monde Diplomatique*, no. 340 (July 1982): 1, 3.
Recounts step by step the preparations for the invasion of Lebanon and the justifications advanced for it.

Kashkett, Steven B. "Iraq and the Pursuit of Nonalignment." *Orbis* 26, no. 2 (Summer 1982): 477–94.
The author develops the Ba'thist ideological support for nonalignment, but stresses Iraq's desire for dominance in the Gulf, the need to pursue a more moderate stance vis-à-vis the Arab world, and the realization of the danger of an overly close attachment to either superpower.

Kassir, Samir. "L'Ascension de M. Bechir Gemayel." *Le Monde Diplomatique*, no. 342 (September 1982): 13.
Speculation on the type of Lebanon that Bashir Gemayel desired.

——. "L'Avenir de l'état libanais: Quel 'consensus national'?" *Le Monde Diplomatique*, no. 340 (July 1982): 4–5.
This article is based upon statements from Israeli officials that a goal of the invasion was to institute a free and independent government in Lebanon; it is a masterful exposition of the internal political situation in Lebanon.

——. "Jordanie: Le moindre mal." *Le Monde Diplomatique*, no. 338 (May 1982): 16–17.
A discussion of the early 1982 situation in Jordan, with special attention to relations with the West Bank.

——. "Solidarité nuancée avec le monde Arabe dans le conflit du Proche-Orient." *Le Monde Diplomatique*, no. 335 (February 1982): 18.
Summary of the relations between the Arab world and Africa during the past ten years.

Kelman, Herbert C. "Talk with Arafat." *Foreign Policy*, no. 49 (Winter 1982/83): 119–39.
This article is based on two interviews with Yasir Arafat. It places the PLO and Arafat in a far more favorable light than many other observers do. Perhaps most importantly, it is a clear statement of the existence of true Palestinian nationalism (by a prominent American Jewish academician) and the implications it has for U.S., Israeli, and PLO negotiations. Kelman is a social psychologist and professor of social ethics at Harvard University. He also chairs the Middle East Seminar at the Center for International Affairs.

Klich, Ignacio. "L'Annexion du Golan compromet les tentatives amorcées pour renouver avec Israël." *Le Monde Diplomatique*, no. 335 (February 1982): 18.
A discussion of the effect on Israeli-African relations of the annexation of the Golan Heights.

Kreczko, Alan J. "Support Reagan's Initiative." *Foreign Affairs*, no. 49 (Winter 1982/83): 140–53.
This is an elaborate review of the compatibility of President Reagan's 1 September peace initiative with the provisions of the Camp David accords signed in 1978. Kreczko is a legal adviser for Near Eastern and South Asian affairs at the State Department.

Kutschera, Chris. "Les vicissitudes de l'opposition democratique irakienne." *Le Monde Diplomatique*, no. 338 (May 1982): 20–21.
A close analysis of the internal political situation in Iraq, with much detail on the Kurdish problem.

_____. "Yémen du Sud: l'étoile rouge pâlit-elle à Aden?" *Le Monde Diplomatique*, no. 343 (October 1982): 22–23.
A detailed discussion of the foreign relations of South Yemen, with attention to currents pushing the country to a reconciliation with its Arab neighbors.

Lepidoth, Ruth. "The Autonomy Talks." *Jerusalem Quarterly*, no. 24 (Summer 1982): 99–113.
An interesting, insightful account of the talks on Palestine autonomy under the "Framework for Peace in the Middle East" signed at Camp David on 17 September 1978. The author, professor of public international law at the Hebrew University, urges that the talks be vigorously pursued.

Mehta, Jagat S. "A Neutral Solution." *Foreign Policy*, no. 47 (Summer 1982): 139–53.
This article reviews the Afghanistan situation and presents a set of proposals to restore peace to the country and to stabilize the region. Mehta hopes to see Afghanistan restored to its traditional nonaligned status.

Morris, Benny. "Mordechai Gur." *Present Tense* 10, no. 1 (Autumn 1982): 27–31.
A journalist's interview with a prominent member of the Labor party in Israel and former chief of staff (1974–78).

O'Brian, William V. "Reflections on the Future of American-Israeli Relations." *Jerusalem Quarterly*, no. 22 (Winter 1982): 85–98.
The author is professor of government at Georgetown University and wrote this article in September 1981. The essay focuses on the decline in support for Israel. It advocates bringing Israel into a NATO-like Middle East coalition.

Podhoretz, Norman. "J'Accuse." *Commentary* 74, no. 3 (September 1982): 21–31.
After a vigorous assault on those writers and commentators who have vilified Israel for its invasion of Lebanon, Podhoretz dissects the use of anti-Semitism and the application of a double standard in dealing with Israel. Letters in response to this outspoken polemic are published in the December issue of *Commentary*.

"La politique de defense." *L'Afrique et l'Asie modernes*, no. 134 (3ᵉ trim. 1982): 70–78.
A summary article by "known experts" on the present military capacity of Saudi Arabia.

Raab, Earl. "Is the Jewish Community Split?" *Commentary* 74, no. 5 (November 1982): 21–25.
An analysis of reactions among American Jews to the invasion of Lebanon and to the Beirut massacres.

Ramazani, R.K. "Who Lost America? The Case of Iran." *Middle East Journal* 36, no. 1 (Winter 1982): 5–21.
Ramazani, one of the leading scholars in the United States who deal with contemporary Iran, argues that American involvement in Iran was initiated and constantly promoted by the shah.

Rosenbaum, Aaron D. "Discard Conventional Wisdom." *Foreign Policy*, no. 49 (Winter 1982/83): 154–67.
The author states lessons learned from the 1982 Lebanon situation and argues that a bilateral U.S. approach is better than a comprehensive solution to the problems of the Middle East.

Rosenfeld, Stephen S. "Dateline Washington: Anti-Semitism and U.S. Foreign Policy." *Foreign Policy*, no. 47 (Summer 1982): 172–83.
The author, who is an editorial writer for the *Washington Post*, concentrates on the issue of anti-Semitism in the AWACS sale and in U.S.-Israeli relations. He takes up the fact of dual loyalty for American Jews, does not avoid mentioning the influence of Menachem Begin on American policy toward Israel, and is able to separate legitimate anti-Zionist thought from anti-Semitism.

_____. "The Middle East—One View." *Present Tense* 9, no. 4 (Summer 1982): 22–23.
A casual review of U.S.-Israeli relations as of mid-1982. The author suggests that not much will change as a result of the invasion of Lebanon.

Rouleau, Eric. "Israel dans l'engrenage libanais." *Le Monde Diplomatique*, no. 341 (August 1982): 1, 5.
On the reactions inside Israel to the prolonged occupation of Lebanon.

Rubinstein, Alvin Z. "Afghanistan: Embraced by the Bear." *Orbis* 26, no. 1 (Spring 1982): 135–53.
This is a detailed account of the Soviet takeover. The author predicts a transformation of Afghanistan into a compliant client state, like Mongolia, and stresses the serious consequences of the occupation to American interests in the Gulf.

_____. "The Last Years of Peaceful Coexistence: Soviet-Afghan Relations, 1963–1978." *Middle East Journal* 36, no. 2 (Spring 1982): 165–83.
The author, a political scientist specializing in Soviet affairs, recounts the close relations between the USSR and Afghanistan. Weight is given to the Pushtunistan issue and especially to the blunders of Daoud as factors leading to the Soviet takeover.

Rubinstein, Danny. "Muhammad Watad." *Present Tense* 10, no. 1 (Autumn 1982): 39–42.
A sympathetic interview with an Israeli Arab who is a member of the Mapam party and a Knesset representative.

Sid-Ahmed, Mohamed. "Une autre 'revolution rectificative' en Égypte?" *Le Monde Diplomatique*, no. 345 (December 1982): 1, 13.

_____. "Changement et continuité en Égypt." *Le Monde Diplomatique*, no. 335 (February 1982): 1, 18.

Takes up the problem of corruption and nepotism in Egypt faced by Hosni Mubarak in his attempt to promote economic progress. The article also delves into progress toward a national reconciliation within Egypt.

_____. "Le Fil du rasoir." *Le Monde Diplomatique*, no. 338 (May 1982): 1, 18.
A discourse on the aftereffects of the transfer of the Sinai peninsula from Israel to Egypt. Special attention is paid to the possibility of a change of policy by Hosni Mubarak (discounted) and to the process of reconciliation between Egypt and the Arab world.

Spiegel, Steven L. "The Middle East: A Consensus of Error." *Commentary* 73, no. 3 (March 1982): 15–24.
The author delineates and argues against what he sees as a new consensus on the Middle East, one that is not shared by the majority of American Jews. This "consensus" embraces the need to settle the Palestine problem, hopes for comprehensive Arab-Israeli solution, sees Saudi Arabia as the pillar of U.S. policy and Israel as a liability, and threatens the Jewish "lobby."

_____. "Religious Components of U.S. Middle East Policy." *Journal of International Affairs* 36, no. 2 (Fall/Winter 1982/83): 235–46.
Spiegel, a political scientist at the University of California at Los Angeles, looks at the influence of both Jewish and Christian groups on Middle Eastern policy and finds little real impact on the decision-making process.

Tucker, Robert W. "Lebanon: The Case for the War." *Commentary* 74, no. 4 (October 1982): 19–30.
An analysis, often at odds with the consensus of scholarly opinion, on why the Israeli army stopped short of the conquest of Beirut and on what the future holds for the PLO after its dispersal from Beirut. This is a closely reasoned, argumentative article. Tucker is a political scientist and student of the American Revolution.

Turquié, Selim. "L'Etroite marge de manoeuvre de la diplomatie palestinienne." *Le Monde Diplomatique*, no. 337 (April 1982): 1, 7.
Contains an analysis of statements issued by the PLO after the visit of French president Mitterrand to Israel; and the impossibility of West Bank Palestinians to achieve autonomy.

_____. "L'Impuissance de l'Europe au Proche-Orient." *Le Monde Diplomatique*, no. 336 (March 1982): 1, 10.
After a summary of the close and important economic ties between Europe and the Arab world, the author explores the diplomatic options available to Europe and especially to France, in the period prior to Mitterrand's visit to Israel, in promoting peace between Israel and the Arabs.

Warburg, Gabriel R. "Islam and Politics in Egypt, 1952–80." *Middle Eastern Studies* 18, no. 2 (April 1982): 132–57.
An interesting and well-documented survey that is recommended for its description of fundamentalism in Sadat's Egypt.

Weissbrod, Lilly. "Gush Emunim Ideology—From Religious Doctrine to Political Action." *Middle Eastern Studies* 18, no. 3 (July 1982): 265–75.
While the author fails to explain satisfactorily why the present government

of Israel supports the Gush Emunim, the article is recommended for its account of the origins and ideology of this movement that justifies a *Jewish* claim to the West Bank.

Wright, Claudia. "Shadow on Sand: Strategy and Deception in Reagan's Policy toward the Arabs." *Journal of Palestine Studies* 11, no. 3 (Spring 1982): 3–36.
The author, a correspondent for the *New Statesman*, presents a critical essay on the principles of U.S. Middle Eastern policy and its implementation, in which she takes up policy toward Libya and toward the Fahd plan, and concludes by dissecting the U.S. national security adviser.

_____. "Tunisia: Next Friend to Fall?" *Foreign Policy*, no. 46 (Spring 1982): 120–37.
This is an analysis of the problems now faced by Tunisia. Major emphasis is on weapons from the United States.

Yariv, Aharon. "Reflections on a Solution of the Palestinian Problem." *Jerusalem Quarterly*, no. 23 (Spring 1982): 24–33.
Argues for a flexible strategy of accommodation to the Palestine problem that will lead Israel to a period of "constrained acceptance" by the Arab states, and proposes six principles for an Israeli initiative toward Palestinian self-determination. The author is director of the Center for Strategic Studies, Tel Aviv University.

Zagorin, Adam. "A House Divided." *Foreign Policy*, no. 48 (Fall 1982): 111–21.
The author, who was *Time* magazine correspondent in Beirut (1980–81), reviews the economic situation of Lebanon following the invasion. With the premise that the Lebanese will not accede to a strong central government, Zagorin puts forward the idea of an American-sponsored cantonal arrangement that would recognize the economic and political fragmentation that currently exists.

_____. "Politics and Violence in Lebanon." *Jerusalem Quarterly*, no. 25 (Fall 1982): 3–26.
A detailed yet very readable account of military factions and political violence in Lebanon since 1975. Special attention is given to the Maronites and to the Phalange-Israeli cooperation. The author closes this highly recommended essay by criticizing the late 1982 attempts to impose an artificial unity on Lebanon, and calls for a "confederal structure" with separate, autonomous areas.

_____. "Smaller and Greater Lebanon—The Squaring of a Circle?" *Jerusalem Quarterly*, no. 23 (Spring 1982): 34–53.
This essay looks at the causes of the establishment of greater Lebanon in 1920 and the political consequences of that act: while the area of Lebanon doubled, the incorporation of essentially Muslim areas caused the problems that confront Lebanon today.

Index

Ottomans, in Lebanon, 71, 72, 74–78
passim
Ould Daddah, Mokhtar, 132, 134
Ould Heydalla, Khouna, 140
Ouled Delim, 129
Özal, Turgut, 168

Palestine Liberation Organization
(PLO): in Lebanon, 80, 81, 82,
86–87, 88, 90, 91, 95–97, 102;
and U.S. Mideast policies, 114–16,
122, 123–24
Palestinians: in Lebanon, 80–82,
85–88 passim, 91, 92, 93; and U.S.
Mideast policies, 113–16, 119, 122
Pasha, Dā'ūd, 77
Pasha, Fu'ād, 77
Peres, Shimon, 120
Pertini, Sandro, 99
Phalange (Lebanon), 77, 81, 82, 84, 85,
86, 87, 88, 91, 93, 96, 97, 98, 101
PLO. See Palestine Liberation Or-
ganization
Polisario Front, 129–48 passim

Qaddafi, Muammar, 143, 144, 148
Qatar, 177; economy of, 188; U.S. ex-
ports to, 180 (table); US. imports
from 184 (table)
Qaysis, 71
Quadruple Alliance, 71, 72, 77

Rabin, Yitzhak, 90, 120
Ras Al-Khaimah, 187
Reagan, Ronald: and Arab-Israeli
peace initiative, 113–25; and Leba-
non, 90, 94, 95, 96, 98, 99, 100, 101,
106; and Western Sahara conflict,
138, 139, 143, 145–47
Réglement Définitif, 77
Reguibat, 129, 130–31
Republican People's party (RPP) (Tur-
key), 152, 153, 155, 156, 158
Republican Reliance party (Turkey),
152
Roberts, Edmund, 189
Romberg, Alan, 94

Sabra camp, 92, 93, 101
Sadat, Anwar, 137
Saharan Arab Democratic Republic
(SADR), 129, 136–37, 141, 142, 143,
144, 147
Şahinkaya, Tahsin, 151

Salam, Saeb, 96
Salem. Elie, 84, 98, 99, 104–5, 106
Saqr, Etienne, 101
Sarkis, Elias, 96, 87, 91, 95
Saudi Arabia, 101–2, 177, 178, 186,
188, 189; economy of, 179–83; and
Lebanon, 87, 88, 90, 94, 100; U.S.
exports to, 180 (table); U.S. imports
from, 184 (table); and U.S. Mideast
policies, 117, 118, 122
Senegal, 137, 142, 143, 144
Shamir, Yitzhak, 97, 101
Sharjah, 187
Sharon, Ariel, 97, 100, 123
Shatila camp, 92, 93, 101
Shiff, Zeef, 97
Shihāb, Fu'ād, 80
al-Shihābī, Bashīr, II, 71, 72, 73
Shiites, 71, 76, 78, 79, 81, 83–87 pas-
sim, 92, 96
Shultz, George, 118, 121
Sierra Leone, 139, 141
Somalia, 137; U.S. exports to, 180
(table); U.S. imports from, 184
(table)
South Yemen, 138
Soviet Union, 103, 106, 179; and
Lebanon, 95, 101; and Turkey, 166,
172; and U.S. Mideast policies,
116–17; and Western Sahara
conflict, 138, 141
Spadolini, Giovanni, 99
Spain, 129, 130, 131, 132, 136
Spanish Sahara, 129
Stanhope, Lady Hester, 75
Sudan, 136, 137; U.S. exports to, 180
(table); U.S. imports from, 184
(table)
Suez Canal, 177–78
Sunnis, 71, 78, 79, 81, 83, 96
Syria, 138; and Lebanon, 71, 81,
85–87, 88–90, 92, 93, 96, 106, 114;
U.S. exports to, 180 (table); U.S. im-
ports from, 184 (table)

Tanzania, 136, 141
Tiyyān, Yusuf, 74
Togo, 144
Toure, Ahmed Sekou, 142
Tripoli, 73
Tuéni, Ghassan, 103–4
Tümer, Nejat, 151
Tunisia, 137; U.S. exports to, 180 (ta-
ble); U.S. imports from, 184 (table)

Turkey: background to military take-over, 152–56; foreign policies, 166–74; military in power, 157–59; new constitution, 160–65; transition to civilian rule, 165–66; U.S. exports to, 181 (table); U.S. imports from, 185 (table)
Turkish Textile Workers Federation, 158

Ulusu, Bülent, 157
Umm Al-Quwain, 187
United Arab Emirates, 177; economy of, 187–88; U.S. exports to, 180 (table); U.S. imports from, 184 (table)
United Kingdom, 182, 188, 189, 190
United Nations: and Lebanon, 86, 91, 92, 93, 94, 95, 99; and Sahara, 130, 140
United States: and Arab-Israeli peace initiative, 113–25; exports to Middle East, 180–81 (table); imports from Middle East, 184–85 (table); in Lebanon, 80, 88, 90–96 passim, 98–102 passim, 105–6; as trading partner with Egypt, Arab Gulf states, 177–91; and Turkey, 159, 166, 169, 174; and Western Sahara conflict, 138, 139, 143, 144, 145–47, 148

United States–Saudi Joint Economic Commission, 182–83

Washington Post, 93–94
al-Wazzān, Shafik, 98
Weinberger, Caspar, 96, 143
West, Francis J., 143
West Bank, 114, 117, 122, 123
Western Sahara, 129–48
West Germany, 182, 183, 188
World Bank, 183, 186–87

Yamani, Muhammad Abduh, 100
Yanbu', 182
Yemen (Aden): U.S. exports to, 180 (table); U.S. imports from, 184 (table)
Yemen (Sana'a): U.S. exports to, 180 (table); U.S. imports from, 184 (table)
Yemenis, 71

Zaire, 137, 142, 144
Zartman, I. William, 131
Zgharta Liberation Army (Lebanon), 82
Zimbabwe, 137, 143

Contributors

Donna Robinson Divine is an associate professor in the Department of Government at Smith College. She received her B.A. at Brandeis University and her Ph.D. at Columbia. She has taught at the City College of the City University of New York and at Yale University. Author of studies on Israeli, Egyptian, and Palestinian politics and history, appearing in the *International Journal of Middle East Studies, Review of Politics, Response, New Outlook,* and *Palestinian Politics and Society* (edited by Joel S. Migdal, Princeton University Press, 1980), she is currently engaged in writing a social history of Palestinian Arabs from 1839–1948.

Caesar E. Farah is a professor of Middle Eastern and Islamic history at the University of Minnesota. He holds a Ph.D. in Near Eastern Studies from Princeton University. He has served in the U.S. Foreign Service as Public Affairs and Cultural Affairs officer in India and Pakistan. He has taught at a number of universities including Indiana at Bloomington before joining the University of Minnesota, and was a visiting professor at Harvard and Cambridge universities. He has authored several books, edited a seven-volume series in Arabic, and published extensively on the internationalization of confessional Lebanese politics in nineteenth-century Ottoman Lebanon. He has lectured widely in Europe and the Middle East. His articles on Lebanon have appeared in the *International Journal of Middle East Studies, Journal of Asian History, International Journal of Turkish Studies,* and in a number of festschrifts and anthologies.

Ragaei El Mallakh, professor of economics at the University of Colorado, Boulder, is director of the International Research Center for Energy and Economic Development and editor of the *Journal of Energy and Development.* The author of over eighty articles and reviews, he also has authored, edited, or contributed to fifteen books, including eight on Arab Gulf states (Kuwait, Qatar, Saudi Arabia, and United Arab Emirates) and four on energy economics and energy-related development. Dr. El Mallakh is currently completing a book on Oman and another on the Yemen Arab Republic.

Robert A. Mortimer is professor of political science at Haverford College. The author of *The Third World Coalition in International Politics* (Praeger, 1980), he has published articles on North African politics and foreign policy in such journals as *Orbis, Africa Report,* and *Current History.* He has taught international relations at the University of Algiers and at the University of Abidjan in Ivory Coast.

Eric Ormsby was curator of the Near East Collections, Princeton University Library, from 1977 to 1983, and is now director of libraries at the Catholic University of America. He is the author of *The Perfect Rightness of the Actual: An Islamic Theodicy* (Princeton University Press, 1984) and coeditor, together with the late Professor Rudolf Mach, of the *Short Catalogue of Arabic Manuscripts (New Series) in the Princeton University Library* (Princeton University Press, 1983). He holds a Ph.D. in Near Eastern Studies from Princeton University.

Ilter Turan is a professor of political science at the Faculty of Economics, Istanbul University. His research interests and publications (in English and Turkish) have been in the fields of comparative and international politics, with particular emphasis on political change and development, political attitudes and behavior, Turkish politics, and Turkish foreign policy. He has been a visiting professor in the Departments of Political Science of the University of California, Berkeley, and the University of Arizona, Tucson.

David H. Partington was educated at Lehigh University, received an M.A. in European history from Rutgers University, and earned his doctorate in Oriental Studies at Princeton University in 1961. Successively employed by Princeton, Michigan, and Harvard universities, he has been since 1970 the Middle Eastern librarian in the Harvard College Library and an associate of the Harvard Middle East Center. The author of numerous reviews, articles, and studies related to bibliography and Middle Eastern librarianship, and articles on Arabic, Persian, and Turkish literatures in the *Reader's Adviser,* he has served on the board of directors of the Middle East Studies Association, been chairman of the Mid-East Committee of the Association of Research Libraries, and is now an editor of *Mundus Arabicus,* an annual devoted to modern Arabic literary topics. He brings to the editorship of the *Middle East Annual* a broad background in Arabic, Turkish, and Persian studies.

Previous Essays